EVALUATING DEMAND RESPONSE
OPPORTUNITIES FOR DATA CENTERS

UNIVERSITÄT
MANNHEIM

Evaluating Demand Response Opportunities for Data Centers

Inauguraldissertation

zur Erlangung des akademischen Grades
eines Doktors der Wirtschaftswissenschaften
der Universität Mannheim

vorgelegt von

Sonja Klingert
aus Karlsruhe

Bibliografische Information der Deutschen Nationalbibliothek
Die Deutsche Nationalbibliothek verzeichnet diese Publikation in der Deutschen Nationalbibliografie; detaillierte bibliografische Daten sind im Internet über http://dnb.d-nb.de abrufbar.
1. Aufl. - Göttingen: Cuvillier, 2020
Zugl.: Mannheim, Univ., Diss., 2020

Dekan: Prof. Dr. Christian Becker
Referent: Prof. Dr. Christian Becker
Korreferentin: Prof. Dr. Anke Weidlich

Tag der mündlichen Prüfung: 11.08.2020

© CUVILLIER VERLAG, Göttingen 2020
Nonnenstieg 8, 37075 Göttingen
Telefon: 0551-54724-0
Telefax: 0551-54724-21
www.cuvillier.de

Alle Rechte vorbehalten. Ohne ausdrückliche Genehmigung des Verlages ist es nicht gestattet, das Buch oder Teile daraus auf fotomechanischem Weg (Fotokopie, Mikrokopie) zu vervielfältigen.
1. Auflage, 2020
Gedruckt auf umweltfreundlichem, säurefreiem Papier aus nachhaltiger Forstwirtschaft

ISBN 978-3-7369-7330-5
eISBN 978-3-7369-6330-6

Abstract

Data center demand response is a solution to a problem that is just recently emerging: Today's energy system is undergoing major transformations due to the increasing shares of intermittent renewable power sources as solar and wind. As the power grid physically requires balancing power feed-in and power draw at all times, traditionally, power generation plants with short ramp-up times were activated to avoid grid imbalances. Additionally, through demand response schemes power consumers can be incentivized to manipulate their planned power profile in order to activate hidden sources of flexibility. The data center industry has been identified as a suitable candidate for demand response as it is continuously growing and relies on highly automated processes. Technically, data centers can provide flexibility by, amongst others, temporally or geographically shifting their workload or shutting down servers. There is a large body of work that analyses the potential of data center demand response. Most of these, however, deal with very specific data center set-ups in very specific power flexibility markets, so that the external validity is limited.

The presented thesis exceeds the related work creating a framework for modeling data center demand response on a high level of abstraction that allows subsuming a great variety of specific models in the area: Based on a generic architecture of demand response enabled data centers this is formalized through a micro-economics inspired optimization framework by generating technical power flex functions and an associated cost and market skeleton. As part of a two-step-evaluation an architectural framework for simulating demand response is created. Subsequently, a simulation instance of this high-level architecture is developed for a specific HPC data center in Germany implementing two power management strategies, namely temporally shifting workload and manipulating CPU frequency. The flexibility extracted is then monetized on the secondary reserve market and on the EPEX day ahead market in Germany.

As a result, in 2014 this data center might have achieved the largest benefit gain by changing from static electricity pricing to dynamic EPEX prices without changing their power profile. Through demand response they might have created an additional gross benefit of 4% of the power bill on the secondary reserve market. In a sensitivity analysis, however, it could be shown that these results are largely dependent on specific parameters as service level agreements and job heterogeneity. The results show that even though concrete simulations help at understanding demand response with individual data centers, the modeling framework is needed to understand their relevance from a system-wide viewpoint.

Acknowledgements

The last mile. The last step. The last word. Done.

As scientists, we are standing on the shoulders of giants. Yet, in our daily lives, we are woven into our personal networks of people. These are the people whom I owe, due to their support in all those little and a couple of big things that kept me going.

First of all, I want to thank my doctoral supervisor, Prof. Dr. Christian Becker. Christian, thank you again for giving me a professional home in your chair when I needed one. The Information Systems group is imbued by your openness and curiosity, trust and cheerfulness which has created a group spirit that makes it a pleasure to collaborate and enjoy after-work-hours together. Thank you for accepting me as a phd-student, knowing that this might be a cumbersome journey. Somehow you felt, when to push me, when to make my life hard by posing questions that were not always welcome but improved the quality of the work. And when to build me up in order not to lose track :-). Thank you so much for your support and your belief in me!

I also would like to thank Prof. Dr. Anke Weidlich for acting as my second reviewer. I was very happy meeting you at my first thesis-based poster publication and hearing later that you liked the approach. This is one of the little things that spurred me to go on.

I am deeply grateful for discussions and comments from Prof. Dr. Hermann de Meer and Prof. Dr. Paul Kühn who both acknowledged the challenges of my background, but still continuously urged me on and gave me valuable advice. I am further indebted to Prof. Dr. Boudewijn Haverkort, who at the global minimum of my hopes invited me to the secluded university cloister of Twente. This was the turning point. Thank you. When it comes to an impact on this work, the importance of my anonymous donor of data is key. Thank you for trusting me and enabling this specific piece of work. The direction of my work would have been different without you. The results reveal the challenges of the demand response potential for data centers in Germany; hopefully for the benefit of all.

This work would not have evolved in the way it did without the works of my former students Sebastian Szilvas and Nils Wilken. Thank you for your spirit and ideas; it has been a pleasure working with you. I would also like to thank Dr. Marco Gerards and Martijn Schootuiterkamp from University of Twente who instructed me with a badly needed maths course.

The Information Systems research group, constituted by Martin Breitbach, Dr. Janick Edinger, Kerstin Goldner, Melanie Heck, Benedikt Kirpes, Markus Latz, Martin Pfannemüller, and Anton Wachner, as well as former members and guests as Dr. Patricia Arias Cabarcos, Dr. Christian Krupitzer, Dr. Jens Naber, Dr. Vaskar Raychoudhury, Dr. Felix Maximilian Roth, and Dr. Dominik Schäfer, was way more than my solid ground in every day work. You always make me smile when entering my office in the morning and supported me in so many small things be it thesis discussions or formatting problems. Thank you everyone!

I have also been part of a different, interdisciplinary research team, the so-called 'UNIMA team', made up of Benedikt Kirpes, Dr. Celina Kacperski, Dr. Florian Kutzner, and Dr. Thomas Schulze. You carried me through the ups and downs of project work and gave me any kind of support and friendship that I needed in order to pursue and finally finish this thesis. Thank you for being as you are.

I am also grateful for having been part of a wider EU project team, that taught me the first steps of science and became friends over the years: These are most of all Maria Perez Ortega, Prof. Dr. Hermann de Meer, Giovanni Giuliani, Marco di Girolamo, and Prof. Dr. Xavier Hesselbach-Sierra. Thanks for your patient guidance, especially in the first years.

In the end, it is my family who are and have always been the backbone in my life. My mother Sieglinde Bohning and my grandmother Ursula Niepelt who raised me to be who I am. My brothers Christoph and Felix Bohning who are always there with wanted and unwanted advice, being simply how and what I need them to be. My children: Janik, and Kensia, and Lisa. You had to be so patient with me. Thanks for changing your attitude of the first years - 'stop working on your phd, we need you' to 'work on your phd, we need you to finish'. Thank you for teaching me what is important in life.

Most of all, this goes to my husband Dr. Arnold Klingert. Arno, you are my friend and mentor. It was a learning curve for both of us, and not only in the factual way. Thank you for taking this journey with me, for fighting against your own impatience and for winning. Thank you for all those lively discussions and for being my personal spell-checker. Thank you for believing in me.

Contents

Appendix i

List of Figures

List of Tables

List of Abbreviations

CAPEX	Capital Expenditure
CDN	Content Delivery Network
COP	Coefficient of Performance
CPP	Critical Peak Prices
CRAC	Computer Room Air Conditioner
CRAH	Computer Room Air Handler
C-State	Sleep State
DSO	Distribution System Operator
DSRM	Design Science Research Model
DVFS	Dynamic Voltage and Frequency Scaling
EP	Energy Price (component of SCR compensation)
FIFO	First In First Out
HPC	High Performance Computing
IDC	Internet Data Center
LMP	Local Marginal Price
LTDF	Longest Time to Deadline First (scheduler)
MOL	Merit Order List
NECP	National Energy and Climate Plan
NYISO	New York Independent System Operator
OPC	Other Power Consumers
OPEX	Operational Expenditure
OTC	Over The Counter (electricity contracts)
PP	Power Price (component of SCR compensation)
P-State	Performance State

PV	Photo Voltaic (power generation)
QoS	Quality of Service
REN	Renewable Energy Sources
RWL	Ratio Workload Shifting
SCR	Secondary Control Reserve Market
SGAM	Smart Grid Architectural Model
STDF	Shortest Time to Deadline First (scheduler)
SLA	Service Level Agreement
TOU	Time of Use (tariff)
TSO	Transmission System Operator
VM	Virtual Machine

1. Introduction

Data centers, as increasingly huge energy consumers, can assume a new role in the future energy system: instead of demanding power and energy as needed, they might adapt their power profile to the requirements of the power grid through more or less automated communication and trading channels. This concept is called demand response, the temporary adaptation of power demand to economic incentives like varying prices or contracts with the electricity power grid service provider. Fostering this concept with data centers as participants is the main goal of this thesis.

Reasons for this approach can be found in a changing paradigm on the power supply side and in characteristics of data center power demand. To date, the power grid was built to accomodate any power demand from any customer at any time, with the sole exception of emergencies. The result is a planned overprovision in the power grid. In Germany for instance, in 2019, 88GW of conventional and 124GW of renewable energy sites[1] were waiting to supply a demand which in 2019 peaked at around 82.6GW[2] [1]. With a growing political interst to enlarge the share of intermittent renewable energy sources, both the frequency and the amplitude of oscillations in the grid are becoming higher and less predictable. Applying former expansion strategies to the grid would therefore lead to disproportionally reduced utilization rates and at the same time increase investment cost. For these reasons new concepts are needed.

There are many candidates for demand response ranging from people's 'smart' refrigerators via electric vehicle batteries to aluminum production. Recently, data centers have been given a lot of attention as potential participants in de-

[1] https://www.energy-charts.de/power_inst.htm, accessed 08/06/2020

[2] These are preliminary data.

mand response schemes: Due to increasingly communication-based production and consumption patterns, they are booming in size, number and power density.

In Germany, for instance, reports indicate that between 2007 and 2017 the overall number of data centers in Germany has increased from roughly 2000 to nearly 3000. Also, within this time frame the number of big data centers has doubled [104]. In the U.S., the development of 'big' data centers is even steeper: Nearly all server shipment growth between 2010 and 2015 was related to hyperscale data centers [183], which will render power draws of over 100 MW per data center more common[3]. The impact of this on the energy and power consumption of the total data center industry is further spurred by an increasing power density inside normal data centers[4][156].

Thus, the digitization of society is resulting in increasing shares of data center electricity consumption at total electricity demand. For Europe, a study commissioned by the EU [36] estimated that electricity used by data centers in 2015 were at 78 TWh, equivalent to 2.5 % of total EU demand. In Germany, in 2017, the overall energy demand from data centers was 13,2 TWh, representing around 2.5% of German final electricity consumption[5]. Globally, power demand by data centers is predicted to represent about 20% of power demand world wide by 2025[6], and in hubs like Frankfurt this percentage is already a fact today[7].

Therefore, due to its sheer size the data center industry is an excellent candidate for demand response. And by their very nature, data centers build on highly automated and often fine-grained computing processes that technically can be tuned to grid requirements in a sophisticated way. At the same time, this enables a high level of automation for implementing demand response schemes at data center sites, should contractual constraints be dealt with. So, not only its size but also the technical characteristics of the data center industry render

[3]http://worldstopdatacenters.com/power/, accessed 08/06/2020

[4]https://www.datacenterknowledge.com/power-and-cooling/new-workloads-cost-pressures-drive-data-center-power-densities, accessed 08/06/2020

[5]calculated based on [105] and [44]

[6]https://www.researchgate.net/publication/320225452_Total_Consumer_Power_Consumption_Forecast, accessed 08/06/2020

[7]https://www.datacenter-insider.de/strom-fuer-die-deutsche-hauptstadt-der-rechenzentren-a-827997/?cmp=nl-86&uuid=00181A4B-B282-4507-B06A3E10CDE5105E, accessed 08/06/2020

it a perfect match for demand response schemes. Therefore, it is not surprising that there is a large body of scientific work examining demand response in data centers. The number of research papers in this field started to grow very slowly after the turn of the century and accelerated around 2010, stabilizing on a high level since around 2015. Most of these acknowledge demand response with data centers as having enormous potential. However, looking into data about demand response with the participation of data centers reveals that there is not much experience with this approach, not even in the U.S., where the concept of demand response was developed and applied long before it became a topic in Europe.

Demand response was first developed in the U.S. as demand side management, i.e. on a mandatory basis and with public intervention rights. In the 1980s a weak power grid was confronted with the formerly unknown load of ubiquitous air conditioning which led to increasing threats of outages. The original idea was that *the utility* could temporarily reduce the load of big power consumers in order to react to temporary problems in the power grid through unexpected increases of power demand [84, 62]. While this concept has been developed and refined to incorporate various scenarios, contractual options and partners, in principle it is a matter of the difference between power and energy: Whenever the instant demand for electrical power deviates from the instant supply, in order to avoid damages to equipment due to electrical imbalances, this gap must be filled, either by supply or by demand flexibility. In the case of demand response, this means that a consumer is required to temporarily reduce or increase their power demand without necessarily changing their overall energy consumption. Whereas energy efficiency projects aim to reduce the energy consumption of processes (i.e. the number of kWh), demand response targets the adaptation of power (i.e. the number of kW) to a temporary problem of size in the power grid. Many industrial processes contain elements that can be temporarily shifted, implying that the *theoretical potential* for demand response is huge. Unfortunately, it can be only partially realized due to economic constraints which turn some technically feasible concepts into economic impracticality. Therefore, the *economic potential* is greatly reduced when compared to the technical potential. In practice, even economically sound solutions might not be implementable, creating even less *practical potential* for demand response.

However, manipulating power demand to accommodate grid requirements instead of customer requirements may lead to unwanted consequences. In the case of data centers these include increased package round trip times, extended job runtimes or even reduced site accessibility. Also contractual constraints might prevent data centers from touching the operation of their system, or data center management might not be ready for the general concept of demand response. These are a few reasons for the considerable *gap* between the technical potential of data center demand response identified in previous research and its practical implementation, discussed by [217, 28, 37].

1.1. Observations

This dissertation takes a step towards closing this gap by analysing demand response with data centers from a broader and economically motivated point of view. It is based on the following observations:

Despite the large body of research dedicated to demand response with data centers, the real economic potential of data center demand response is only partially represented.

- On the one hand, many research papers deal with very specific scenarios so that the results cannot be generalized and the external validity is low.
- On the other hand, many research papers only address a small subset of flexibility options and associated incentives in a data center so that the flexibility potential of a data center is underestimated.

This partially explains the gap between the theoretical and practical potential of demand response with data centers.

1.2. Hypotheses

In order to avoid the constraints identified through the above observations, the following hyphotheses are made:

- The economic potential for data center demand response can be represented well by a combination of methods that connect an economics-inspired generic framework of demand response with data centers with concrete instantiations.
- The broad view of the framework represents the (technical and) economic potential with a high degree of external validity.
- The specific view of a concrete instantiation represents a high share of the total flexibility of the modeled data center.

1.3. Research Questions

It it the aim of this thesis to support these hypotheses by working on the following research questions:

1. How can demand flexibility in data centers be modeled in order to theoretically encompass power management strategies at all levels of their architecture?
2. How can the high level of abstraction of modeling demand response with data centers be reconciled with technical and economic characteristics of specific data centers?

1.4. Contributions

To answer these research questions, this dissertation will produce the following results, starting with a high level of abstraction that is successively broken down to represent the characteristics of a specific data center:

1. A *modeling framework for demand response* with data centers will be created in the form of multi-strategy, multi-market optimization. It is inspired by micro-economics, and it views the power flexibility of a data center as the *'output'* of a *'production function'* that needs the *'input'* of power management strategies.
2. This framework is validated in a hierarchical approach by first designing a *generic simulation architecture Sim2Win* that models demand response with a variety of different data center types and demand response schemes.
3. In a second step this generic architecture is instantiated into one *specific simulation system Sim2Win-HPC*, which simulates the impact of involving a specific German HPC data center on two German power flexibility markets.

1.5. Structure of the Work

To lay down the contributions of this thesis and how they are being developed, chapter 2, explains the background, introducing data centers, the power grid, and issues involved with demand response schemes. Chapter 3 is dedicated to scientific work related to the presented thesis. It focuses on optimizing and simulating demand response with data centers. As a framework for demand response with data centers is to be designed, this chapter also refers to other research that aims at modeling flexibility of electricity consumption in general. This paves the way for the introduction to the methodology chosen for this thesis and the explanation of the modeling framework in chapter 4. As a first level of evaluation the simulation architecture Sim2Win is illustrated in chapter 5, and in the second part of this chapter the simulator Sim2Win-HPC is presented in detail. Chapter 6 explains the set-up of the simulation scenario, the planning of the simulation runs, and it documents the results which are discussed at the end of the chapter. Finally, chapter 7 concludes the thesis, summarizing the results and providing an outlook for future work.

2. Background

2.1. Data Centers

There are a great variety of data centers. They not only range in size, business model, and workload, but also in other issues as housing characteristics. These are, for instance, notable in the case of the Barcelona Supercomputing Center which was constructed inside a former chapel (see figure 2.1) .

In order to derive a definition of a data center many authors view data centers from a buildings perspective and focus on the housing aspect of the IT equipment. *Hintemann* [103] or *Barroso and Hölzle* [25] define a data center as 'a building (or buildings) designed to house computing and storage infrastructure in a variety of networked formats.'[25, p.47]. Others provide broad definitions based on the computing infrastructure as *Ghatikar et al.* [89]. As the focus of this thesis is the power flexibility of data centers these definitions fall short of providing a good basis. The requirements for defining a data center in the context of this work are:

- To reflect the overall dependence of a data center's power demand on the workload
- To reflect the impact of operating the physical infrastructure in different modes on the power demand of the data center
- To focus on dynamic, influenceable characteristics of the data center rather than on static characteristics (e.g housing).

Therefore this thesis builds on the definition by *Oro et al.* that encompasses the housing, the infrastructure, and the usage of the DC:

Figure 2.1.: Barcelona Supercomputing Center is constructed inside a former chapel (Photographer: T. Schulze)

> *'A data centre could be defined as a structure, or group of structures, dedicated to the centralized accommodation, interconnection and operation of IT and network telecommunications equipment providing data storage, processing and transport services, together with all the support facilities for power supply and environmental control with the necessary levels of resilience and security required to provide the desired service availability'* [160, p.430].

2.1.1. Power Metrics

From the great variety of data center power metrics only the most well-known and widely used 'Power Usage Effectiveness' (PUE) is shortly introduced. The main reason for its usage is the overall high availability of data relating to this metric. Also it is applied in many data center power models and will here be used in this context. For more information on data center power metrics that are used to understand how different characteristics in a data center manifest in its power consumption see e.g. [61, 174, 47, 220]. Metrics that are dedicated to the flexibility of data centers are introduced e.g. in [128, 14].

The PUE was developed in 2007 by The Green Grid, a U.S. based green data center organization [174]. It is defined as

$$PUE = \frac{TotalFacilityPower}{ITEquipmentPower}, \tag{2.1}$$

where $TotalFacilityPower$ is the power measured at the electricity meter of the utility, i.e. including cooling power, power distribution losses and lighting. $ITEquipmentPower$ is the power that is used to operate the hardware components of a data center in order to process the workload, i.e. server, storage and network power. Theoretically, the PUE ranges from 1.0 to infinity. PUE values have been decreasing over time, mostly due to new cooling technologies. Today many data centers in Europe range around 1.8 [18]; hyperscale data centers even get close to unity[1]. The main drawback of the PUE is that it is not comparable between sites due to different cooling necessities in different geographical locations. It is not even comparable within one data center historically. The reason is that as equipment is being replaced, cooling demand typically does not scale accordingly so that the formula's denominator does not vary in step with the nominator. In the short run, however, it can be used for power modeling, especially if the PUE is calculated dynamically and not averaged over the year.

2.1.2. Data Center Service Models

One main criterion to differentiate data centers and understand the demand response opportunities of specific data center is the service model, i.e. the value proposition a data center offers to their customers. It is the core part of the business model of a data center and highly impacts their options for power

[1] https://www.datacenterknowledge.com/archives/2016/09/27/latest-microsoft-data-center-design-gets-close-to-unity-pue, accessed 08/06/2020

management needed to participate in demand response schemes. This thesis uses the following categories and terminology, loosely aligned with [39, 81, 161]:

Wholesale colocation: offering housing, access, security, power and resilience to customers that own the dedicated servers inside. Wholesale in this case means long-term contracts with one or only few customers.

Retail colocation: offering the same or comparable features to multiple customers that typically own the servers housed.

Cloud infrastructure services: offering infrastructure as a service (IaaS) or (development) platform as a service (PaaS). In some cases this is combined with a colocation service.

Hosting (application hosting, web hosting, software as a service (SaaS)): offering to host applications for the customer, e.g. specialized customer applications, web applications or off-the-shelf SaaS. It is up to the customer to manage and run the software. Supercomputing services might be offered in this context.

Application Management: a data center that actively manages applications for their customers. An example is a service provider computing tax dues from the payroll data delivered by the customer and transferring back the results. The emerging trend of edge computing can be subsumed in this category.

2.1.3. Data Center Workload

Given the infrastructure, the main determinants of a data center's power profile are the *outside temperature* and the *workload.*

The degree to which outside temperature and workload influence data center power depends on the involved technologies, infrastructure setting and buildings' characteristics. For data centers housed in regular buildings (not e.g under the sea[2] or underground[3]), the correlation between cooling power and outside temperature is high: Own findings for a German HPC center with direct liquid cooling technology, based on 2014 data, indicate a correlation between the cooling power and the outside temperature of 0.4 - nearly the same value as for the correlation between the cooling power and the IT load (i.e. aggregated server power and other power consumption like network and lighting). These findings are corroborated by literature, e.g. by [200] who also detect a high correlation between non-IT load (i.e. mostly cooling) and outside temperature. However, the weight of this impact on the total facility power further depends on the PUE. In cases when this is very low the impact of outside temperature on the overall data center power is negligible compared to the workload. As a consequence, in the case of low PUEs the power profile of the data center, i.e. the dynamics of the changing power, is dominated by the workload profile. As PUEs are - notwithstanding the shortcomings of this metric - continuously decreasing on average (see e.g. [18] for Europe and [183] for the U.S.), the focus in this work is set on analysing the workload profiles in order to derive workload models for modeling data center demand response in the later part of this thesis.

From an aggregated perspective, there are flat and variable data center power profiles. Using the metric of an 'average daily load factor', i.e. the ratio between the average and the peak data center load, *Ghatikar et al.* [89] classified data center power profiles into flat loads and mixed-use loads, which according to their terminology represent data center loads where the presumably *flat* IT workload profile is impacted by the surrounding offices.

However, today this is only partially representative: in many cases the workload profile itself has valleys and peaks which are the result of varying utilization, due to office hours or seasonal demand patterns. This was monitored by [32] who for 10 days in 2010 sampled utilization rates from servers in 500 places

[2] `https://news.microsoft.com/features/under-the-sea-microsoft-tests-a-datacenter-thats-quick-to-deploy-could-provide-internet-connectivity-for-years/`, accessed 08/06/2020

[3] `https://www.datacenterdynamics.com/analysis/the-king-under-the-mountain/`, accessed 08/06/2020

around the world. They found that the average CPU utilization was below 50% and characterized by two extrema of very low times below 12% and above 98% and thus supported prior research from [24].

Interactive and Batch Workloads

These observations are connected with the general distinction in literature between *batch* and *interactive* workload (see e.g. [21, 138, 141] and [45] as fundamental analysis). Batch-workload consists of jobs with a distinct power profile (often averaged) and execution time, which are collected in a queue and executed using scheduling algorithms as 'first-in-first-out' or 'shortest-time-to-deadline-first'; the reason is that the implementation of an optimization is in many cases infeasible due to complexity [151]. Batch workload often computes heavy-load scientific work in a high performance environment. Until recently the scheduling objective was mostly either performance optimization or load balancing, thus resulting in a flat workload and data center power profile. In contrast, interactive workload, like web-based searching requests, depends on the activities of users. This means that it forms diurnal and weekly patterns and therefore is often modeled based on historical data [169]. These two basic workload categories can be further refined, by adding a 'data workload' category [161], or by being decomposed into even more fine-grained types [46]. These additions, however, are not considered in this thesis as they do not offer added value for the management of the power profile.

In many cases, batch workload and interactive workload are modeled differently. This is due to discrepancies with the statistic or stochastic properties of arrival, certainty, processing time and deadlines. As a differentiation, Feitelson [76] talks of 'rates' rather than 'sizes' for dynamic vs. static workload, i.e. a continuous stream of tasks vs. some specific amount of work which is done and completed after being processed. As figure 2.2 shows, batch and interactive workload can be viewed as extremes on a continuum: both types have a processing time that is not immediate, despite the fact that interactive workload

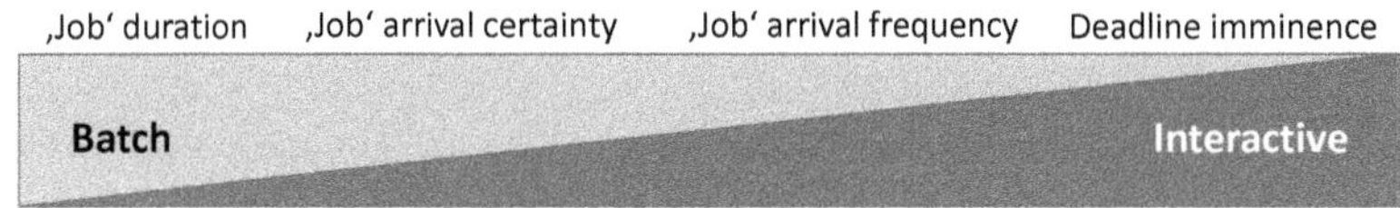

Figure 2.2.: Schematic illustration of batch versus interactive workload

requires 'instant feedback'. That means, also HPC jobs may be running for a very short time and/or carry an immediate deadline, e.g. in the case of medical modeling. In the same way, as illustrated by figure 2.2, the uncertainty and frequency of workload arrival are fundamentally not different for the two types.

So, in principle, all kinds of workload can be modeled using the same approach. A more detailed overview of modeling approaches for both batch and interactive workloads will be given in section 5.2.1.

Workload Descriptions

Before workload can be modeled, it needs to be described and analysed. Analysing the aggregated workload, meaning the workload profile, can be done using a set of different metrics, as for instance the 'peak to mean ratio', i.e. the ratio between the average and the maximum load or the 'peak to minimum ratio', i.e. the ratio between the peak and the minimum load.

Dis-aggregating the workload allows a more fine-grained view on its composition, namely a compound of jobs with starting times, average power consumption, ending times, number of nodes occupied, and CPU frequencies applied. Apart from basic job descriptions workload is also characterized by request arrival rates, by utilization rates on servers or by any other kind of metric that aims at representing the combination of data, computing instructions, and requirements for memory, compute and networking actions. This workload description can be used as a first step and basis for modeling and fitting data with a model. This is the approach that is mostly assumed in literature, of course involving data pre-processing and often normalization and/or scaling of data traces (e.g. [54, 141, 175, 214, 142, 4, 200, 191, 172]).

2.1.4. Service Level Agreements

The final section of this introduction is dedicated to the execution of the service provided by a data center. It is important to differentiate between the nature of the service itself, e.g. payroll computation or delivering web-based streaming services and the *'quality of service' (QoS)* required by a customer for characteristics that are non-functional to this service. Among others, QoS can have timing aspects as e.g. a certain maximum round-trip time, aspects regarding the service access, or the maximum error rate of a result. In publicly owned data centers, QoS levels may be monitored, but typically have no legal consequences as they are not contractually fixed. In a commercial environment, however, QoS levels required as the 'correct' execution of a service are typically laid down in specific technical contracts, or *'service level agreements' (SLA)*. Thus, an SLA can be defined as a formal technical contract between a data center as service provider and a customer which determines *how* a specific service must be executed. Typically, SLAs are negotiable for each type of service and customer. Opposed to strict SLAs with strict QoS levels, in the context of 'green' data centers, also 'GreenSLA' are being discussed, which are defined in dependence on the energy context of a data center. This makes them applicable for the case of demand response with data centers whenever a service provider aims at extending their flexibility by collaborating with their customers and sharing the corresponding benefit. More information on this concept can be found, amongst others, in the former work of the author of this thesis [38, 130]. An overview on SLA parameters and negotiation issues is given e.g. in [3, 78].

The challenge raised by SLA in the context of demand response is the impact of power management on the SLAs' QoS parameters. These can be just monitored, serve as constraints, or be used for the calculation of a penalty that has to be paid to the customer, reducing the data center's demand response benefit.

2.2. The Electrical Power System and Demand Response in Europe

2.2.1. Introduction to the Electrical Power System

Today's electricity system of Europe is the result of an about 20-year-long process aiming to transform the formerly vertically integrated, public-utility-based system. Under this system the utility owned and managed the power grid, generation, transportation and selling of electrical power (see e.g. [182, ch.2], [199, ch.11]). This process is called 'unbundling' and aims at splitting the responsibility and economic units of the above mentioned issues; it started on a European level with the 96/92/EG directive in 1996. This was reinforced with the directive 2009/72/EC of the Third energy package 2009 and as of today is not completely finished.

Figure 2.3 gives a schematic overview about the physical infrastructure of the German power grid, but the general idea can be more or less applied to any grid in Europe. At the upper level, the highest voltage transmission grid transports electricity generated by large bulk generation sites throughout Germany and connects to the surrounding countries. This part of the grid is organized by the transmission system operator (TSO), who is solely responsible for balancing power inside the grid. In some European countries like Spain and France there is just one TSO; in Germany the four TSOs Amprion, Transnet BW, Tennet, 50Herz emerged from the four biggest utilities, today named RWE, EnBW, Eon and Vattenfall. The distribution grids, managed by distribution grid operators (DSOs) distribute the power to the lower level; both electricity consumption and production sites are connected to it. Distribution grids are very heterogeneous regarding size, organizational form, and technical status; in Germany, currently, there are more than 800 DSOs [40]. Europe as a whole has 90% of the DSOs still vertically integrated whereas the unbundling of TSOs is complete. The reason is that on a TSO level the unbundling requirements are stricter than for DSOs [58].

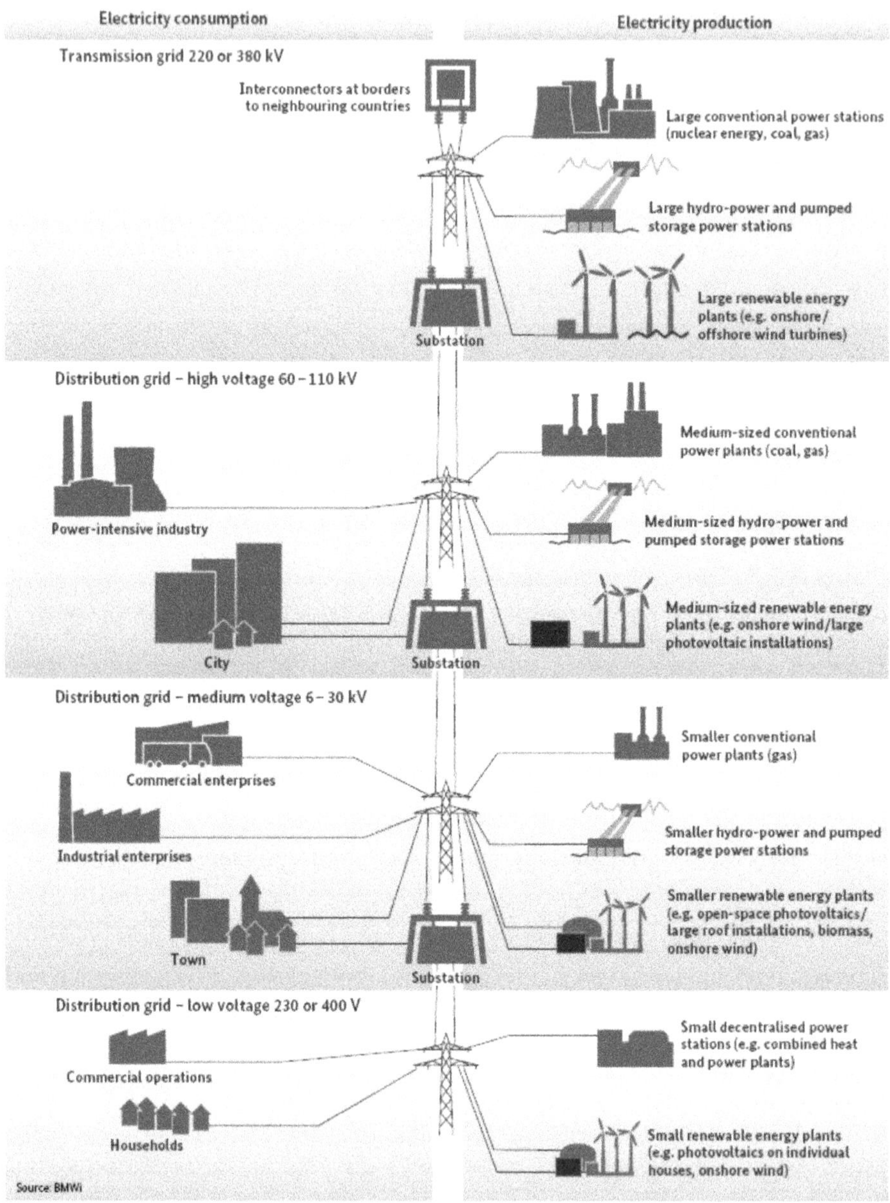

Figure 2.3.: Schematic representation of the German grid and grid levels [75]

As can be seen from figure 2.3, dating from 2012, until very recently the grid separated strictly between electricity consumers and producers. Due to the increasingly distributed character on the electricity production side, this dichotomy is not being kept up: consumers even on the low voltage grid can become so-called *'prosumers'*, both producing *and* consuming electricity and thus frequently changing directions of energy flow in a grid that formerly was uni-directional.

Figure 2.3 shows the physical connection of the electricity production side, i.e. distributed and bulk generation and the consumption side, i.e. households and industry through the power grid. These basic units are connected not only physically, but also through a set of communication and market interactions grounding on incentive structures and business options.

Due to the political objectives of increasing the shares of renewable energy sources (REN) the complexity of this 'system of systems' is constantly increasing, mostly due to rapid and uncontrollable fluctuations through the growing shares of intermittent REN. Therefore a model representing this complexity was needed. It was provided through the development of the Smart Grid Architectural Model (SGAM). This was developed in the context of the EU decarbonisation policy as a means to fathom the implications of this emerging situation and the corresponding need for flexibility [49].

The SGAM model (see figure 2.4) decomposes complexity by differentiating between five layers starting with a 'component layer' which is composed of infrastructure elements using the electricity grid. These are grouped in domains (generation, transport, consumption) and aggregation zones. The whole contents of figure 2.3 is thus represented in the lowest layer of figure 2.4. On top of the component layer, the 'communication and information layers' map protocols and data models to the physical entities below. The 'function layer' represents the use case, as for instance an aggregator offering the aggregated demand response potential of various load entities to the grid operator. On top of all, the 'business layer' represents the sum of rules & regulations whether they come

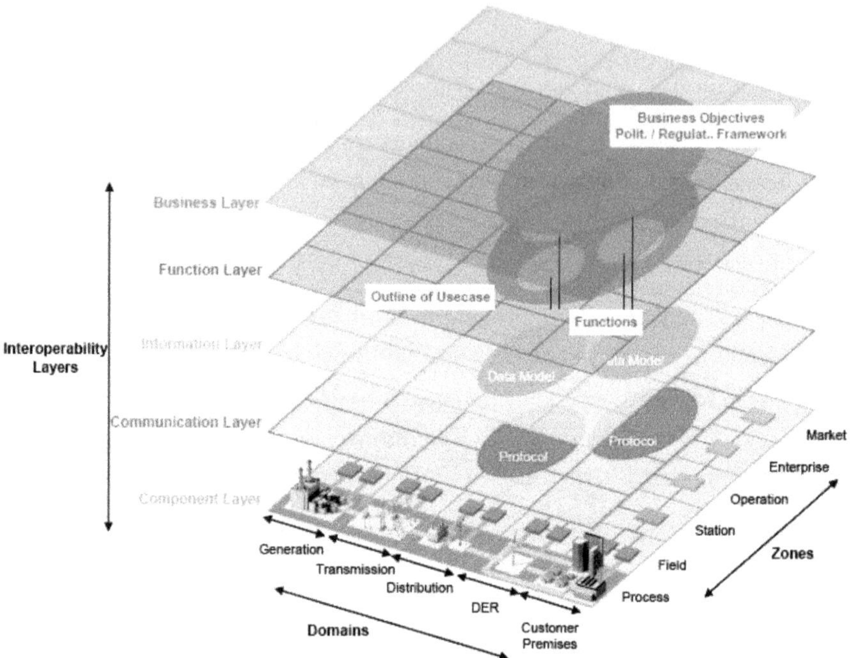

Figure 2.4.: The Smart Grid Architectural Model (SGAM) matches business rules on the top layer with infrastructure elements on the lowest layer [49]

in the form of legal acts from a public entity or in the form of guidelines and business rules from a private organisation. This model was amended by a set of new actors and future roles which are linked to the different layers and domains [196].

This cube, composed of physical, communication, legal and business structures, defines the meaning of 'electricity system' in the context of this thesis. Although technically speaking the electrical energy system is only a part of the energy system (also containing e.g. heating), in this thesis the terms 'energy system', 'electrical energy system', and 'electricity system' are used synonymously.

Electricity Related Goals

As shortly mentioned in the preceding section, the reasons for the current changes and challenges in the energy system originate in political decisions: one of them being the unbundling process, another the increase of REN sources. These political decisions were taken on the basis of a set of overall goals with regards to the electricity system and climate change. Due to their implications for the necessity of demand side power flexibility and demand response schemes, some major goals will be reiterated in this section.

The key EU targets related to the presented thesis concern climate objectives. The target year is 2030 and the comparison basis are 1990 levels; they were devised for the following categories in 2009 and 2014 and updated in 2018[4][70].

- Reduce greenhouse gas emissions by at least 40%
- Achieve a share of at least 32% of renewable energy sources (REN) at final energy consumption
- Increase energy efficiency by at least 32.5%

A simulation study illustrates the high ambition of these goals: in order for the EU to achieve a share of 27% REN at final energy consumption, the study concludes that the share of REN in gross generated electricity would need to reach 47.3%. Furthermore, a 30% REN share would entail an increase in European REN electricity consumption by 92% compared to 2016 [23].

The overall climate goals are being turned into national goals as 'national energy and climate plans' (NECP) accounting for the diversity of the EU member states. For Germany, which is the example scenario in the presented thesis, by 2030 the share of REN energy at gross final energy consumption and at final electricity consumption are to be increased to 30% and 50% respectively [74, 85]. Germany's starting position to reach their goals is comparably good: The German DSO Bayernwerk, for instance, in 2019 stated that already today around

[4]https://ec.europa.eu/clima/policies/strategies/2030_en, accessed 08/06/2020

400 hours/year they fully cover the demand of their customers by RENs[5].

The main challenge of high REN levels in a power grid system is the physical necessity to have a strict balance between the intake and the provision of power at all times. This implies that electrical power cannot be stored, but that this balance needs to be maintained by flexibility of supply and demand. Today's energy systems with their overlay of regulation and market mechanisms can absorb REN levels of 40-50% by activating existing flexibility options. At levels beyond these, the required system flexibility will increase drastically. Demand response is one concept which will play a central role in this future energy system [163].

2.2.2. Electrical Power Markets

The market layer on top of the physical electricity infrastructure can have basically two organizational approaches: it can be a *pool-based market* as the NordPool group or as the Spanish electricity market or an *open trade market* as in several member states of the central EU, e.g. Germany, France, or Italy.

In the pool-based market design all supply and demand of a certain time span are submitted to one specific market operator who then determines the price based on the bids creating a *'merit order list' (MOL)*, i.e. a list of supply bids ordered according to their price and volume. All transactions take place via that market, and there are no bilateral contracts. In order to calculate the market price, through a modeling approach, the market organizer also takes the physical flow of the electricity into account, so that the prices include not only the economic interplay of supply and demand for energy, but also physical power characteristics and constraints thus including network cost. This model's main advantage is that the basic pool market is very liquid; its main disadvantage that the market outcome depends largely on the quality and nature of the network modeling based price algorithms.

[5] `https://www.bdew.de/verband/magazin-2050/tomorrowland-die-verteilnetze-der-zukunft/`, accessed 08/06/2020

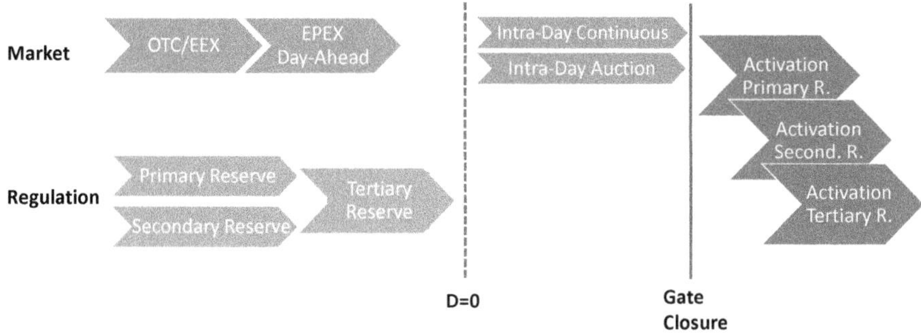

Figure 2.5.: Timeline-based interaction of wholesale and regulation markets, based on [199, 121]

The open-trade market design consists of a set of different markets that are operated subsequently with partial overlaps. This design is amended by regulation services that close the gaps between supply and demand bequeathed by the markets in cases of unexpected supply and demand after the trading is completed. That means after gate-closure in the regular trading-sphere the TSO takes over the control of adjustment until close to real-time. For more detailed information on these market designs see [199, ch.11],[80, 121].

The open-trade market design is the foundation for the demand-response scenario in this thesis. The interaction of the different entities is therefore explained in more detail using the specific design of the German market (see figure 2.5).

As mentioned above, there is a market sphere and a regulation sphere which amend each other [226, 57, 109], [199, ch.11]: The market sphere (blue icons in figure 2.5) consists of so-called Over the Counter (OTC) contracts, which are individual contracts between suppliers and demand side agents. They can have different timings; many of these are contracted months ahead. For market tradeable long-term bids, there is also the futures exchange market EEX. The counterpart to these are the EPEX spot markets: on the day-ahead market, hourly bids for the following day are placed until 12 a.m. In 2012 its volume amounted to more than 40% of the total trading volume; so, contrary to the intra-day market (around 3% in 2012) it is highly liquid [121]. The intra-day market in Germany is comparably new: it consists of intra-day auctions and an intra-day continuous market where bids for 15-minute-slots can be traded until 45 minutes before the actual delivery of electricity at the latest. After this gate-closure there is no more room for market activity, then regulative power is called.

In Germany, there are three kinds of regulation that are enacted once the frequency in the German TSO grids goes beyond the allowed band around 50Hz: primary, secondary, and tertiary regulative power, represented as dark green arrows in figure 2.5. They differ with regards to response time and activation time. Primary reserve, often delivered by spinning masses, needs to be fully activated within 30 sec and can be kept running up to 15 minutes in order to bridge the time until secondary reserve takes over. In order to restore frequency into the allowed band, secondary reserve is called, which needs to be fully operational after 5 to 15 minutes. Both of these are operated automatically, whereas tertiary reserve, which can be kept operational for several hours, is actively called in case secondary reserve is not sufficient. The study of Consentec [57] explains these regulatory concepts in detail; the German TSOs are required to publish activations on a transparency platform[6]. Since 2018 the auctions for reserve power (represented in lighter green arrows in figure 2.5) take place on a weekly basis for primary reserve and on a daily basis for secondary and tertiary reserve in Germany [226]. This makes the tertiary reserve product the most attractive for the suppliers of power flexibility, however, this is also the market with the least attractive remunerations.

In order to understand demand response concepts, the basic remuneration concept of regulatory power (e.g. [226, 57, 121]) needs to be explained: The delivery of electricity as primary reserve power has been hard to trace until recently, so that suppliers of primary regulative power are rewarded exclusively

[6]`https://www.regelleistung.net`, accessed 08/06/2020

for the capacity offered, i.e. they receive a price per kilowatt offered. For secondary and tertiary reserve power, both the option and the delivery are rewarded: the supplier receives price for power (PP) for the time of offering the capacity and a price for the electricity (EP) which is finally delivered when called in case of need.

As in the pool-market design the basic methodology of the auction process for regulation power is a list of suppliers ordered according to the size of their power bids (€/kW) until the last offer necessary to fill the total reserve power needed (MOL). Suppliers are then rewarded as pay-per-bid. Whenever regulative power is called, the reserve is activated according to the electricity price offered (€/Mwh), starting with the least costly offer.

The regulation or reserve power on TSO level introduced above is just one part of the *ancillary services* that guarantee the reliability of power provision. On DSO level, voltages drops are controlled via the supply of reactive power. Other ancillary services are congestion management and the management of cold starts and the re-building of grid functionality after blackouts.

2.2.3. Demand Response

As explained in the preceding section, due to physical constraints demand and supply of electrical power are mapped perfectly on the level of the electrical power grid. Therefore the economic sphere needs to be amended by a set of regulation services that take over control once market gates are closed.

Traditionally, the physical balancing between electrical demand and supply was provided by generation units able to respond quickly as e.g. gas power plants. However, in step with the increasing share of intermittent REN at electricity production the necessity for flexibility is increasing (see section 2.2.1). On the other hand, an increasing power demand through the digitization of society and through the electrification of mobility also leads to temporarily and geographically varying pressure on the power grid. The cost of the growing volatility is high already - according to the latest report of the German National Regulation Authority [41] in 2018 more than 5.2GWh of REN had to be curtailed due to local congestion issues resulting in reimbursement cost of around €500m. All ancillary services together in 2018 cost Germany around €1.8bn of which regulation power was around €123m [41].

At the rise of air conditioning in the U.S. in the 80-ies of the last century the challenges of grid management led to the idea of using not only the flexibility of power generation, but also the flexibility of electricity consumption to balance the grid [84], thus generating the idea of (originally mandatory) *'demand side management'*. Adding pricing and further market participation rules, this evolved into *'demand response'*. Demand response in this thesis is defined as

> *'[V]oluntary changes by end-consumers of their usual electricity use patterns - in response to market signals (such as time-variable electricity prices or incentive payments) or following the acceptance of consumers' bids (on their own or through aggregation) to sell in organised energy electricity markets their will to change their demand for electricity at a given point in time. Accordingly, demand response should be neither involuntary nor unremunerated'* [69, p.3].

Contrary to the original understanding of demand response by the U.S. Federal Energy Regulation Commission from 2006 [72], this definition by the EU commission allows for both up- and down regulation of power. 'End-users' in this context are electricity consuming entities, 'customers' according to the SGAM model (see 2.2.1), i.e. private, public, industrial, or commercial electricity consumers. This power flexibility can then be offered on power markets where it is sought for; in this thesis they are generalized as *'power flex markets'*.

The general idea can be illustrated by an emergency grid event in Texas on a very hot summer day at the beginning of August 2011 shown in figure 2.6: The 'emergency interruptible load service', i.e. a specific demand response product, was activated in order to implement a load reduction of 400MW over the course of 2.5 hours (violet line) which was more than met by the real load reduction

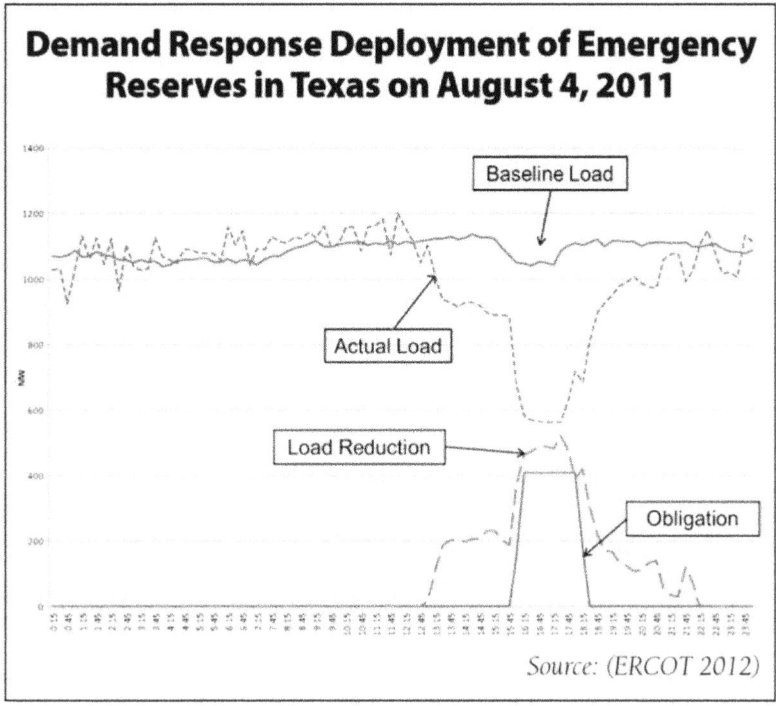

Figure 2.6.: An ERCOT Demand Response Event [112]

(green dotted line). The difference to a pre-calculated 'baseline' consumption is shown in the upper part of figure 2.6. The participants in these demand response schemes in those days in the U.S. were typically big industry sites as aluminum production plants or paper mills that can postpone some thermal processes.

In order to reflect different contractual obligations it is helpful to differentiate between explicit versus implicit demand response [195] (also called incentive-based vs. price-based). *Explicit demand response* means to offer and implement power flexibility based on a specific demand response contract, whereupon a predetermined adaptation must be enacted when called by the grid operator. Whereas *implicit demand response* is the voluntary reaction of an electricity consumer to dynamic prices without being contractually bound to such a reaction. Demand response can be dispatchable and non-dispatchable [112]. This differentiation has a high overlap with explicit vs. implicit demand response. The main difference is the viewpoint: The latter differentiation stresses the point of view of the operator and their ability to see demand response as a power resource (see section 2.2.3).

Today, demand response has a long tradition in the U.S., whereas in Europe the maturity of demand response programs and markets is very heterogeneous due to a variety of regulation issues. The U.K., France, and Ireland are considered to be spearheading European demand response, whereas Germany and the nordic countries are lagging behind; and in some countries like Spain and Poland demand response is still in its very infancy [195].

Typical scenarios for offering flexibility can be found in processes like grinding, smelting or cooling in the cement, aluminum and refrigeration industries [184]. Meanwhile, also smaller and even private equipment is being used for demand response schemes; in that case, however, not each owner is a demand response contract partner, but the contracts are mediated via a so-called 'aggregator' [195, 193, 49]. Demand response with a data center as a 'consumer' is rarely referenced in practice. An introduction to this specific case will be given in section 2.2.3.

Demand Response Functionalities

Demand response can take up various roles which are partially dependent on contractual obligations [112]: the stricter the ties in the demand response contracts as in the case of many explicit demand response schemes, the more dispatchable the connected load behaves, and the more it can be treated as power system resource. This is important, e.g. in the case of unexpected demand spikes. Based on ramp up times and other characteristics, this power resource can be mapped to different ancillary services and is thus viewed primarily as a resource for regulation services and also for congestion management.

Focusing on shifting aspect in power management of demand response participants stresses its potential as a storage option; a functionality that gains more importance as the share of intermittent renewable resources at the electricity generation is growing.

One issue that needs to be considered when evaluating demand response suitability as a power resource or storage option is the impact of *timing*: required ramp up times are decreasing fast, so that the automation of demand response (e.g. through openADR [184, 89, 134]) gains more importance the more demand response is going to play a vital role in the next generation power system. This is reflected in the concept of 'demand response 2.0' [62, 134] and also a challenge for data center demand response.

Stakeholders in the Demand Response Eco-System

The demand response eco-system consists of a variety of different roles and stakeholders [93]; a first description was developed in the course of creating the SGAM model [196]. On the demand side of flexibility, there are actors from the distributing and trading functionalities on the business layer of the SGAM model; notably grid operators on all levels and traders (in the case of implicit demand response), often also vertically integrated utilities. Regarding grid operators, currently in Europe mostly TSOs implement explicit demand response programs. Extending these to the DSO level and thus bringing the flexibility closer to where it is needed is currently being widely discussed [194, 94] and is evaluated in a European research project [153]. On the consumer side, traditionally only huge industries were requested to take part in demand response schemes. In order to be admitted to ancillary services programs they need to undergo laborious prequalification processes; even to source electricity directly at the exchange market as the EPEX, consumers must be able to buy electricity in volumes of at least 100kW. But since the evolvement of a more distributed, REN-dominated power system the option to aggregate smaller consumers is being researched (e.g. [190, 192, 83] and implemented in various EU member states, although at different stages of maturity [195]. European companies active in this business model are for instance Entelios, Next-Kraftwerke, EnergyPool, or EDF.

More discussions about the roles in the demand response eco-system can be found in [196, 184, 135].

Demand Response Potentials

Identifying a potential for demand response either on individual or on aggregated level requires a concept of 'demand response potential'. In energy efficiency literature the differentiation into theoretical, technical, economic and practical/market potential of energy savings was devised [120], where each subsequent potential is a subset of the previous. This concept was mapped to the demand response scenario by *ETSO* [68], *von Roon et al.* [210, 211] and *Gils* [90]. They define as theoretical potential the theoretical contribution by all facilities and devices suitable for flexibility, as technical potential the flexibility of those facilities and devices controlled by existing ICT infrastructure. The economic potential is the part of the technical potential that can be realized under the current economic framework in a cost-efficient way. And the practical potential is the subset of the former which actually can be implemented accounting for business rules, social norms and the legislative framework (see figure 2.7).

To a high degree this differentiation explains the gap between demand response potentials assessed by literature (e.g. [90, 210]) and the demand response flexibility provided to a power system (e.g. [195, 41]). Many works focus on the theoretical potential; only rarely the difference between a theoretical, device- or process-level potential and the economic potential is discussed.

Based on the identification of suitable processes for load shedding (i.e. reducing power persistently thus saving energy) and shifting (i.e. reducing power temporarily) *Gils* [90] identifies an EU hourly average load reduction potential

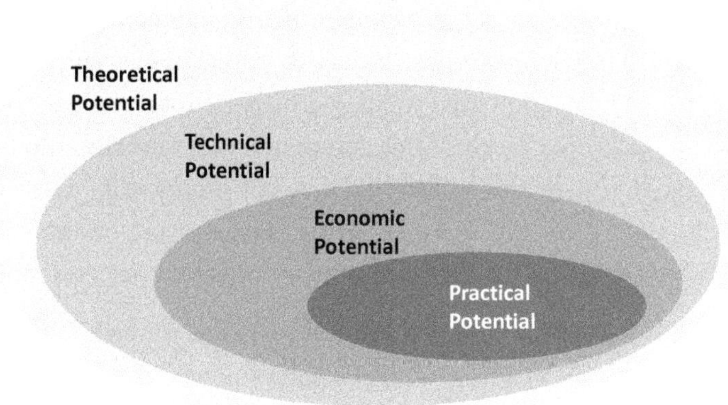

Figure 2.7.: The different concepts of demand response potentials (retraced from [211])

of 93GW and a load increase of 247GW, meaning around 10% of most EU country's peak load on average. The processes with the highest shares of average potential load reduction are pulp and paper (7%), steel (9%), cement (6%), commercial ventilation (15%), and refrigeration/freezers in private households (17%).

Contrary to this bottum-up approach, another study chose a top-down approach starting with the electricity consumptions of the three sectors households, industry, tertiary and disintegrating these into processes [208]. Thus also looking into the technical potential for demand response in Europe, their results indicate a load reduction potential of 52 GW, representing on average 9.4% of the peak load estimated by ENTSO-E for its 34 represented countries. Interestingly, these two studies, carried out independently but in parallel, reach similar conclusions.

Analysing the economic potential for Germany, *Bergaentzlé et al.* in 2013 [33] estimated a 3% cost reduction through load shedding of 3.5% from the evening peak at 7pm to the afternoon at 4pm. Apart from cost savings, this would avoid coal-fired peak generation and thus have a positive climate effect. For Southern Germany alone, based on a questionnaire among more than 300 companies, *Klobasa et al.* [133] estimates a peak reduction potential of around 1GW. This is a considerable technical potential compared with the total average consumption load of 14GW. A further result of this questionnaire is that the absolute amount of the envisaged cost reduction through demand response for these companies is more important than the share at their electricity cost budget. This study concept comes closest to the idea of a practical demand response potential.

In the U.S., however, where demand response has a much longer tradition, already today demand response plays a significant role in peak power management: in 2017 5.6% of peak demand were reduced by the activation of power flexibility through a variety of demand response schemes [73]. Since 2006, data of demand response activities have been monitored and published yearly [72].

Data Center Demand Response

With the growing role of data centers in business and society a discussion was started about the power consumption of data centers and how to increase energy efficiency. Recently, there has been a growing concern regarding the impact of data center operation on power grids not only because of the increasing 'weight' of individual data centers (exascale data centers are estimated to go way beyond 100MW) and the industry as a whole (see figure 2.8), but also with regards to vast power swings [198] that might be connected with operation due to a high difference between idle and full operational power. The SuperMuc I in LRZ, for instance, has an idle power of around 700kW, but can use up to 3.4MW under Linpack in turbo mode [186]. Sometimes these data centers are fully utilized with one huge batch job - if that ends unexpectedly this might lead to a voltage drop that threatens the local power quality.

Towards the end of the first decade of this millennium, demand response with data centers was brought up in the discussion. *Qureshi et al.* [171] were

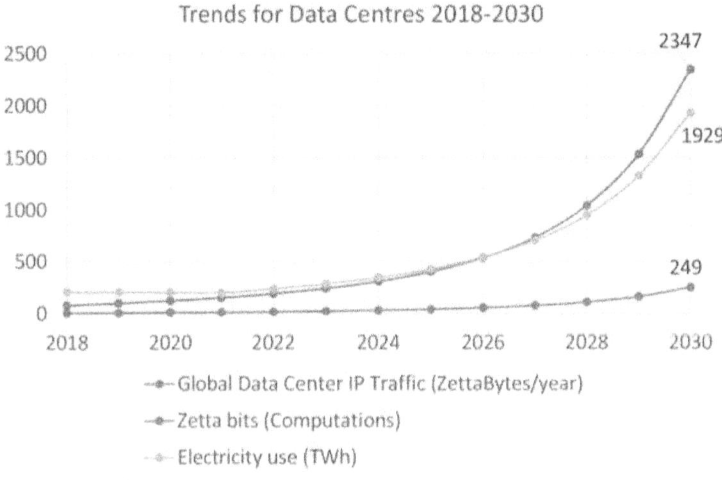

Figure 2.8.: Extrapolation of data center industry trends in traffic and data generation as well as power consumption [12]

among the first to give a theoretical foundation of capitalizing on geographical and temporal price differences of distributed data centers by routing an interactive load accordingly. Shortly after that, aiming at explicit demand response schemes, *Ghatikar et al.* [89] at Lawrence Berkeley National Laboratory (LBNL) explored general demand response opportunities for data centres, also performing experiments in four data centres. The results of above mentioned experiments are used as a basis for many research papers (e.g. [217, 144, 15]), sometimes as an assumption for data center loads' flexibility in settings other than LBNL's , e.g. [15].

A selection of the large body of research that addresses various issues considering data center demand response will be introduced in section 3.1. Issues relate to the power management strategies applied inside that data center, the requirements from both explicit and implicit power flex markets but also the physical integration into the smart grid. In order to deeply analyse demand response opportunities for data centers, chapter 4 will introduce a general model of a data center in the context of demand response and a modeling framework that addresses the three different potentials: technical, economic, and practical.

Barriers to Demand Response

The gap between the theoretical potential for demand response in an industry and its practical potential and implementation is due to a set of barriers to demand response which can be analysed alongside the four different categories of demand response potentials. This means that barriers to demand response relate to

- the gap between the theoretical and the technical potential, i.e. technical barriers as the lack of monitoring or communication technology implemented to suitable processes;
- the gap between the technical and the economic potential, i.e. economic barriers as high fees or low remunerations for demand response under the current market conditions;
- the gap between the economic and the practical potential, i.e. practical barriers as missing knowlegde, adversarial regulations or social norms.

The lack of the access to monitoring and ICT communication equipment is an issue that is continuously loosing importance due to a growing prevalence of corresponding equipment. An example is the roll-out of smart meters, that in Europe was initiated in 2014 and lead to a heterogeneous coverage ranging from nearly 100% in Finland, Sweden and Italy, to a very hesitant deployment in Germany of only 2-15% [170, p.50ff].

In general, the economic benefit of investment into demand response technologies and its implementation depends to a high degree on the value of electricity and the stiffness of the grid. Electricity cost consist of generation and distribution cost, fees and taxes, with varying degrees of their shares over Europe.

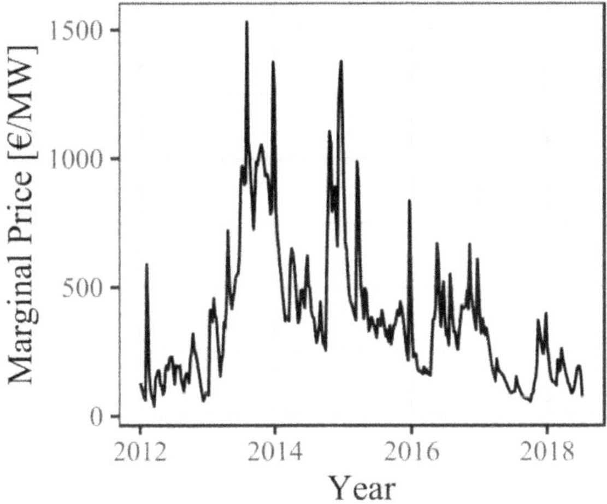

Figure 2.9.: The development of prices in the secondary reserve market from 2012-2018 [116]

In Germany, for instance, fees and taxes have about equal weight as electricity generation, grid management and sales cost [43]. Additionally, electricity generation and distribution cause so-called *'external cost'* that are not covered by the prices paid for consumption [150, 181]. For electricity provided by hard coal, for instance, the external cost exceed the private cost by a factor of 3 [150]. This implies that the electricity bill today underestimates the real value of electricity and therefore only very partially incentivizes the realization of power flexibility through demand response. This has implications for all prices related to generating and managing electricity, including of course, remunerations paid for reserve power.

Independent of the absolute level of the value of electricity, prices for power flexibility are extremely volatile as figure 2.9 shows for the positive week-day product in the secondary reserve market. Entering into costly prequalification procedures and finding that prices are not worth it reduces the economic potential of demand response.

Additional to pricing issues, major obstacles to the implementation of demand response schemes for all types of consumers are regulation and legislation [184], but also business models and social norm issues:

Even though the EU Commission launched the so-called 'Clean Energy Package' in 2016 that strengthens the role of demand response in Europe, in most member states the regulations are prohibiting the tapping of its potential [202, 135]. In some markets demand response as a power resource is not eligible for regulation, in some countries there are no power flex markets at all for explicit demand response; some markets are closed to aggregation and some have not clearly defined roles [123] and billing processes [65], or they are requiring very strict and costly prequalification procedures [137] as mentioned above. A regularly carried out study that assesses the market maturity for demand response in EU member states finds for 2017 that Germany is still lacking good access of demand flex resources to electricity markets [195]. One reason for this is that the reserve markets are aimed at large generation units and that network fees are still static.

Apart from these tangible issues, intangible barriers like general attitudes in society still prevent a higher adoption of demand response, e.g. a lack of awareness and information but also a status-quo bias, loss aversion and bounded rationality [137, 168].

3. Related Work

The core topic of the presented thesis is 'data center demand response'. This will cover the major part of this chapter, and section 3.1 is dedicated to organizing and explaining this research field.

Research that addresses modeling power flexibility in general is the other focus of this chapter as it provides insights for the presented modeling framework for data center demand response from a more general perspective. Work in this rather small research area is discussed in section 3.2.

A different strain of research is *data center energy efficiency*; it is interrelated with data center demand response, because in many cases, power management strategies have an impact on data center performance and thus on energy efficiency. This very large research area is not elaborated further in this thesis; the focus of the work remains the *temporary shift of power consumption*, not the reduction of energy consumption. Likewise *balancing the power demand of data centers with intermittent renewable power supply* meanwhile is a widely-researched area. The latter is also not explored explicitly here as it primarily focuses on creating a physical match between data center power demand and REN supply, *independently of any demand response program* issued by an actor in the energy system.

3.1. Data Center Demand Response

One of the first works about power adaptive data centers was *Qureshi et al. in 2009* [171]. They became aware of the opportunities of regionally and temporally different prices and simulated the effects of rerouting network traffic.

For their simulations they used interactive workload data traces of 9 locations of the content delivery network (CDN) Akamai employing the very simple, but efficient utilization based power model of [71]. They concluded that a data center like Akamai could easily save 2% of their aggregated utility bills without compromising on QoS or increasing bandwidth and up to 30% if their power demand were fully elastic, i.e. independent on QoS. As a next step, optimization approaches capitalizing on basically the same scenario appeared: In *2010 Rao et al.* [173] used a queuing based approach to optimize cost in a mixed integer linear problem formulation, assuming both job arrival and servicing rate. They corroborated the findings of *Qureshi et al.*, calculating a cost reduction between 17-30%.

After these first endeavors to analyse the power flexibility of data centers in an implicit demand response scenario, general introductive papers emerged as for instance [89, 88, 127, 35, 30, 217]. As mentioned, *Ghatikar et al. 2012* at LBNL in California [88] executed a set of experiments: they explored the impact of different power management strategies in three university data centers and one commercial data center. For some specific cases they measured 25% of load reduction on data center level and 10-12% reduction on building level.

Meanwhile, a large body of modeling work exists in this area[1], and the here referenced literature is just the selection of the most relevant works in the context of the discussed research questions. Important is therefore research that aims at providing a general concept of demand response opportunities of data centers. Concrete scenarios, however, are the groundwork of the concrete instance of the modeling framework, so that selected papers of this field are also introduced.

This section is mainly organized according to the method applied, either optimization or a simulation approach analysing the outcome of a set of different scenarios. Other important criteria are the power management strategy/ies applied, the types of power flex markets targeted, the optimization criterion

[1]A google scholar search on March 10th, 2020, of the terms 'data center' and 'demand response' produced 6,190 hits

and the question if and how SLA cost are integrated. In order to take account of all these criteria, the works will be summarized in tables at the end of each section.

3.1.1. Optimizing Data Center Demand Response

The First Phase

In *2011 Liu et al.* [143] introduced the classical concept of geographical load balancing using geographical price differences as incentives to adapt scheduling and thus change the load. Comparably to *Rao et al. 2010* [173] they applied a queuing based model to inject traffic data into a cost function that depends on the number of active servers, as a representative for the power consumption, on regionally differentiated prices, and on the traffic arrival rate. They introduce delay cost based on the queuing and the routing delay into the optimization problem that aims at choosing the routing policy and determine the number of active servers that minimizes the sum of energy and delay cost.

This basic problem setup, i.e. a federation of data centers like internet data centers (IDC) or CDN with interactive workload that can be (re-)scheduled geographically was re-used by a high number of later optimization research papers, some of which are referenced here. *Wang et al. 2012* [214] and 2013 [215] use this setting with an approach of moving virtual machines (VMs) instead of routing requests. [214] models emergency demand response as a version of explicit demand response where the reward is based on different 'locational' marginal prices (LMP), which are unknown in advance. They set up a cost minimization mixed integer linear problem which takes into account SLA cost of reduced QoS during migration and is constrained by a threshold profit which must be achieved. In [215] *Wang et al. 2013* the setting is changed insofar as they add more detail to the time-based impacts of migration and integrate the risk that the expected reward is lower than anticipated.

Contrary to these, *Li et al. 2013* [140] apply migration to batch workloads in a data center federation using dynamic prices which are tied to the intake of renewable energy sources so that the benefit is not only economic but also ecological. They develop two interdependent models, one of which represents data center cost including the extra migration energy cost and the other determining the renewable-based geographically differentiated price.

Starting with this, the idea of explicit demand response was discussed more intensely, in different data center settings, and using various adaptation strategies. *Ghamkari & Mohsenian-Rad 2012*, for instance, present a profit maximization framework, viewing the rewards from the participation in ancillary services as an alternative way of benefit generation [86] at the expense of creating SLA cost. Using a queuing based approach they analyse the behaviour of one data center facing adaptation requests which include a volume dependent compensation function. To this the data center reacts via consolidating workload on few servers and shutting down unused servers. This commonly modeled power management strategy is often disputed as it contradicts general data center policy to keep all servers running independent on the utilization [91].

Similarly, *Ghasemi-Gol et al. 2014* [87] develop a load shedding approach via switching on/off servers to adapt to both regulation requests and hourly changing prices on the day-ahead market in a scenario comparable to [86]. Contrary to the latter, they minimize the total electricity cost, substracting the rewards received through the participation in an ancillary services scheme. Furthermore, they do not take into account SLA cost. Using trace-based inter-arrival times the model of [87] achieves an energy cost reduction of up to 13% for the case of participating in ancillary services compared to dynamic prices. *Mahmud et al. 2013* [149], also focusing on server consolidation and shut-down, are one of the few that view data centers as price makers in an implicit demand response setup, not price takers due their huge power consumption (assuming 50MW). Controlling the number of active servers, they model the price that the data center predicts based on a linear regression of historic data and a feedback activity on that price. In this assumed setting they estimate a cost reduction of around 2%.

Very differently from that, *Yao et al. 2014* [222] envision a scenario where the data center does not need to adapt their workload, but reacts via 'smart' charging or discharging of batteries whenever the dynamic utility energy prices are specifically low or high. Modeling the server power consumption utilization based, they derive an energy cost minimization model considering constraints from both latency and battery models.

Colocation Demand Response

At the end of this first phase of modeling data center demand response, a new set of papers appeared that turned attention to the fact that the thitherto utilized workload power management models were inapplicable in a major number of cases where the data center operator is not allowed to touch the workload: the case of colocation service providers, data centers that rent out space to their customers who run their own workload on dedicated servers. Thus the challenge arose to overcome the so-called 'split incentive', i.e. the situation that the colocation service provider is incentivized to adapt power under demand response schemes whereas under the predominant business models the tenants are not.

This was first explained and modeled by *Ren & Islam 2014* [175]. They present an incentive mechanism for tenants based on a reverse auctioning process in order for them to adapt their demand whenever the colocation provider receives a signal to reduce as much power as possible. One assumption is an extremely low utilization rate in colocation data centers which was has been backed by data many times, e.g. by [91], and allows tenants to consolidate workload and shut down idle servers. Data center power demand is modeled through the number of active servers. Arrival and service rates are utilized to model delay, with different classes of delay-tolerance. In a simulated data center with 3 tenants, involving data traces from hotmail and Wikipedia, the authors show that the tenants' power demand can be decreased by 50% without compromising on assumed delay constraints. This general approach has been studied frequently since, always capitalizing on the idea of non-intrusive methods to stimulate the collaboration of tenants.

Ahmed et al. 2015 [4], using a similar modeling setup and power management strategy as in their former work [175], focus on the novel type of contract needed between the tenants and the colocation provider for the case of emergency demand response where the colocation provider must abide to the power reduction signal. In order not to incur penalties the data center needs to provide the gap between the target power consumption and the power flex contribution from its tenants by turning on a costly diesel generator. The paper develops algorithms that balance the tenants' delay costs and the colocation provider's generator cost with the demand response renumeration under the uncertainty that the colocation provider is not informed about the tenants' power reduction potential. *Tran et al. 2016* [205] aim at minimizing the tenants' adaptation cost accrued proportionally to the delay created assuming two different types of tenants: price-takers and strategically bidding tenants who both react to incentives by reducing the number of active servers. This is optimized under the constraint that the colocation provider again must fulfill the power reduction request issued from the grid provider.

A different area of demand response entailing a different strategy is suggested by *Islam et al. 2015* [114]. They set up the scenario of a colocation data center with dynamic cooling demand and intermittent on-site PV power generation in an implicit demand response scheme with time-varying prices including high peak power prices. This is used as an incentive for requesting the tenants' collaboration to avoid increasing peak power. As in [4] the colocation operator needs to take into account the unsure collaboration effort of the tenants. In this scenario the colocation service providers' overall cost is minimized, made up of energy and power costs as well as the rewards paid to the tenants. The objective is to determine the reward that needs to be offered to the tenants. Evaluating the resulting algorithm leads to a cost reduction for the colocation operator of 27%; tenants can reduce cost by up to 15%. This idea of profit sharing goes into the same direction as the research introducing 'GreenSLAs' [209, 130, 3].

Later, *Islam et al. 2016* [115] introduce to the topic of oversubscription in the context of colocation data center demand response. This means the phenomenon that colocation providers rent out more power than contracted with their utility, knowing very well that tenants tend to under-utilize the power infrastructure due to a low server utilization rate. Thus implementing an overall power cap, [115] work towards minimizing the tenants' SLA cost who can adapt their power by tuning the CPU frequency and who issue individual supply bidding functions.

Temporal Workload Management

A different scenario and research area is the temporal scheduling of jobs which has a long history beyond the demand response use case. In *2012 Liu et al.* introduced demand response to the temporal scheduling topic by integrating renewable supply, energy storage, dynamic pricing and dynamic cooling demand into workload scheduling algorithms [141] . They focus on one data center that aims at minimizing all cost associated with job scheduling: the energy bill impacted by dynamic prices and the cost of lost revenue due to the delay-tolerant batch job part of the workload that is not executed by a specific point in time. Assuming that interactive workload needs to be serviced instantly, for each timeslot they generate a schedule for the batch jobs and the energy storage usage that takes into account dynamic cooling, prices and the deadlines from the interactive service. They do this first in a generic model without instantiating power and delay functions and for the evaluation apply the linear, utilization based power model developed by [71] combined with a queuing delay calculation model.

Temporal workload shifting has been explored widely since then, e.g. lately by *Tipantuña and Hesselbach 2018* [203], *Jiang et al. 2018* [119], and *Bahrami et al. 2017* [19]. *Tipantuña and Hesselbach 2018* [203] offer a scheduling approach of reducing power demand in a demand response event by minimizing the 'residual power' which is the difference between the planned power profile and the available power issued by a grid operator. They implement this in a data center with a batch workload using a combinatorial scheduling algorithm that computes all potential time-shift combinations of all services. Apart from the high computational load, the drawback of this approach is that whenever the residual power threatens to become negative, specific jobs are evicted. *Jiang et al. 2018* [119], in an implicit demand response setting with the aim of avoiding peak power cost suggest a scheduling algorithm that minimizes the power consumption of servers over time. They model a utilization based server power function for a cluster of heterogeneous servers. Each job has a specific deadline and resource requirements. This information is used in a non-linear integer programming problem which is solved by decomposing it into a temporal job scheduling and a 'spatial' task assignment sub-problem. Considering a time horizon of 4 hours and 400 Map and Mapreduce jobs lasting up to 250 seconds with deadlines up to more than 50 times the job duration, they show that both peak power and energy consumption are reduced compared to alternative scheduling algorithms.

Bahrami et al. 2017 [19] address the scheduling problem using an alternative modeling approach: they construct a game theoretical model representing the situation of a data center strategically choosing a utility and at the same time a scheduling strategy in order to minimize their electricity cost. In this case, however, the dynamic prices offered by the utility depend on both the demand of this utility - which itself depends on its customers' demands - and the demand of all other utilities. This implies that the scheduling decisions of the current data center, which influence their choice of utility, depends on the scheduling decisions and power demands of the other data centers in the eco-system.

Other Power Management Strategies

Dynamic Voltage and Frequency Scaling (DVFS), typically realized as scaling the CPU frequency, is a power management strategy that is often used in the context of implicit demand response, either to comply with time-varying prices or to prevent peak power cost. An example for this is *Shoukourian et al. 2015* [185] who explore a 'software defined power cap' in order to avoid peak charges, at the same time capitalizing on the slightly different power consumptions of officially identical nodes in the high performance setting of the German Super-Muc data center. They analyse the details of the hardware setup in order to find the most efficient and effective combination of frequency, node and application which still respects the power cap minimizing the overall energy cost including the power charge component.

The power management strategies implemented in the context of demand response nearly exclusively abstract from the applications which are executed by the data centers. In 2013 a European project, All4Green [29] introduced the idea of a middleware software that adapts specific QoS characteristics in order to comply with event-based power caps and elaborated a proof-of-concept using experiments at the European HPlabs. *Xu & Li 2014* [221] explore a comparable approach minimizing the energy and power consumption of a data center applying 'partial execution'. This means that web crawling service as e.g. search applications are halted a little prematurely. While still delivering sufficient results they are avoiding over-proportionally increasing energy consumption needed in order to produce 'final' results. They achieve this, like All4Green, by tuning the SLA according to the current situation under a time to completion constraint. Using Wikipedia request traces and a simulated data center setting they show that their algorithm can reduce peak demand by 12.17%.

Applying a Set of Power Management Strategies

All models described until here have in common that the adaptation of the data center power profile is achieved by applying one power adaptation strategy. To the best of the author's knowledge, this was changed by *Liu et al. in 2013* [145]. They use temporal workload shifting as well as turning on backup generators and consuming local REN as power adaptation strategies to react to uncertain events of 'critical peak prices' (CPP) where the price is known in advance, however the time-slot for which the utility broadcasts this price can only be assessed. Minimizing energy, power, fuel and utility cost under the uncertainty of the events they develop algorithms that - fairly robust to prediction errors - provide cost savings of up to 40%. One year later, the team around Zhenhua Liu, *Liu et al. 2014*, compared the system wide savings created through data center demand response with the cost of an equally sized storage system [144]. As a metric for the effectiveness of both technologies they use the improvement of voltage violations. Assuming a 20MW data center with 20% power flexibility they calculate that this can replace a 0.67MWh battery system. Furthermore, they suggest novel, prediction-based explicit demand response programs targeted specifically at data centers and evaluate these suggestions through a model minimizing system-wide curtailment cost.

Le et al. 2016 [138] focus on integrating capacity planning and operating, i.e. minimizing CAPEX and OPEX cost by jointly analysing requirements for both. In order to use this general approach for demand response schemes, the authors rely on both scheduling the batch part of the mixed workload in a simulated data center and ramping up the diesel generator when the contribution from batch scheduling is either too low or infeasible due to deadline constraints. In an experiment with HP's Net-zero Energy Data Center the study simulates a set of power flex markets like a time-of-use (TOU) tariff[2], CPP and the spinning reserve scheme where participants are rewarded based on pre-defined rates, but must reduce their power consumption after a signal. In the context of the spinning reserve scheme, the emulated Net-zero Energy Data Center can reduce its power during the event by 30%. In this scenario workload scheduling plays the most important role, contrary to the CPP scenario, where the adaptation is achieved mostly by using the Diesel generator. However, this is due to the temporal workload distribution of the data trace, as the original data center's power demand is much higher in the CPP event hour than in the spinning reserve

[2]This is a tariff with time-varying prices for a specific, low number of blocks

event hour. This detail shows that both adaptation processes and results depend heavily on the parameter configuration.

In the model of *Cupelli et al. 2018* [60] a data center engages in dynamic pricing or in an event based explicit power flex market using three different strategies: the data center can schedule the workload at different times, it can change the cooling set-point and additionally charge or discharge batteries. The approach aims at minimizing the difference between planned and target power profile, comparable to [203], but contrary to the latter, they model the thermal characteristics of a specific data center testbed to which end the model processes a high number of physical data. *Chen et al. 2019* [52] present EnergyQare, an approach that includes both a bidding strategy for the provision of load-following, constant regulation services and a policy that executes a set of different server activities at runtime. Taking into account transition times, sleeping servers are woken up, idling servers are put to sleep or assigned to jobs, and finally the CPU frequency can be changed. Using these power management techniques and respecting QoS, EnergyQare determines the optimal combination of average power consumption and reserve power provision at each time step. In a general data center scenario [52] demonstrate that it can provide 50% of their average power consumption as reserve power reducing electricity cost by 44%. The results, however, are highly dependent on the deadline parameters but do not include a sensitivity analysis.

In another setting the electricity bill of a data center depends on its average power consumption and on the reserve power that it provides to a fast demand response scheme with signal updates every couple of seconds. In this scenario *Zhang et al. 2019* [224] develop a cost minimization model where the data center uses both a scheduling strategy and DVFS. They minimize total power cost, which is the sum of the energy bill and a penalty in case of provision failure, less the benefit from the reserve power activation. Defining a set of different job types with respective QoS constraints and specific queues the model assigns different weights to each job type so that the levels of average power consumption and reserve power are optimized. The suggested algorithm reduces the total cost by 14-51%.

Nasiriani et al. 2018 [157] apply a game theoretic approach to model a so-called 'differential pricing' scheme for cloud data centers engaging in an implicit demand response scheme. 'Differential pricing' is based on the observation that different market participants display different price elasticities, i.e. the percentaged reaction of demand in proportion to the percentaged price change. Due to this observation the authors price cloud data center customers in accordance with their price elasticities whenever the cloud provider aims to adapt to dynamic wholesale electricity prices. The tenants then (dis)charge virtual batteries or drop workload thus accruing SLA cost proportionally. The impact of this collaboration maximizes the overall system benefit, leading to both an increased profit on the data center side (+31%) and a higher tenant utility (+18%).

Modeling Frameworks for Data Center Demand Response

A lot of research on data center demand response starts from a specific power management strategy or a set of strategies in a specific data center and a specific power flex market setting. This leads, however, to distorted results from generalization. Some approaches may exaggerate benefits when the respective power management strategy, although very beneficial in the referenced setting, cannot be applied in the majority of scenarios. On the other hand, benefits may be belittled when focusing on one strategy where a set of strategies could be applied. Therefore models are needed that aim at identifying the total potential of data center demand response by analyzing all sources of power flexibility and evaluate these on both implicit and explicit power flex markets.

To the best of the author's knowledge, there are but two research groups that are working on this endeavor: *Wang et al. 2014* [213] develop a 'hierarchical framework for data center power cost optimization'. They start from the observation that there is a high complexity both on the part of *'IT knobs'* to control the data center power profile and on the part of the power flex markets.

They analyze data center flexibility as being the result of two basic phenomena: workload related activities either reduce or postpone some portion of the power demand or they do both at the same time. Power flex markets in general, from the point of view of the data center exhibit either peak prices or time-varying prices or a combination thereof. A comparable, more detailed analysis of the power flex markets, is offered by a former work of the author of this thesis, *Kirpes & Klingert 2016* [124], who differentiate 6 power flex market pricing components. Using their observation *Wang et al.* develop an optimization framework where they minimize total cost of electricity plus any revenue loss, which is a linear non-decreasing function of delay, under capacity constraints. The off-line version of the problem is approximated using an algorithm for dropping demand and evaluated using three real world demand traces from MediaServer, Google, and Facebook.

In the context of the EU research project Geyser *Cioara et al. 2016* [54] and *Cioara et al. 2019* [55] analyze all types of power flexibilities in the data center, not only workload related ones. The first work focuses on the description of the Geyser market places consisting of two versions of an auction-based energy market place and a merit-order based ancillary services market place. Additionally, they present a non-linear programming problem minimizing both the difference between the adapted power demand and the target power demand *and* between the adapted power demand and the original power demand, initiated by a demand response signal. The power demand in the objective function depends on the workload, on cooling and on both a thermal storage and a battery. Interestingly, the authors do not base the power demand of a component on its origin, e.g. jobs submitted, but rather the demand of one time-slot depends on its historical development and, in the case of workload power, on shifting ratios.

The cooling related power management strategy is not evoked by the manipulation of the cooling set-point, but by the charging or decharging of a thermal power storage. Regarding explicit demand response the evaluation presents solutions for some specific events, as e.g. for an ancillary service request due to an unforeseen demand peak in the local electricity grid where the data center reacts through reducing its power demand by 32%. In this first version of the model there are neither prices nor cost. In the later work building on a similar optimization problem, contrary to the first version, *Cioara et al. 2019* [55] for the case of geographical workload shifting account for relocation cost and for associated delay cost. However, as in that work temporal shifting is not included, delay cost for extending the time of sojourn of jobs in the system are still not integrated.

To sum up, even though the authors state that they include in 'a holistic and integrated manner all major DC [data center] components that consume electrical energy' [55, p.3], on the theoretical part of the approach they model concrete power management strategies instead of formulating a high level model that leaves room for further instantiation of basic activities, as in *Wang et al. 2014*, who unfortunately are restricted to workload-based power management. This means that *Cioara et al.* do not fully embrace the challenge that they had set themselves.

Table 3.1 summarizes the main characteristics of the research presented in this section.

3.1.2. Simulating Data Center Demand Response

A different method of evaluating the impact of data center demand response on both the data center and the overall eco-system is *simulation*. Instead of striving for an optimum, simulation analyses a set of *different optional 'futures'* based on a common structure but different, controlled parameter settings. The modeling framework for data center demand response presented in this thesis is evaluated through simulation. Therefore, a small set of simulation approaches in this area are presented in this section.

Simulation of Software or Server Related Power Management Strategies

The first work by *Qureshi et al. 2009* [171] was introduced at the very beginning of this section. It capitalizes on the regional and temporal price differences in geographically distributed data centers and addresses the concept of implicit demand response by rerouting traffic.

In *2012, Aikema et al.* [6] presented a work that implements temporal shifting of batch workload and the manipulation of servers' performance states (P-states; the combination of frequency and voltage pairs) as techniques to enable the participation of data centers in the ancillary services market. Using the scenario of the ancillary service products sought for by New York Independent System Operator (NYISO), they see the highest revenue opportunity through services where the participant is rewarded for the general offer of power adaption, even though it might be activated only partially. The data center simulator is composed of a pricing module that contains any pricing information, a workload event generator that decides on workload related activities, an ancillary event generator that starts from the event signal from the grid operator, and a cluster controller that orchestrates all activities. The server power model is frequency based; upon an ancillary service request, any running tasks are assumed to be suspended within a 10 sec reaction time, and new tasks are not admitted until the end of the event. This strategy neither takes into account the required adaption sizing nor associated SLA cost. Alternatively the authors discuss the option of data centers using their backup generators for ancillary services events, which seems a non-disruptive method at first glance, but in reality is rejeced by data center operators. Injecting data traces of the parallel workloads archive and using ancillary services market data from NYISO, the authors find amongst others that they can reduce the electricity cost of the simulated data center taking part in the emergency demand response scheme by up to 50% not only implementing the workload related strategies, but also activating the backup generator.

Table 3.1.: Optimization research. EX/IM: explicit/implicit DR, TTC: time to completion, DL/D: deadline/delay

Authors	Strategy/ies	DR Area	Objective	SLA cost?
[173] Rao 2010	geogr. scheduling	IM (reg.& dyn.prices)	min (elect. cost)	QoS constr.
[143] Liu 2011	geogr. scheduling	IM (reg.&REN-dyn. prices)	min (elect. & delay cost)	yes
[141] Liu 2012	temp. scheduling	IM (dynamic pricing)	min (elect. cost & revenue loss)	DL constr.
[214] Wang 2012	geogr. VM migration	EX (emerg. DR®. prices)	min (cost w. profit constraint)	yes
[86] Ghamkhari 2012	serv. cons., shut down	EX (events)&IM (dyn.pr.)	max (profit: DR reward - cost)	yes
[149] Mahmud 2013	serv. cons., shut down	IM (dyn., feedbacked prices)	min (elect. & delay cost)	yes
[140] Li 2013	geogr. migration of batch jobs	IM (REN-based dyn. prices)	min (electr. cost incl. migration)	no
[215] Wang 2013	geogr. VM migration	EX (dispatch & reg. prices)	max (profit: DRreward-cost-PPF)	ass: no D
[145] Liu 2013	temp. scheduling&generator integr.	IM (CCP)	min (cost: energy, power, fuel)	DL constr.
[175] Ren 2014	tenants' serv. cons., shut down	EX (reduction max)	max (tentants' energy reduction)	D constr.
[144] Liu 2014	unspecified	EX (bidding strategy)	min (DR cost incl. PPF)	no
[222] Yao 2014	battery management	IM (reg.& dyn.prices)	min (elect. cost)	DL constr.
[87] Ghasemi-Gol 2014	serv. cons., shut down	EX (ancil.serv.)& IM (dyn.pr.)	min (elect. cost-ancil.serv.reward)	delay constr.
[221] Xu et al. 2014	partial execution	IM (peak charge)	min (energy&power consumpt.)	TTC constr.
[213] Wang 2014	WL delay &dropping	IM (dyn. prices)	min (elect. cost&revenue loss)	no
[114] Islam 2015	DVFS at tentants	IM (peak charge)	min (elect. cost&rewards paid)	D constr.
[4] Ahmed 2015	tenants' serv. cons., shut down	EX (energy)& IM (peak ch.)	min (tenants' load reduct. cost)	yes
[185] Shoukourian 2015	DVFS	IM (power cap)	min (energy cost)	no
[54] Cioara 2016	temp. sched.&cooling&battery	EX (events)& IM (day ahead)	min (power consumption)	DL constr.
[138] Le 2016	temp. scheduling&generator integr.	EX (spinning)& IM (dyn.pr.)	min (elect. cost: CAPEX&OPEX)	DL constr.
[205] Tran 2016	tenants' serv. cons., shut down	EX (required reduction)	min (tenants' load reduct. cost)	yes
[115] Islam et al. 2016	tenants' DVFS	IM (peak charge)	min (tenants' QoS cost)	yes
[157] Nasiriani 2018	tenants' WL dropping&battery mgmt	IM (dynamic pricing)	max (profit & tenants' utility)	yes
[20] Bahrami 2018	temp. scheduling	IM (dynamic pricing)	min (elect. cost and PPF)	D constr.
[203] Tipantuña 2018	temp. scheduling	EX (synthetic events)	min (supplied power - DC power)	no
[60] Cupelli 2018	temp. scheduling&cooling&battery mg.	EX (target load profile), IM	min (realized-target power profile)	yes
[119] Jiang 2018	temp. scheduling	IM (peak charge)	min (server power through time)	DL constr.
[52] Chen 2019	serv. cons., shut down & DVFS	EX (reg. service requests)	min (elect. cost-regul.reward+PPF)	QoS constr.
[224] Zhang 2019	temp. scheduling, DVFS	EX (reg. service requests)	min (elect. cost-regul.reward+PPF)	QoS guaran.
[55] Cioara 2019	temp.sched.&migration&cool.&batt.mg	EX (target load profile)	min (realized-target power profile)	'yes'

Chen et al. 2014 [51] view data center demand response from an electrical engineering point of view, analysing the impact on the grid frequency; the nature of the regulation service applied is then determined in dependence of the total deviation from the nominal frequency of - in the U.S. - 60Hz. The data center reacts to ancillary service requests through either temporally shifting or shedding the workload which is comparable to the view of *Wang et al.* [213] who understand adaptation as either shifting, shedding or combining the two. These strategies are enacted through manipulating server consumption by applying DVFS or putting them into a sleep mode from which they can be awoken creating a time and power penalty which is taken into account as a delay constraint. Using artificial traces based on a poisson process and a delay constraint where at least 95% of the jobs need to be executed at maximum in twice the minimum time to completion the authors simulate the participation of a 1000 server data center in different regulation services. As a result, assuming a 'typical' server utilization rate, the simulated data center can reduce their cost by 59.9% by participating in a regulation service scheme. Unfortunately it is not clear, to which extent the set of data center and workload assumptions represents the data center landscape. This work was obviously preparatory for the development of EnergyQare 5 years later [52] (see section 3.1.1).

In a co-simulation approach that links data center activities to a smart grid model *Mäsker et al. 2016* [151] simulate the result of a set of different batch workload scheduling algorithms on the electricity cost assuming that local electricity prices are proportional to the local REN generation. The two main schedulers analysed in this work are the so-called 'green scheduler' and 'enhanced green scheduler'. The difference between them is the level of certainty: whereas the green scheduler takes into account current REN forecast information in order to schedule according to expected REN based prices, the enhanced version fakes complete knowledge and thus serves as a benchmark for the reliability of the REN forecast information. With HPC data traces in a very rudimentary simulated data center environment and a deadline policy which restricts the waiting time for a job to 4 days, the green scheduler results in an improvement of REN energy usage of 42.7% vs. 26% using the FIFO scheduler. The enhanced green scheduler with full knowledge of the imminent prices reaches 46.3% which is only slightly better than the forecast based scheduling approach.

Ahmed et al. 2017 [5] also analyse the impact of different batch scheduling strategies, but contrary to [151] without a co-simulation. As [151] they assume a FIFO scheduler as the baseline situation, switching to an HPC-DR scheduler that implements job evictions of active jobs during demand response events. These, however, are only enacted in case the power savings achieved through an optimization of frequencies for the affected jobs, is not sufficient to stay within the targeted power cap. Consequently the power model for a job running on a specific processor is frequency based and assessed through a regression for the utilized small set of applications emulating three different HPC systems. As [6] and many others, also *Ahmed et al. 2017* use a workload trace from the parallel workloads archive, i.e. a different one than the ones used to create the power models. Assuming demand response events happening in 20-80% of the simulation timeslots where the power cap is suddenly reduced to 80% of original peak power, the authors find that the jobs' time to completion increases between 4.4-21.0%. Unfortunately there is no information about the number of jobs evicted.

Fridgen et al. 2017 [79], like the very first papers in the area, use the setting of distributed data centers computing an interactive workload in order to simulate geographical scheduling. In this case, however, the incentive to migrate workload is not dynamic pricing but the participation at event-based demand response schemes. The example implementation envisions two data centers situated in two balancing power markets. Similar to the evaluation simulation presented in this theses, the bidding procedure into the power flex market takes place outside the simulation, i.e. the bids have been placed and accepted and must be implemented in case of activation; the reward is paid independently of activation. As soon as an activation of positive balancing power takes place, the 'receiving' data center increases the capacity in order to assimilate the workload from the other data center, and then the central controller dispatches less workload to the 'giving' data center and more to the 'receiving' data center If necessary the 'giving' data center reduces power further, e.g. by switching off idling servers. The simulation does not specifically model server power, but uses an energy efficiency parameter that determines which power in relation to the current capacity is necessary to compute one request. The evaluation reflects a scenario of two 50MW Google data centers envisioned in Germany and Finland, assuming that both data centers can provide 15 MW. With regards to the economic benefit of the data center, using a lower and an upper bound of a positive balancing power price, the simulation assesses a net income of €1.4m for the upper and a little less than a million € for the lower bound accordingly. This simulation set-up represents a very specific situation using data from the German and the Finnish power flex markets and anylizing the details of power exchange; however, on the part of the data center the model remains superficial, so that in theory the power could be provided by any other industry.

Simulation of Physical Infrastructure Related or Mixed Power Management Strategies

As for the case of optimization, some simulation approaches implement more than one power management strategy, however none of them apply a simulation on job level. *Tang et al. 2013* [200], for instance, use a very simple, linear-regression based model of the workload and cooling demand in a small 300kW university data center that does not compute critical tasks. For an assumed demand response event they manipulate the cooling set-point and the utilization rate of servers; in essence this means that workload is being dropped, and neither deadlines nor SLA cost are applied. The workload data traces in the form of utilization rates on servers are partitioned into low, medium and high utilization rate periods so that the reduction potential for each period can be analysed separately. The authors are also taking into account that the cooling infrastructure scales less with server power in low utilization periods than in others. In order to activate more power than achievable through dropping workload, in times of demand response events, the data center could additionally increase the cooling set-point from regular 26°C to 35°C. In high utilization periods, this data center could thus reduce their power demand by 30%. This simulation has hardly any external validity, as it is targeted solely at the said data center. It has however the high advantage of using real data of a real data center, so that workload data and power data are connected and internally valid.

In *2014 Aksanli & Rosing* [8] proposed a model for a data center to offer regulation services using a data center's batteries. The general setting is a data center that already employs their batteries in order to avoid power peaks and thus increased power charges. In the case of regulation services, additionally the batteries are used to deliver positive or negative regulation power without imposing any disruptive activities on the data center workload operation. Their model is based on a data center's average power consumption which can then be increased or decreased by a potential contribution to regulation services. From this they calculate a lower bound for the regulation reward and an upper bound for the contracted regulation power that they have to deliver. They rely on a utilization based server power model to determine data center power demand and connect it with a battery model where capacity and degradation cost are integrated. As most simulation research, also the model of *Aksanli & Rosing* targets a very specific case.

Also *Arnone et al. 2017* [15] focus on non-IT, non-workload related power management in a data center to simulate the physical interaction of a data center and the power grid in the context of primary and secondary reserve power schemes. What singles out this work from others is the utilized data: contrary to other research (with the exception of [200]) this paper uses data from a real data center and data from the real distribution power grid in Italy where the data center in located. The simulation is not economic-based, but physical, assessing

Table 3.2.: Simulation research. EX/IM: explicit/implicit demand response, TTC: time to completion

Authors	Strategy/ies	DR Area	SLA cost?
[171] Qureshi 2009	geogr. scheduling	IM (reg.&dyn. prices)	QoS constr.
[7] Aikema 2013	temp. shifting, DVFS	EX (ancil. services)	no
[200] Tang 2013	WL dropping, cooling mgmt.	EX (load reduction)	no
[8] Akansli 2014	battery management	EX (peak mgmt.)	n.a.
[51] Chen 2014	serv.cons., shut down, DVFS	EX (reg. serv.)IM(peak)	QoS constr.
[151] Maesker 2016	temp. scheduling	IM (REN-dyn. prices)	TTC constr.
[5] Ahmed 2017	WL dropping, DVFS	EX (random events)	TTC monit.
[79] Fridgen 2017	geogr. scheduling	IM (bidding strategy)	no
[15] Arnone 2017	cooling, battery mgmt.	EX (frequency control)	no

how data center reactions in the case of power flex market signals impact both the data center and the distribution grid. For an event of primary reserve power the techniques employed are parameter manipulations of the lighting and the cooling demand. Additionally, the power demand in the offices is reduced by either a 5% or a 10% , and the data center can ramp up their backup generator. Secondary reserve power is provided solely by switching on the data center's back-up generation. The authors simulate different situations of calamities in the distribution grid where the data center should respond with said activities, and they show that this can be accomplished. However, no cost or benefit issues are taken into account; this is an exclusively physical simulation.

Table 3.2 sums up the main characteristics of the simulation research papers referenced in this section.

3.2. Modeling Flexibility in General

There may be some characteristics of demand side flexibility which are independent of the industry of the supplier. Therefore, in order to create a framework for data center demand response, additionally to research in that area, also papers that contemplate power flexibility in general need to be analysed.

Niedermeier et al. 2016 [158] discuss the suitability of integrated power planning for an unspecified load to continuously adapt to the intermittency of the electricity supply by RENs. The authors start from the scenario of an omniscient planner who, due to the involvement of different entities, needs to split the overall planning task into creating a power plan, i.e. a target power profile, and scheduling the load accordingly. The flexibility of this load is modeled alongside the three characteristics of demand response events: frequency of changes, size of changes and notification time. Based on this the intake of RENs is maximized for a specific power plan under the constraint of cost which depend on above mentioned characteristics of a demand response scheme. They evaluate their approach using both data centers and electric vehicles as examples.

A different approach is offered by *Barth et al. 2018* [26], who try to capture all possible features of flexible loads in a linear optimization problem. Contrary to [158] they focus on the characteristics of the flexibility of loads instead of the cost incurred in general by determinants of demand response schemes. The basis of their model are jobs of any kind, be it computational tasks or production tasks of any industrial process. These jobs have a set of different attributes as duration, deadlines, resources needed, interdependency with other jobs or ramping requirements, and the flexibility of these jobs is defined as 'slack'. The authors formulate a mixed-integer linear program that minimizes the difference between the locally produced electricity and the power demand, using said attributes of the 'jobs' as constraints.

An EU research community around the FP7 project MIRABEL[3] developed the concept of so-called 'flex-objects' which are the combinations of a power profile of an electrical production or consumption process and the associated time-frame of starting this process. The power profile of the process consists of time 'slices' each of which contains a minimum and a maximum power consumption/production. The flexibility inherent in a flex-object is defined as the product of time and amount flexibility. All this is explained in detail by *Šikšnys et al. 2015* [190] and *Šikšnys and Pedersen 2016* [189]. The main problems are

[3] `https://goflex-community.eu/Projects.html`, accessed 08/06/2020

the aggregation of flex-objects into larger, aggregated 'macro'-flex-objects that contain the flexibility of the aggregated objects and can be scheduled easier due to reduced complexity. The corresponding counter-activity is the disaggregation, which takes place after the scheduling of the macro-flex-object has taken place. This general idea can be compared to the definition and characterization of 'jobs' in [26], however here the focus is not the optimal scheduling, but the control of complexity in the face of a high number of objects or jobs and on the observation that a power production process is can be viewed as a counterpart to power consumption which can be characterized by the same criteria.

3.3. Relating this Thesis to the Presented Research

Despite building in general on the experiences of the related research introduced in this chapter this thesis exceeds these approaches by introducing a unifying modeling framework for data center demand response and an evaluation through an architectural framework for simulation.

There is a small subset of research in 3.1.1 however, which like the presented thesis aims at creating a framework for modeling data center demand response. *Wang et al. 2014* [213], for instance, even though presenting a 'hierarchical framework for data center power cost optimization' restrict themselves to workload related power management strategies. They also do not account for the interdependence of different power management strategies, and even though they do offer a variable and abstract model that they link with a simulated real world situation, this high level of complexity is missing. Also, as opposed to the suggested framework, they do not account for the option to invest into more than one power flex market at the same time. However, in the offline model version they explicitly formulate a stochastic dynamic programming, a feature that is currently not included in the here presented approach. In a different strain of work *Cioara et al. 2016* [54] and *Cioara et al. 2019* [55] aim at analysing all types of power flexibilities in data centers, not only workload related ones. As mentioned before, they, too, fall short of offering a generic model.

The thesis presented here explores flexibility beyond the referenced research insofar as it creates a model on a high level of abstraction linked to a general data center architecture, in order to encapsulate all possible power management strategies. It leaves the formulation of concrete strategies to the evaluation which at the same time is an instantiation of the problem not only with regards to parameter setting but also with regards to the definition of power management strategies and power flex markets.

Also the simulation approach presented here stands out from other simulation approaches. By offering a demand response enabled data center simulation architectural framework it goes beyond the specific scenario implemented in the concrete simulation system. Other power driven data center simulators are available [125, 11], but to the knowledge of the author none offers the variance of starting points for power management and interaction with the power system as the one presented in the context of this thesis.

The simulation research papers presented in section 3.1.2 with the highest overlap to the simulation instance created for this thesis are *Mäsker et al. 2016* [151] and *Ahmed et al. 2017* [5] as both of them simulate the impact of different scheduling approaches. However, *Mäsker et al. 2016* [151] though offering an interesting scenario located in Germany, however, neither takes into account effects of data center power consumers other than serves, nor, what is a major difference, delay cost. Comparing the simulation of *Ahmed et al. 2017* [5] to the simulation instance presented in this thesis shows that *Ahmed et al.* are restricted with regards to the available power management strategies. Also, the data traces used for evaluating the impact of demand response are different from the ones used to create the utilized power models. Evicting jobs that have consumed already some energy and restarting them after the demand response event from the beginning seems like a rather inefficient policy.

Contrary to the presented appraoch, most simulation works use workload traces from a different source than the data center power models apart from

Arnone et al. 2017 [15], whose simulation experiment is unfortunately not data center specific and *Tang et al. 2013* [200] whose model is regression based, offering no explanatory power with regards to workload or cooling models.

Analysing research that models power flexibility independent on the flexibility provider helped at delimiting the contributions provided here. *Niedermeier et al. 2016* [158], similar to this thesis, aim at modeling flexibility in a very simple way, just using three parameters. This is a very interesting framework but it takes a different point of view from the one presented in this thesis. Whereas in [158] demand response events are analysed with regards to their impact on cost, in this thesis the detailed reaction of the data center as a whole is in the center of attention. *Šikšnys et al. 2015* [190] and *Šikšnys and Pedersen 2016*[189] dealing with 'flex object' also exhibit a very different viewpoint on power flexibility: First of all, obviously, the current thesis analyses exclusively power consumption processes. But furthermore, contrary to both latter approaches, data center demand response modeling framework presented here does not focus on *scheduling* flexible processes, but rather on extracting inherent flexibilities by modeling different means to create flexibilities in the power consumption of a data center.

Finally, *Barth et al. 2018* [26] at first sight seem to pursue a similar approach as the one presented here, albeit not specific to a consumer. The main difference of the latter is that it focuses on the power flexibility, i.e. the 'slack' as defined by [26], whereas *Barth et al.* model the static and the dynamic part of the system, albeit without including cost, without the elasticity to different rewards as formulated in the current model, and without the link to demand response schemes.

4. Modeling Demand Response with Data Centers

Having introduced necessary background information about the topic of this thesis and the related work that it connects to, the first part of this chapter 4.1 presents *methodology considerations*. The second part *Data Center Modeling* (4.2) is dedicated to the understanding of a data center; this forms the groundwork on top of which the concept of demand response is added. Subsequently in section 4.3, the idea of *demand response potentials* is mapped to the use case of a data center. The chapter culminates in the presentation of a *Modeling Framework for Data Center Demand Response* in section 4.4.

4.1. Methodology Considerations

As a first step the research is put into the context of the affected disciplines. Figure 4.1 illustrates that this thesis is impacted by questions and methods used in energy informatics, energy economics and information systems: Around a decade ago *energy informatics* started tackling the challenge of balancing the electricity injected into and extracted from the power grid using methods as optimization and simulation. This issue is the bedrock of this thesis. The economic side of demand response and demand flexibility is part of the research in *energy economics*. Energy economics deals with questions of pricing electricity under different market settings, of market design and regulative and business rules. Also, amongst others it evaluates the economic potential of flexibility and analysis its barriers. Economic methods and questions will help modeling demand response strategies on all levels of the data center architecture. Finally,

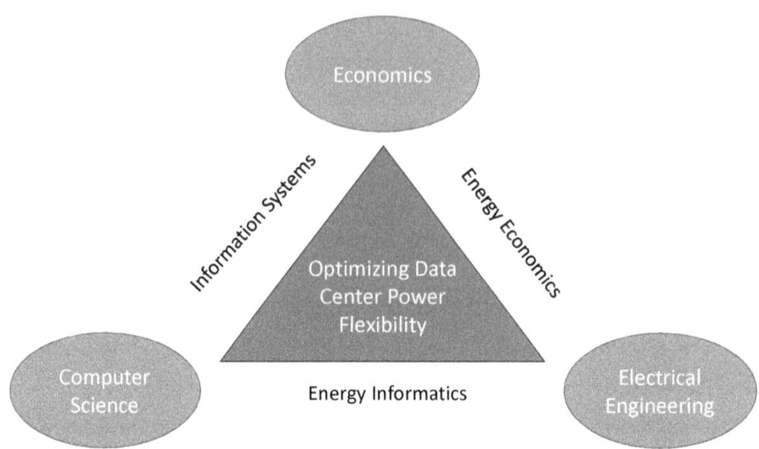

Figure 4.1.: Positioning the Presented Research in Scientific Disciplines

information systems researches into the creation of artifacts that support the management of organisations. The presented work creates artifacts to assist the applicability of demand response schemes in a data center thus advancing the concept of demand response with data centers and linking to all types of demand response potentials.

This section will explain the approach through a top-down process: at a high level of abstraction the general methodology is introduced, and this methodology is mapped with a specific approach to answer the current research questions.

4.1.1. Generic Research Methodology

A generic definition of a research methodology is given by *Novikov and Novikov 2013* [159] who state that the focus of research methodology is the organization of research activity which essentially contains a design phase, a technological phase, and a reflexive phase. In the design phase, a concept including problem statement and the criteria for the assessment of the validity of results must be drawn up. Then a hypothesis, i.e. a 'model of future scientific knowledge' [159] p.78, must be constructed which in the technological phase is probed either theoretically and/or experimentally. The technological phase begins with research implementation: This is where theoretical models are developed and subsequently tested, and as a result the hypothesis is either supported or rejected. This phase finishes with evaluating and approving the results. The reflexive phase deals mainly with research communication and discussion in the research community.

Methods of research, as deduction, induction, analysis and synthesis, are activities within this research process to reach the objectives defined in the course of the research process (see e.g. [159, 139, 92]). They must be amended by basic empirical methods as literature research, observations, testing, or measurements [159]. How these methods are applied and instantiated depends on the research question and research context (e.g. availability of data and tools).

4.1.2. The Specific Approach

For the research questions of the presented thesis (see chapter 1), which are in short:

a) How to comprehensively model power demand flexibility in data centers *and* represent the power market side? ?

b) How to reconcile such a high level of abstraction with specific data centers and markets?

the following considerations help selecting a suitable set of methods:

Even though there is a lot of research that evaluates data center flexibility either in terms of a theoretical potential or in terms of economics, the works are generally dealing with very specific data center and market settings. From these, often statements about a general potential are induced [144, 86, 145, 50, 19] which may over- or underestimate the real potential that is impacted by a great heterogeneity of data center characteristics, by business models, and regulative contexts. Also assessing the potential within a data center, business rules or the influence of the workload composition are hardly ever mentioned, SLAs often neglected [144, 213, 203, 19].

What is therefore needed is a generic model of demand response with data centers that comprises typical potential technical and economic options. On the other hand, such a general approach should be enabled to also represent specific data centers aiming to know *their* flexibility potential and opportunities to turn them into an economic benefit. A solution to the first endeavor is to create a modeling framework that encompasses options for all categories of power management strategies and power flex markets (see introduction in section 2.2.2). In order to comply with the second requirement this framework needs to be able to instantiate for a specific data center in a specific market environment.

An approach that suffices the requests from both research questions is therefore the following:

> To create a comprehensive model of demand response with data centers at a high level of abstraction as a framework. Based on that, to further design a generic simulation modeling architecture as a first step in a hierarchical evaluation. As a second step to apply this architecture to generate a simulation system tailored to one specific setting.

This framework model is realized as a micro-economics based optimization approach that integrates any kind of data center into a generic set of power flex markets. This implies that this model should be able to represent power management strategies on all layers of the data center architecture and should be enabled to integrate any kind of power flex market.

In order to evaluate the general applicability of this model, a hierarchical evaluation procedure is carried out in two steps: A generic architecture for an event-based simulation model is generated that is able to implement the strategies expressed in the overarching modeling framework and serves as a blueprint for a real implementation. In order to be encompassed by the modeling framework also this simulation architecture should be designed in a modular way that allows adding and removing strategies as for a specific data center these depend on their chosen business model and technical conditions. The same applies to the power flex markets: aside from the adaptation to local programs the generic architecture should enable the addition and removal of flex power markets.

In a second evaluation step this generic architecture needs to be corroborated by an empirical evaluation using data from a real data center to instantiate into a concrete simulation system. The objective of this evaluation is to show the existence of a consistent chain of artifacts between the overarching comprehensive modeling framework, the generic simulation architecture and the specific simulation system based on a real data set. For the considered data center, applying the specific simulation system reduces their knowledge gap how to make use of opportunities on the local power flex markets.

Through this hierarchical scheme the presented thesis tackles all three demand response potentials: the theoretical and technical potential through the integration of power management strategies on all layers of the data center architecture, the economic potential through the integration in various types of power flex markets and the consideration of data center cost, and the practical potential through the applicability to all types of data centers and the showcase for one specific data center.

This scientific approach matches well with the research methodology developed within the information system discipline: The design science research model (DSRM) by *Peffer et al.* [167] and *Hevner et al.*[101, 102] as shown in figure 4.2.

Therefore, the work-flow of this thesis was carried through along the lines of the DSRM and is mapped to the six DSRM phases in the following way: The first step in the DSRM *Problem Statement and Motivation* is the groundwork

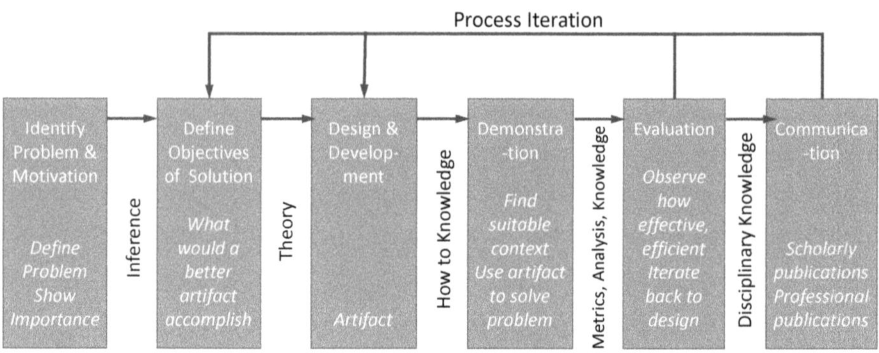

Figure 4.2.: Design Science Research Model [167]

of this thesis laid out in the chapters 'Introduction' (chapter 1), 'Background' (chapter 2) and through the analysis in the 'Related Work', chapter 3. Step 2 *Objectives* is partially treated in the 'Introduction' (chapter 1) and presented in more detail in the requirements analysis (section 5.1.1) in chapter 5. The *Design & Development* phase is realized through creating the general model of demand response with data centers in section 4.4. The *Demonstration* phase is realized as a hierarchical evaluation, as explained before: First, the framework is applied to creating a generic architecture for a simulation model of demand response with data centers Sim2Win. This is then instantiated as a concrete simulation system Sim2Win-HPC that reflects the situation of a German HPC data center (section 5.2) offering its flexibility on two power flex markets in Germany (5.2.7). Subsequently this simulation system is evaluated for this realistic case in chapter 6.

Communication, as the last step of the DSRM, is being undertaken with journal and conference publications as well as through this thesis.

In order to follow this procedure, in the next sections the comprehensive model of demand response with data centers is introduced.

As explained in section 2.2.3, demand response with data centers essentially means that a data center first assesses flexibilities in its power profile depending on the remuneration from the (implicit and explicit) power flex markets. Then these flexibilities are offered on the subset of available power markets that are accessible to the data center and where an economic benefit is expected. Modeling this interaction implies that as a first step a data center without demand response activities needs to be understood and modeled. Only as a second step, data center activities in order to integrate in demand response schemes can be modeled.

Therefore, the next section presents a generic model of data centers that allows to represent power management strategies which are the source of power flexibility before the comprehensive modeling framework for demand response with data centers is introduced.

4.2. Data Center Modeling

The understanding of a data center in this thesis builds on the operation-based definition of *Oro et al. 2015* ([160], see section 2.1). The envisioned data center model needs to focus on integrating power flexibility into data center operation and be designed in a way that power, operation and OPEX views can be mapped with other architectural frameworks (e.g. [129]). In order to do this, first a data center typology is created for the specific scenario of demand response and then based on this an architectural framework is developed. The latter is used to give an introduction to existing power, workload and cost models that allow for the integration of power flexibility.

4.2.1. Data Center Typology

In order to understand the role and assess the demand response opportunities of a specific data center as defined in [160], some further characteristics need to be analysed. They are best subsumed using an archetypical characterization of data centers that has been developed as a former work of the author in order to characterize the flexibility options of data centers [126]. The typology is based on the following parameters:

Data Center Service Model The data center service model is the core service or sometimes the set of core services that a data center offers to their customers. Typical data center service models are colocation and cloud services, hosting and application management. These will be explained in more detail in the section 2.1.2.

Ownership The ownership determines to a great degree the rights of a data center to shape its power profile by managing the workload. Main categories are:

- Enterprise data center: it is owned by a company whose sole purpose is to execute the workload imposed by the mother company.
- Commercial data center: a data center whose core business model is selling IT services to their customers (also called a 'public' data center).
- Public sector/publicly owned data center: a data center that belongs to a public entity and delivers IT services to the state and its citizens.

Tier level The Tier level is a broadly used classification of data centers created by the Uptime Institute [207]. It defines 4 'tiers' alongside the categories redundancy, maintenance, uptime, fault resilience and recovery as well as power and cooling, all of which are evaluated from the point of view of the overall reliability of a data center. Each higher category fulfills all requirements of the lower categories and adds new ones or imposes stricter regulations. As opposed to tier 1, for example, tier 4 data centers are fully redundant, fault tolerant (meaning that there is no impact of faults on IT operation), and have no maintenance down-times. The topology criteria are amended with a document that requires methods for operational sustainability linked to the tier levels [206].

Workload In case a data center has the rights to manage the workload, the nature of the workload (see section 2.1.3) determines if, how, and to which degree a power management strategy can be applied. The main differentiation is batch vs. interactive workload. The relevance of workload characteristics for demand response will be explored in more depth in section 2.1.3.

Figure 4.3 shows the result of applying the described dimensions to create a typology. Columns show different ownership characteristics, and rows represent different core value propositions. Each column is further split into a 'high' (summarizing Tier 3 and Tier 4) versus a 'low' (summarizing Tier 1 and Tier 2) tier level, as the tier classification plays a major role in operational requirements and therefore has a high impact on a data center's options for power management. Finally, in the cases where workload management is part of the value proposition, extra rows for interactive and batch workloads are added. Except for the greyed-out area all combinations of the suggested dimensions are imaginable.

In reality, it is difficult to consistently locate a specific data center in one cell. For instance in cases where a data center offers a set of different service models instead of one, occupying several of the cells which makes them hard to locate. However, this typology enables a first assessment with regards to the nature of power flexibility. This can be linked with power management strategies and thus demand response activities as will be shown in sections 4.2.5 and 2.2.3.

Today, enterprise data centers still make up more than half of the data centers, but the outsourcing trend is persistent [39, 161]. This outsourcing trend benefits both colocation and cloud computing data centers, some of which are huge hyperscale data centers like Amazon or Google data centers. For colocation, predictions are between 7-15% growth/year, cloud computing is forecasted to grow even faster, at around 16%/year[1]. For Germany, *Hintemann et al. 2018* assess that the share of colocation data centers, in terms of IT space, will

[1] `http://www.datacenterdynamics.com/content-tracks/colo-cloud/three-data-center-trends-for-2018/99760.fullarticle`, `https://www.researchandmarkets.com/research/3v9rnq/global_colocation?w=5`, both accessed 08/06/2020

Ownership / Service	Enterprise Data Centre	Commercial Data Centre	Public Sector Data
Wholesale colocation			
Retail colocation			
Cloud infrastructure			
Hosting	Batch	Batch	Batch
	Interactive	Interactive	Interactive
Application Management	Batch	Batch	Batch
	Interactive	Interactive	Interactive

Figure 4.3.: A data center typology structuring according to core service, ownership, Tier level, and workload type

increase from 25% in 2015 to 45% in 2020 [108]. At the same time the share of cloud data centers will grow to around 1/3 [104]. All of this, as mentioned previously, will be at the expense of traditional and enterprise data centers.

4.2.2. Data Center Architectural Framework

Even though there is no typical data center, each data center contains a set of typical components which are uniquely constructed and connected and thus form a unique data center following the definition introduced above. The structure of a generic architecture used as data center model differs depending on the objective: it can be energy flow based, infrastructure (IT and supporting components) based, level of abstraction based or of course building physics based. The first three points of view play an important role in understanding the focus of this thesis, and therefore they are merged to form one generic architecture.

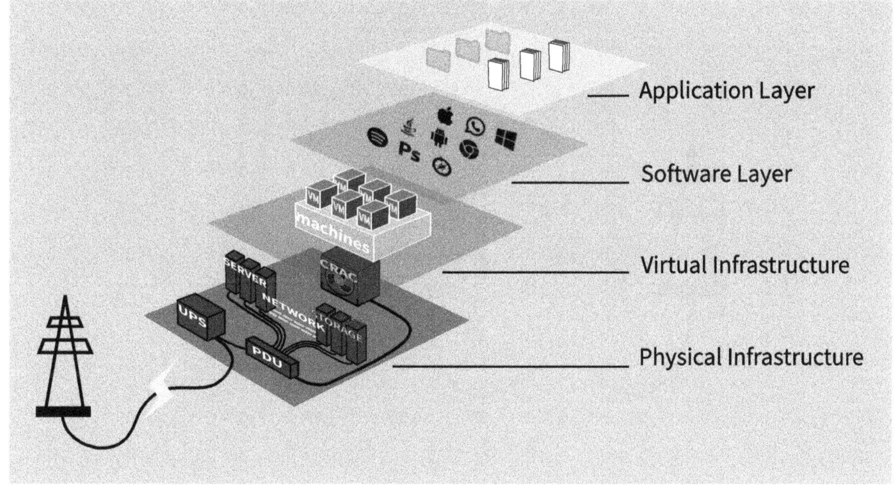

Figure 4.4.: Data Center Layers of Abstraction

The proposed generic architecture (see figure 4.4) decomposes a data center modeling view into four layers on a different level of abstraction. On the ground layer the physical infrastructure is depicted; the virtualization layer that re-organizes the physical infrastructure in order to satisfy the current functional or contractual needs is positioned on top of it. The third layer is the software layer that represents the connection point between the top layer, i.e. the applications running in the data center, and the physical infrastructure layer or - if existent - virtualization layer. The layers are described in more detail in the subsequent sections.

The Physical and Virtual Infrastructure Layers

The ground layer of the architectural framework represents the physical data center infrastructure with the following basic components (see figure 4.5): The inter-connected IT infrastructure is made up of servers, storage and network de-

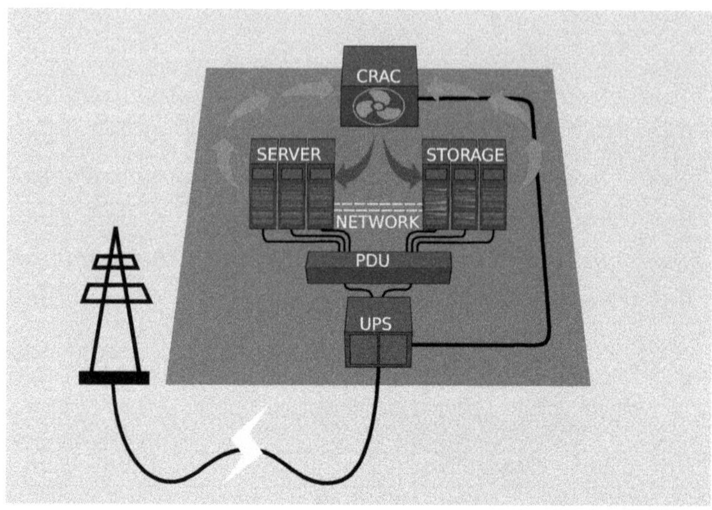

Figure 4.5.: Data Center Infrastructure Components with basic Power and Energy Flows

vices like routers and cables. The IT infrastructure can be rather homogeneous as in HPC sites where heterogeneity stems solely from different procurement cycles or heterogeneous as in many colocation data centers. It is fed with electrical power (represented by black lines in the image) through power distribution units (PDU) which itself draws power from the uninterruptible power supply (UPS) that acts as contact point between the physical data center infrastructure and the electricity supply in the form of on-site generation or the public grid. Often, for safety reasons, there are several IT clusters separately protected by several UPS units for a partial or full redundancy. Finally some cooling equipment is located inside and often partially outside of the data center construction; in most cases this is connected either directly to the power grid or to the UPS, separately from the IT infrastructure. It takes up the heat produced by the IT infrastructure (red arrows), e.g. through the heated air (in the case of liquid cooling this can also be done directly inside the server infrastructure), cools it down and sends the cold air (or liquid) back to the IT infrastructure (blue arrows).

Viewed from a higher level of abstraction, directly above the physical infrastructure layer there may be a virtual infrastructure layer, which contains a virtual network and/or virtual machines (VMs). The VM layer increases security and energy efficiency through a higher utilization of the underlying physical server infrastructure so that (theoretically) non-utilized servers theoretically can be put into idle or sleep mode. Also VMs allow for a simplified re-location or temporal shifting of the workload that is computed inside the virtual servers.

The Software and Application Layers

On top of the virtualization layer, the software layer orchestrates virtualization processes and mediates between the final applications and the virtual or physical infrastructure. Of course the software layer is again composed of different levels of operating systems, middleware and software closer to the applications that form the final workload of the data center, i.e. the core of data center operation and thus in many cases the value creation layer.

This application layer in most cases drives data center operation. In the case of HPC data centers this is to a high degree composed of batch jobs, in all other data centers the workload is a unique mixture of batch and interactive processes. [25] differentiate between platform-level software, i.e. the operating system, common firmware etc. and cluster-level infrastructure software, i.e. the resource managing software at cluster level, the two of which are comparable to the here referred 'software layer', and finally application-level software which are the specific services that the data center is operated for. For the current viewpoint the reason for the differentiation into the two software layers is the interaction with the customer which is of course higher at the application layer. This means, whenever the adaption of the data center power profile interferes with the application layer software, it is necessary to directly interact with the customers with regards to QoS considerations.

This layered approach can also be used to understand the general types of value proposition, or service model, introduced in section 2.1.2: Both wholesale and retail colocation data centers offer services on the level of the physical and IT infrastructure layer. Therefore their options to offer power flexibility are greatly reduced compared to data centers that offer services on a 'higher' architectural level as data centers focusing on hosting services in the cloud computing service chain or directly managing the applications for their customers.

4.2.3. Workload Modeling

Data center power consumption is driven by the workload. Without workload a data center needs not be operated. Therefore it is not surprising that the data center power profile is closely linked to the workload that it computes (see section 2.1.3), be it on the software or the application layer. This relationship is not linear as it is interfered by outside temperature, by the management of the server clusters (e.g. with regards to the creation of hotspot or the on and off powering of servers), and by the inertia of equipment like the cooling or network setup. In summary, however, the correlation between the computed workload and the total power profile of the data center is high (e.g. [79]). This is supported by own findings: The pearson correlation coefficient between the job power and the derived total data center power consumption of the available HPC data traces is 0.83. This relationship on the other hand is highly sensitive to the mapping of the characteristics of the IT system and the workload [76, 185], as performance and efficiency are interrelated. These considerations show that using the workload to manipulate a data center's power profile has a high impact.

Modeling the impact of the workload (and workload changes) on the power consumption of servers requires two steps:

1. The workload data needs to be made usable to be fed into the model.
2. A link must be created between the workload description and the power consumption of the servers that compute it.

This section deals with the first step. Section 5.2.3 will be dedicated to the second step for the concrete simulation instance of the demand response model.

In order to use workload information in a system, workload data can be either injected directly or it can be modeled based on the data. In the presented case the second option was chosen, mainly in order to enable a sensitivity analysis asking questions about the impact of different compositions of the workload by controlling specific workload features. The observations behind this decision was that jobs in the available data trace contained have an extremely high heterogeneity which lead to the question how the results of the real-world simulation would depend on this fact. The concrete workload model for the simulation system Sim2Win-HPC will be presented in section 5.2.3. Here, based on *Feitelson 2015* [76] some general modeling approaches are explained, all of which are consistent with the presented modeling framework.

The least refined way of modeling data center workload is to combine and replicated real traces, creating *synthetic workload.* This approach is often used for testing models of data center demand response (e.g. [205, 145]); however it is generally *not* used to evaluate the sensitivity to workload patterns or composition.

Descriptive workload models are the second modeling approach; they focus on the statistical properties of data traces as a whole [76]. On a high level of abstraction the *shape* of the workload is mapped with (a set of) distributions, e.g. a bell curve or a Poisson distribution, and fitted with a certain number of the moments of these distributions. When these distribution based workload models are used in a system, the *components* of the workload in terms of jobs and job descriptions are lost. On the other hand, sensitivity analysis can be implemented easily. Sometimes, capitalizing on the differences in the distributions is used to evaluate the sensitivity of results to the workload [222]. Examples for fitting distributions to real data traces are given by *Postema et al. 2018* [169]; sometimes data are not even fitted, but Poisson distributions and their parameters assumed [224]. This latter approach was used frequently for modeling inter-arrival times of interactive workload until the early 90s when extensive studies showed that the Poisson distribution often is not representative for the phenomenon [122].

The third type of workload models are *generative models*, which according to *Feitelso 2015* means to model the behaviour of the workload trace from the inside by understanding how this trace is created [76]. This is why *Feitelson 2015* also calls this an *indirect* modeling approach. Thus, in the end, if modeled with sufficient detail the original workload trace is closely followed. For the case of interactive workload this implies to understand user behaviour, e.g. due to diurnal requirements. Also this approach often starts with statistical descriptions, e.g. based on the data analysis of user sessions ([147, 76, 46]). By changing the parameters this modeling approach can be used to control workload manipulations in experiments e.g. for performance evaluation.

Another starting point to build generative models is to cluster the workload data into logical entities. Frequently applied clustering algorithms are the k-means or MapReduce algorithms. *Mathew et al. 2015*, for instance, use clustering for data pre-processing, in this case regarding time and geographic location of interactive workload requests [152].

Based on historic traces, finally, *predictive workload models* are created using data analytics based prediction methods as machine learning to extrapolate historic data. In addition to the generative modeling approach they include uncertainty. An example where these methods are typically used is energy efficient scheduling in the cloud [201, 164].

The modeling framework for demand response with data centers is not limited to a certain workload model. Principally, all kinds of models could be applied, as long as they can be linked to the power consumption of the servers and other workload dependent power consumers. The simulation instance Sim2Win-HPC that serves as evaluation for the proposed modeling framework uses a k-means based clustering algorithm on the available data trace.

Apart from the necessity to choose a general workload modeling approach, also the level of detail of the model must be determined. Obviously this means to select a specific point on the trade-off curve between precision and complexity, which is formally represented by the Bayes information criterion (explained in [76]). It depicts the changing ratio between an increase of goodness of fit and the complexity of the model. However, obviously the level of achievable goodness of fit is always dependent on data quality and the level of detail in data. Hence '...it is important to outline that the difficulty in obtaining workload data is a critical factor that limits the exploitation of workload characterization.'[46, p.48:30]. For the simulation system Sim2Win-HPC this turned out to be one of the main issues.

4.2.4. Data Center Infrastructure: Power and Energy Models

The groundwork for adapting data center power to the requirements of the power grid through demand response schemes is a power model of the considered data center. Data center power modeling can be understood along the lines of the data center architectural framework presented in section 4.2.2 in figure 4.4: Many data center models focus on the infrastructure layers and try to capture the energy or power used by their different components or aggregations of these components in infrastructure-based power models. Another group of data center models analyses the energy or power consumption of a data center from the point of view of the application layer, e.g. the jobs in an HPC site or the interactive workload in a cloud or colocation data centers. In the end, of course, these need to connect to different components of the infrastructure architecture. Overviews about data center power and energy modeling are given in [61] and [32].

The main requirement for power models used for modeling demand response with data centers is that they offer *steering knobs* to manipulate the power profile of a data center taking part in one or more demand response schemes. Therefore, for a general model of data center demand response that offers the implementation of power management at all layers of the generic architecture (see 4.2.2), power models are needed that on the one hand represent infrastructure components but on the other hand integrate workload models as needed. The power models used in this thesis are based on literature for two reasons: firstly, the chosen models have all been corroborated by many research papers and secondly they are generally applicable in the context of the demand response with data centers and specifically in the exemplary use case. Also, the modeling focus is on *power* models as demand side management is primarily a question of temporarily increasing or reducing power, and not on energy models. However, in some cases the power modification necessarily impacts the energy consumption of e.g. a job, so that both aspects of electricity need to be modeled.

As mentioned in section 4.2.2 the infrastructure level consists mainly of the components severs, network, and cooling. This means that power models are needed for all of these components that grasp the inter-dependencies on infrastructure level. They also need to sufficiently offer starting points for tuning the power in cases of demand response events by interlinking the different levels of the architecture to capture the impact of workload changes on aggregated data center power. The following sections present an appropriate selection of useful power models on infrastructure level and their connection points with the software or application layer.

Server Power Model

There is a great variety of server power models that directly or indirectly depend on the workload as the ultimate goal of operating a data center. One option are utilization based models, like the classical model of *Fan et al. 2007*

[71] that directly uses 'utilization u' as a variable:

$$P_{serv}(u) = (P_{max} - P_{idle}) * u + P_{idle}, \tag{4.1}$$

where P_{serv} is the server power consumption, P_{idle} is the power consumption of the server when it is idle, P_{max} is the maximum power consumption of the server, and u is the current utilization of the server. This simple linear power model works quite well with many different servers, and comparing it with the non-linear version of the model it needs much less calibration, traded-off for only little improvement in accuracy [71, 176]. In order to calculate utilization of a server from the workload injected, a plethora of different workload models can be applied, many of which are based on queuing theory. A different approach is to mediate workload and utilization via the CPU frequency used to compute this load. This is possible especially, where the workload data include frequencies. In order to be able to use CPU frequency as a knob to operate power adaptation strategies, a model building on the work of *Elnozahy et al. 2002* [66] suggests itself. Server power is here defined as

$$P_{serv}(f) = A * f^3 + P_{idle}, \tag{4.2}$$

where A is a server and application specific constant that represents server capacitance and the activity of the server gates, P_{idle} is the server's idle power, and f is the CPU frequency of the server. To derive the power consumed by all servers, these need to be added up in the case of inhomogenous servers or multiplied by the number of homogeneous servers n. For one server and one application this power models works well, however, in the case of heterogeneous workload and/or a heterogeneous server infrastructure either the constant A needs to be modeled based on workload and server characteristics or some fitting activities need to be employed.

The modeling framework for demand response with data centers is not limited to a certain server model. The simulation tool used for evaluation applies the frequency based server power model (equation (4.2)), even though the model had to be fitted due to the heterogeneity of the jobs in the data trace. Using this model, however, has the advantage, that two power management strategies, frequency scaling and workload shifting, can be implemented at the same time.

Cooling Power Model

Cooling power may be the most complex component in data center infrastructure from a physical point of view as it is the result of the interaction of a plethora of different factors: buildings physics, wet bulb and dry bulb temperature, workload characteristics and scheduling, rack positioning inside the data center and many others (e.g. [166, 59, 188]). Again a model that offers starting points for power manipulation is required considering that also cooling can be viewed as a source of manipulation of the data center's power profile. Also influences like outside temperature and buildings physics, although important for a general cooling power model, can be neglected for cooling power models in the context of demand response as these determine the general level of cooling power. Additionally, for a model relevant for demand response, only short-term changes are relevant.

In the use case of data center demand response, cooling models can play both an indirect or a direct role: indirectly, cooling models represent the effects of changes from other components, most notably the server component e.g. through workload changes or shutting down servers. However, cooling models can also be used to directly manipulate the power profile of a data center through the required server inlet or room temperature (depending on cooling equipment), i.e. *the cooling set-point.* In order to offer as many steering points for a data center's power demand as possible, this kind of model is sought for in this thesis. This requirement greatly reduces the number of available cooling models as very often the inlet temperature, if taken into account at all, is a parameter and not a variable. A power model that fits with this requirement is based on the metric *'coefficient of performance'* (COP) of the cooling equipment which is defined as

$$COP = Q/W, \tag{4.3}$$

where Q is the heat removed and W the amount of work needed for heat removal [154]. Q is agreed to be equivalent to server power P_{serv} and W is generally represented by power consumed through the cooling infrastructure [154, 218, 188]. The COP typically relates to a specific cooling technology, whereas a related data center metric, the power usage effectiveness (PUE), equation (2.1) introduced in section 2.1.1, relates to the data center as a whole. Where the COP has been used for manipulating cooling power consumption in a whole data center [87, 10] this was done in cases of a homogenous cooling technology. COP is a promising way to go for modeling demand response with a data center, as in 2005 a widely cited work by *Moore et al.*[154] discovered a quadratic relationship between COP and the Computer Room Air Conditioner (CRAC) supply temperature, i.e. the temperature CRAC emits into the room which at the same time is a knob at cooling equipment, i.e. an active manipulation option. The cooling power model based on this is:

$$P_{cool} = 1/COP(T_{sup}) * P_{serv} * n, \tag{4.4}$$

where P_{cool} is cooling power, COP is the coefficient of performance, T_{sup} the supply temperature of the CRAC, P_{serv} the server power and n the number of servers assuming that all servers are homogeneous. Instead of $P_{serv} * n$ in non-homongeneous cases $\sum_i P_{servi}$ is used. For a complete infrastructure power model of the data center, this component is added to the aggregate server power, but of course it is also dependent on the latter.

Often however, traces for a COP depending on the output temperature or the cooling set-point are not available. As a way out, dynamic PUE data which correlate both on the workload and the outside temperature can be used as a power model. Such a power model, as a major drawback does not allow to tune

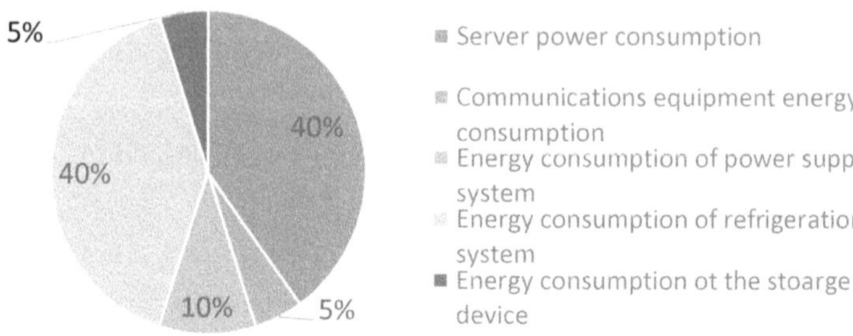

Figure 4.6.: Components of Data Center Power Consumption [177]

the energy profile based on cooling manipulations, but is added to aggregate server power accounting for the interdependence of cooling and servers, so that server-based manipulations of the data center trickle down onto the whole data center power. In this latter case, a formula that is used frequently (e.g. [114, 145]) is:

$$P_{cool} = P_{serv} * n * (PUE - 1) \tag{4.5}$$

This is also the version on which the cooling model builds that was used for the simulation instance of the modeling framework. The reason for this is data availability.

Other Power Consumers/Network Power

Server and cooling power generally account for about 80% of data center power [172, 106]. Other power consumers (OPC) are storage equipment, network equipement, power distribution and lighting.

As figure 4.6 shows, the shares or power supply, network, and lighting are mostly low compared to server power (computing and storage): in the show-case, power supply accounts for 10%, network and lighting both 5%. However, again it should be pointed out that there is no such thing as a 'typical' data center, so also the shares of the power consumers vary greatly. There is a great body of work specifically modeling network power consumption, and some of these also offer actuators to change the power demand of the network, e.g. [125, 118]. Basically, formula for network power devices like switches and routers consist of a high number of components that have a static power consumption; only 5-15% of network power consumption devices are dependent on the network load . This leaves options to either dynamically turn on or off parts of the network with obvious implications on the scheduling in the data center or to control power through adaptive link rate mechanisms (ALR), so that the following formula is a good basis for modeling network power [125, 148]:

$$P_{switch} = P_{chassis} + n_{linecards} + P_{linecard} + \sum_{r} n_{ports,r} + P_r, \tag{4.6}$$

where $P_{chassis}$ and $P_{linecard}$ are static hardware power elements and $\sum_r n_{ports,r} + P_r$ the dynamic power part depending on the active ports $n_{ports,r}$ with the configuration rate r. As the share of network power at total data center power is comparably low, and the share of the influenceable part of network power even lower, the necessity of integrating network power management into the portfolio of demand response power management strategies is debatable.

Depending on data availability and the real share of OPC-power in a data center the components might be bundled and similar to the PUE be modeled based on server power consumption using linear regression:

$$OPC = n * P_{serv} * frac_{OPC} \tag{4.7}$$

This is the approach used in the simulation system developed to evaluate the modeling framework; the data traces available did not include any networking, lighting or power distribution power data. In the overall comprehensive model OPC are implicitly accounted for: in case the underlying data center power modeling differentiates into server and OPC power models with actuators as e.g. switching off unused network devices corresponding power management strategies can be expressed.

4.2.5. Data Center Power Management

Power flexibility in data centers can be achieved through a set of different power management strategies. Contrary to energy management strategies, there are no research papers that offer consistent typologies of power management strategies encompassing the *whole* and *any kind of* data center. Therefore, in a previous work, the author of this thesis categorized power management strategies using the layers of the data center architectural framework (section 4.2.2) as criteria [126]. Additional criteria are the impact of a power strategy on the internal (inside the data center site, in line with the architectural model) or external energy consumption as well as, in the case of software strategies, different workload characteristics and timings of the adaptation activity.

Figure 4.7 illustrates this categorization, sorting the strategies in rows according to the architectural layers.

On the physical infrastructure level the following power management strategies are currently discussed:

- *Cooling set-point manipulation* on infrastructure level changes not only the power draw of the cooling system but also the energy consumption by increasing or decreasing the inlet temperature for servers. The efficiency of this measure is dependent on the cooling technology (via the coefficient of performance (COP) [154, 166]) and the IT load (see e.g. [225, 187]). It might be partially or fully compensated when an internal fan takes over the cooling task.
- Using *backup generators* to support the grid in times of external demand spikes or low power production affects the power draw from the grid but it does not change the energy consumption inside the data center. This model [54, 217] is the one which is applied in reality[2] for explicit demand

[2] https://www.webair.com/webair-and-enernoc-turn-data-centers-into-virtual-power-plants-through-demand-response/, accessed 08/06/2020

<table>
<tr><th rowspan="2">Data Center Layer</th><th colspan="6">Energy Impact of Power Management Strategy</th></tr>
<tr><th colspan="2">Changed Energy Consumption</th><th colspan="2">Constant Energy Consumption</th><th colspan="2">External Energy Consumption</th></tr>
<tr><td>Physical Infrastructure Strategies</td><td>Cooling Setpoint Manipulation</td><td>Battery Storage, PCM</td><td colspan="2">Generator Integration</td><td colspan="2"></td></tr>
<tr><td>IT Infrastructure Strategies</td><td>DVFS (CPU/Memory)</td><td>Server/Cluster Power-on/off</td><td colspan="2"></td><td colspan="2"></td></tr>
<tr><td rowspan="2">VM Strategies</td><td colspan="2">Server consolidation/WL dropping</td><td colspan="2">Temporal Management</td><td colspan="2">Geographical Management</td></tr>
<tr><td>Before Execution: Scheduling</td><td>During Execution: Shifting</td><td>Before Execution: Scheduling</td><td>During Execution: Shifting</td><td>Before Execution: Scheduling</td><td>During Execution: Migration</td></tr>
<tr><td rowspan="2">Software Strategies</td><td colspan="2">Server consolidation/WL dropping</td><td colspan="2">Temporal Management</td><td colspan="2">Geographical Management</td></tr>
<tr><td>Before Execution: Scheduling</td><td>During Execution: Shifting</td><td>Before Execution: Scheduling</td><td>During Execution: Shifting</td><td>Before Execution: Scheduling</td><td>During Execution: Migration</td></tr>
<tr><td>Application Strategies</td><td colspan="2">Partial Execution
Functional Adaptation</td><td colspan="2"></td><td colspan="2"></td></tr>
</table>

Figure 4.7.: Categorization of power management strategies

response, even though it is the least specific to data centers - any industry with backup generators can participate in programs like this. For instance, using backup generator testing for ancillary services is sought for by aggregators like RWE in Germany[3] or ENERNOC in the U.S[4].

- *Energy storage in batteries or phase changing materials (PCM)* changes the power profile of the data center through the charging and de-charging processes as described in [191, 8]. Depending on the size of the energy conversion losses, it can also be sorted as a power management strategy that changes energy consumption.

On the level of hardware, there are generally two approaches:

- *Dynamic Voltage and Frequency Scaling (DVFS)*, in essence consists of

[3] https://news.rwe.com/flex2market-allows-back-up-generators-to-tap-into-the-electricity-market/, accessed 08/06/2020

[4] https://www.enernoc.com/sites/default/files/media/pdf/brochures/br_generators.pdf, accessed 08/06/2020

manipulating the clock speed with which computation or memory access is being carried through. Especially regarding the CPU clock, this strategy has been given a lot of attention; the reason is a high impact of the dynamic part of the power contribution of frequency in power models: The power impact is cubic [178], whereas the impact on execution time depends linearly on CPU utilization (see server power model 4.2). This power saving strategy is discussed in detailed in the related work section and in the context of the simulation system Sim2Win-HPC (see section 5.2.3).

- *Powering on/off servers* to save power and energy seems very obvious at first glance. This strategy is not dichotomic, but can also include the activation of different sleep states (C-States). However, due to a high technical and contractual complexity this is still a challenge, so that an EU research project was set up to deal with this strategy [28]. A lot of research is dedicated to the efficiency and implications of shutting down servers temporarily, often in combination with workload consolidation and using this approach as a flexibility option for demand response e.g.[86, 87, 88, 175].

In principle, hardware strategies can apply to the data center as a whole, to clusters, servers or even to specific applications.

Software related power management strategies can be described through three different characteristics as figure 4.7 illustrates:

- The first issue is the *decision-making time. Scheduling* deals with decisions that are taken before or at the time of starting a task or a job whereas *migration* is implemented after computation has started, and it carries additional issues like time-consuming migration overheads, the question of hot or cold migration amongst others.
- Secondly, the *impact on the energy consumption* of the site matters. If decisions are targeted at consolidating workload on few servers, even though this may be a temporary activity, in most cases it leads to a *shedding*

of load, i.e. an overall energy saving effect. In case software is shifted temporarily and resumed later (or executed earlier from a queue), the energy consumption remains constant or is only slightly changed due to overheads. And in case, software is shifted geographically, as in the case of federated data centers, there is for example no need to assess the risk of a later peak, because the energy consumption is shifted to an external site.

- And finally, these strategies can relate to either workload (WL) in terms of jobs and tasks or to virtual machines (VM), each of these carrying different challenges and options.

Software related power management strategies belong to the by far most tilled research ground; a taxonomy on job scheduling in distributed systems in 2016 covered over 1000 papers [146].

Finally, there are some strategies that relate to the applications themselves. These are only a few, and they have not been researched by many research groups:

- *Partial execution* of software means that the application is stopped prematurely on demand. The idea is to use this for applications with a concave-shaped quality profile with regards to CPU-time input which leads to a constantly decreasing energy efficiency. Examples are web crawling or searching algorithms. This strategy has been discussed mostly in the context of increasing the system output via scheduling computation time for specific applications and has for instance been implemented in Microsoft's search engine BING [99]. One work, however, uses this strategy for shaping the power demand curve of a data center [221].
- *Adaptive applications* are applications that are created in a way that they adapt their functionality to the energy context. This means that these applications consist of a bundle of mandatory and optional features which are combined dynamically according to the requirements of the power

system and within the boundaries of the SLA [64, 48]. The finally realized version of this kind of context-aware application is then dependent on temporary, external power conditions. The idea is obviously implemented in many applications that exist with basic and upgraded functionalities (e.g. the so-called 'freemium' business model); however, to date, it is not used for data centers offering power flexibility.

All aforementioned strategies can be used to manipulate the originally planned power profile of a data center in the case of requests to increase or reduce their power demand (explicit demand response) or to match their power profile as much as possible to a dynamic pricing vector (implicit demand response).

4.2.6. Data Center Cost

In general, data center cost can be differentiated into various categories: fixed vs. variable cost, static vs. dynamic cost, cost that are affected through demand response and others. Real estate and infrastructure cost make up a huge part of the total cost of ownership, however this section addresses OPEX cost in a data center that are potentially affected by power management strategies. Personnel cost are deemed constant and therefore excluded here, which leaves:

- energy cost
- power cost
- SLA cost
- other cost

Power and Energy Cost

The energy bill of a company, payable to a utility, in most countries is made up of cost for energy, i.e. a static or dynamic price per kWh as well as cost for the power connection which is usually dependent on the peak power in a billing period. The way that these cost are structured is subject to tariffs, which can be static (fixed price per kWh in all timeslots), variable (time-slot based pre-fixed price per kWh) or even dynamic, i.e. variable and not known very much in advance. Alternatively, a company of a certain size, can source electricity directly at the wholesale markets as the stock market where prices are always dynamic or through over the counter (OTC) contracts in order to secure large amounts of variable or even static prices. Basic information can be found in [182], information about tariffs in the context of demand response programs in [204, 9], and an analysis of electricity contracts of HPC data centers in [56]. Cost can be therefore calculated as

$$C_{energy} = \sum_{t=1}^{T} pe_t * kWh_t + pp * \max_t(kW_t) \text{ with } t = 1...T \ , \tag{4.8}$$

where the cost of energy C_{energy} are simply the addition of the energy price in timeslot t pe_t multiplied with the corresponding electrical energy kWh_t and the peak power $\max_t kW_t$ multiplied with the peak power price pp.

In the context of demand response the power and energy cost are an important framework condition. On the one hand, they make up the financial frame that serves as a baseline for comparing the economic result of engaging into power flex markets. On the other hand, they might be changed through the implementation of power management strategies insofar as these impact the overall energy consumption or the power peak.

SLA Cost

The second cost category that is at the core of an analysis of the economic benefit of demand response strategies in a data center are SLA cost. SLA as contracts that determine a required level of QoS were introduced in section 2.1.4. SLA cost apply as soon as the QoS level that is fixed by the contract is undercut or exceeded. In many papers, SLA cost are a fixed price for each 'unit' of surpassing the QoS requirement; in case of delay, the nearly exclusively modeled QoS characteristics, this means that SLA cost increase over time [175], but in some cases they are just assumed to be proportional to the energy reduced [4] or the workload not computed [60]. They can be differentiated according to different types of workload, however, also the QoS definition itself can be service dependent. A very generic model introduced by [82] for the case of a delay is:

$$Pe = y * db, \tag{4.9}$$

where Pe is the penalty, y a fixed penalty rate and db the delay calculated as the absolute difference between the deadline and the expected termination. db could also be interpreted as the degree to which any other SLA characteristic has been surpassed.

In the current implementation of the simulation system Sim2Win-HPC the cost is calculated not only depending on the time slots surpassed but also dependent on the size of the workload in terms of nodes occupied. It builds on formula 4.9, which needed to be adapted to fit the scenario. The procedure and formula are explained in detail in section 5.2.6. SLA cost calculations for 'GreenSLA' [128], i.e. the energy aware, dynamic versions of usually static SLA (see section 2.1.4), are introduced in [38].

Other cost

Among the other cost server wear and tear cost can be considerable, depending on the power management strategies applied: whenever this strategy relates to shutting off servers, these cost apply; in all other cases they are not applicable. They come in pair with cost for wake-up times and times to shut down the servers, during which no service requests can be processed. In cases where these cost are modeled, the wear-and-tear cost resulting in a reduced life-expectancy of a server and e.g. expressed in a lower mean time between failures are mostly represented as constants [175]. Server transition times are in some cases modeled via the extra electricity cost [53]. Other cost as licensing cost for management software or virtualization cost are regularly not included into

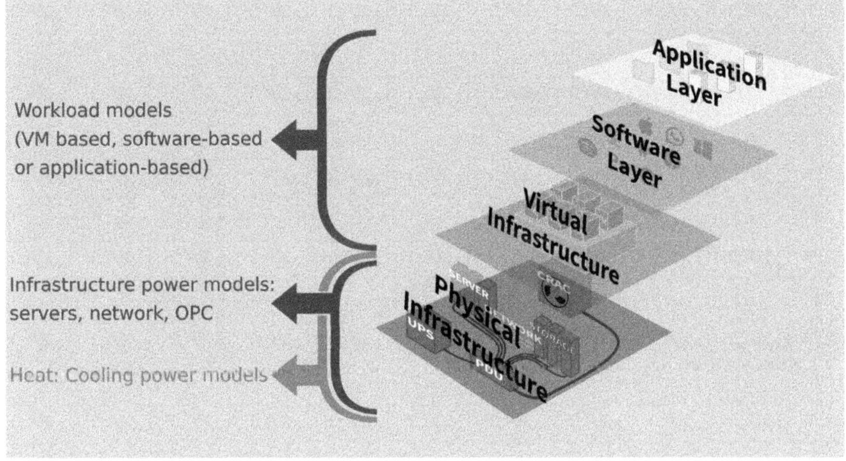

Figure 4.8.: Data center power and workload modeling

demand response models. In the presented comprehensive framework model they could be integrated into the cost for power management strategies.

4.2.7. Summary

In essence, based on a new architectural framework for data centers in the context of demand response the previous sections explained, how to model this scenario from different point of views: first power models of a data center in general were introduced, then the data center was viewed from the point of view of the workload computed. The categorization of power management strategies analysed the data center from yet a different angle; and finally the question how demand response strategies enacted inside a data center affect the OPEX cost. The figures below summarize the results and link them to the architectural based model of a data center (see section 4.2.2).

Figure 4.8 illustrates that the only layer of the architectural framework where power is physically used and transformed into heat, is the physical infrastructure

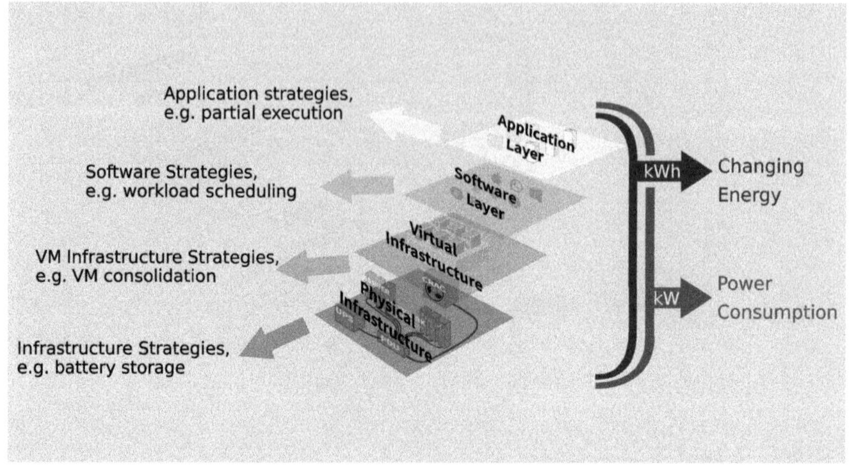

Figure 4.9.: Data center power management strategies

layer, although the other layers are the source of this power consumption. To the best of the author's knowlegde, in all demand response models the physical infrastructure layer remains unchanged. It also refers to the introduced workload models, positioning them on the virtualization and the software layers.

Figure 4.9 maps the power management strategies introduced in 4.2.5 with the layers of the generic architectural model. It should be noted again that data centers that can pursue power management strategies on a 'higher' level of the architectural model, can also pursue strategies on a 'lower' level, but not vice versa.

Finally figure 4.10 summarizes the section that introduced the cost elements of a data center's engagement in power flex markets and maps these to the affected layers of the general architectural model.

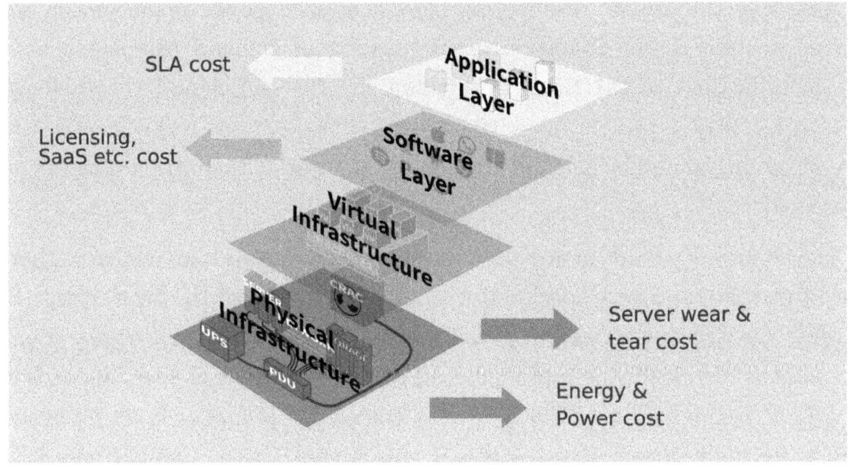

Figure 4.10.: Data center cost items

4.3. The Potentials of Data Center Demand Response

Before designing the modeling framework for data center demand response it is helpful to again differentiate between the theoretical/technical, the economic and the practical potential of demand response as introduced in section 2.2.3. This will allow to position the different elements of the framework.

4.3.1. The Theoretical and Technical Potential of Demand Response with Data Centers

Demand response means to change plans; the originally planned power profile of the data center is manipulated in order to meet the requirements of a power flex market. In general, a data center can change their power profile by implementing any of the power management strategies introduced in section 4.2.5.

Assessing the impact of applying aforementioned power management techniques to data center operation in the context of demand response leads to the identification of the theoretical potential. To understand the challenges related to this assessment, some exemplary considerations regarding the cooling set-point manipulation and the temporary workload shifting strategy are presented.

The cooling set-point manipulation is a good example for an endeavor that is hard to control and very specific to the technical set-up of the data center. Regarding the size of the flexibility that can be offered, manipulating the cooling set-point is obviously the more 'efficient' the less efficient the cooling technology, i.e. the higher the PUE of a data center. This makes it an interesting option for many legacy data centers in Europe with a comparably high PUE: in a 2017 sample of 289 European data centers, the average PUE was 1.8 [18]. However, in many cases a data center as a developing entity relies on heterogeneous cooling equipment; and cooling operation is therefore often based on experience. Due to an uncertain outcome, management tends to avoid changing settings. Especially, as also the net impact is unclear: increasing the server inlet temperature leads, for instance, to a higher activation of the server fans [166]. To which degree this counteractive effect compensates the aspired result further depends on the spatial distribution of servers in the room, on hot-spots from different computation intensities as well as on the share of occupied space in the compute room. The reason is that, contrary to other thermal buffers used for demand response as e.g. a cold store, servers in a data center produce heat themselves. If this exceeds certain limits, it threatens server health [10, 155], so that the storage time span for cooling is rather short. As a conclusion, applying cooling set-point manipulation to market their power flexibility might be a beneficial strategy for a data center with a high PUE, a homogeneous cooling infrastructure, and a rather sparse population of the server room. The best market to target would be a primary reserve market where continuous, extremely short and fine-grained adaptations are required. However, all these are general considerations that, as could be shown, are highly sensitive to the details of the real scenario.

The same applies to software related power management strategies; their impact on power flexibility, but also on the quality of data center services is dependent on many factors as for instance the composition of the workload, the server utilization and the feasibility which is not guaranteed in the case of heterogeneous server infrastructures and hardware requirement of the workload. General statements are therefore again misleading. With regards to frequency scaling, assessment is easier, as most of today's servers offer frequency scaling knobs and have a clearer model of the result of changing the frequency on the servers' power consumption. The impact on the quality of service, on the other hand, depends a lot on the nature of the workload; e.g. in case of a high level of task or job interdependence it is hard to make estimations on total execution time. Frequency scaling and temporal software strategies are the power management techniques that will be more thoroughly analysed throughout this thesis.

Integrating a data center's back-up generator into the power grid is a rather straightforward power management strategy that has no anticipated impact on data center operation. It is therefore comparably simple to estimate the technical potential of data center demand response for this strategy. This was done for the German data center industry for the year 2014 by the Borderstep Institute: using the results of their surveys, this study estimated an installed power generation capacity in data centers of around 700 MW for said year [108]. In 2014 this was thus the upper limit of a theoretical demand response potential with data centers in Germany, considering that the back-up generators enable a data center to run independently from the power grid for some hours.

The technical potential of demand response with data centers is the subset of the the theoretical potential which is enabled through the availability of technical infrastructure for power control and especially for the communication with the energy system. One issue in this context that is continuously being overlooked is the fact that a data center is dependent on its equipment supply network. The less this supply network offers technical equipment that helps at implementing power management strategies, the wider the gap between the theoretical and the technical potential. Examples are manifold, be it UPS batteries that only recently allow frequent charging and discharging, specifying upper and lower state of charge levels because demand response with data centers is slowly becoming a real-world topic. Or be it options to manipulate CPU frequency, which are also only slowly becoming best practice [2]. As technical equipment is not the subject of this thesis, these issues will not be further elaborated here.

4.3.2. The Economic Potential of Demand Response with Data Centers

The economic potential of demand response with data center is impacted by both the cost of implementing demand response inside the data center as well as by the income generated from the accessed power markets, that means

- the cost of power management inside the data center
- the cost structure inside the data center
- market entrance cost and market fees
- the remuneration from the power flex market.

The cost of implementing the power management strategies inside the data center are composed of cost for initiating this new strain of income and of cost for operating in this new mode (OPEX). These were introduced in section 4.2.6.

Apart from power management cost, the general cost structure inside a data center plays an important - often neglected - role with regards to the economic impact of demand response. There is a broad range of the energy cost share in data centers: in some cases energy cost corresponds to around 10% of total cost [136], in other cases - especially when the PUE of the data center in consideration is high - energy cost can make up more than 50% of total cost [97]. As [25] shows, the energy cost share is influenced by many factors, be it industrial energy price, server prices or location (due to cooling needs). It is evident that the economic impact of engaging in demand response increases with the share of the energy bill at total cost.

Market entrance cost can be considerable as in the case of prequalification cost for entering into the German reserve market. When an aggregator collects the flexibility of different industrial partners the prequalification cost are lower, but on the other hand the flexibility income needs to be shared with the aggregator. Finally, the remunereration for the offered flexibility influences the economic benefit of data center demand response. Unfortunately, often this reward is uncertain, as in the case of dynamic prices on the wholesale market or of bidding results in some explicit demand response power flex markets.

The example of demand response using backup generators in German's data centers introduced in section 4.3.1 also coarsely assesses the economic potential: Considering that in 2014 the estimated 700MW installed back-up generators had been used in the secondary reserve market, according to *Hintemann et al.* they would have achieved a benefit of around €44.000 per MW offered throughout the whole year. Starting from a estimated average price of 0.14 €/kWh and a total energy consumption of 10TWh in German data centers in 2014 [107], the overall energy cost were around €100m. Contrasting this with an upper limit income of €30.8m, at first this looks like an economically interesting option. According to the same study, one-off entrance cost would have been €3000-5000 for communication and control equipment [108] and thus acceptable. Unfortunately, the study neither considers the cost for the diesel fuel, nor the number of activations of the considered back-up generators. However, even though the study is not very detailed, this small example shows that the economic potential of demand response with data centers is worth considering.

4.3.3. The Practical Potential of Demand Response with Data Centers

The gap between the economic and the practical impact of demand response with data centers has its origin in three different aspects:

- legislative regulations,
- organizational and business constraints inside the data center,
- human behaviour and an inherent inertia to stick to once adopted behaviour patterns
- lack of knowledge about demand response opportunities.

Legislative barriers with regards to demand response in general have already been mentioned in the introduction to demand response (see 2.2.3). In essence these are market entrance barriers; on the data center side, there are other specific guidelines as for example the EU general data protection regulation (GDPR) which in some cases might prohibit geographical workload shifting or server consolidation. As a different example, labour protection law with regards to temperature might reduce the options of the cooling setpoint strategy.

The first paper to raise the issue of real-world organizational and business challenges to demand response in the context of data centers was presented in 2014 by *Wiermann et al.* [217]: Among others they specifically pointed out issues of market complexity (see 2.2.3), risk management, and the necessity to give the control of e.g. the UPS to an outsider. In most programs nowadays, however, it is up to the data center to implement an adequate power management strategy in the event of a demand-response requests. The entails different control issues because in some data center service types management has only limited control of the 'knobs' of power management strategies. One example is a colocation data center that provides just the housing and grid connection to the servers of their customers; this business model excludes workload related power managment strategies (see section 3.1.1). Apart from this specific situation of colocation demand response, also other service models limit the economic potential for demand response for data center operation due to contractual ties. This issue is explored in more detail in a former work of the author of this thesis [126].

The challenge associated with changing human behaviour patterns have been discussed only rarely in the context of data center demand response. With regards to energy efficiency, some research deals with general attitudes in the data center community that prevent even the shut-down of servers which have been inactive for a long time [77, 216]. Also some surveys illustrate that even in the face of economic benefit, management is often hesitant to deploy energy efficiency solutions [31, 100]. This is closely linked to the final issue, a lack of knowledge about demand response opportunities including the general awareness of the necessity to adjust power demand to power supply. This work aims at both raising the awareness of data center management for demand response opportunities and give them the means to understand its relevance in the context of a specific data center.

The modeling framework presented in the next section in principle addresses all types of demand response potentials; it focuses on the technical and the economic potential though, only introducing some starting points for modeling some barriers that form the gap between the economic and the practical potential.

4.4. A Modeling Framework for Data Center Demand Response

The proposed modeling framework of demand response with data centers builds on the modeling groundwork explained in the previous sections. It is realized as an optimization model on a high level of abstraction, which serves as envelope for the simulation approach used later for evaluation.

The framework focuses on the optimization of the mix of power management strategies in the face of different power flex market conditions. It takes the view of a data center *'selling'* its power flexibility, asking in turn for a compensation that at least outweighs the invested effort. Thus regarding power flexibility as a *(service) product* that the data center produces and then sells to a market opens up possibilities to interpret it using methods from microeconomic theory. There, very generically, creating a product is represented through a production function which describes how an *input* into the production process is converted into an *output* sold on the market. Interpreting the variables of power management strategies as the input into a *flexibility production function* has the advantage of illustrating the dependency of flexibility on the degree to which specific current settings are changed.

Basically, this point of view can be motivated with the situation of Amazon suffering from the huge block of fix cost of servers sitting idle eleven months of the year, waiting for Christmas. Then Amazon explored selling unused capacities and thus invented a new service product based on flexibility (albeit not on power flexibility): the cloud.

Using production functions to represent this point of view, adding or removing power management strategies is then simply a question of adding or removing 'products' in the 'aggregate power flexibility product function' (in short *'power flex function'*). As will be shown, this modeling approach potentially allows to also include issues that help at closing the gap between the economic and the practical potential. The main idea of this modeling framework is to change the mindset of demand response with data centers from specific scenarios using specific power management strategies to an overarching concept where power flexibility is viewed as the result of a set of different strategies, combined in the most efficient way. Additionally it helps to separate physical concerns from financial concerns through the differentiation into power flex functions, quality impact functions, and cost functions. Real world application can then be linked and subsumed under this concept. This means that the optimization framework can be concretized through different methods, e.g. linear or non-linear optimization; however, it can also be reconciled with other methods as e.g. simulation (as will be shown), as long as a system incorporates options to apply a set of strategies to different types of data centers instead of limiting the scenario.

4.4.1. Requirements

At the beginning of this chapter, in order to answer to the research questions in 1.3 the need for a comprehensive modeling framework for demand response that represents any type of data center on any power flex market was expressed.

In order to fulfill this need, such a modeling framework must fulfill the following set of requirements:

- **R1:** In order to be enabled to represent any data center the framework must allow to represent all types of workload.
- **R2:** In order to be enabled to represent a data center's all-encompassing power flexibility, the framework must allow to use power management strategies at all layers of the data center architecture (see section 4.2.2).
- **R3:** In order to be enabled to represent any data center service model the framework must allow to add and remove power management strategies as needed, optimizing among more than one if needed.
- **R4** In order to represent the decision basis inside a data center, both cost and technical dimensions of data center operation need to be accounted for.
- **R5:** In order to express the offering of power flexibility on any power flex market, these markets need to be represented by a set of constituent components.

4.4.2. Assumptions

The microeconomic-inspired approach of creating a framework for demand response with data centers offers a very broad conception, so that most limitations are derived from assumptions on the level of the application of this framework, e.g. using specific formula for modeling the power consumption of data center infrastructure components. An exception is the baseline assumption that the 'behaviour' of a data center can be consistently described using mathematical tools. This implies that even though the behaviour of data center managers and operators may be subject to bounded rationality and other limitations, e.g. due to social norms in the data center community as described in [77, 216], it is consistent and not erratic.

4.4.3. The Data Center Side

As explained, micro-economic enterprise theory views an enterprise as an organizational unit that creates a product (*'output'*) using resources (*'inputs'*) and a production technology represented by a production function. Producing evokes cost; the products are priced according to a specific market structure. In the case of perfect competition, an optimum is reached where marginal cost equal marginal revenue [13].

Power Flex Functions

The concept suggested in this thesis is to translate the idea that a data center offers power flexibility to a set of power flex markets into the creation of a new data center 'service': the aggregated power flexibility (i.e. the *'output'*) created through one or more *'power flex (production) functions'*. The *'inputs'* into the power flex function are thus the necessary power management tuning inside the data center. The more inputs are used, the more power flexibility is generated until a maximum capacity is reached. A power flex function can take positive or negative values based on the direction of adaptation offered to the market: In the case of power reduction, the flexibility offered to the market is positive, if the data center increases its power demand, the power flex function is negative. This is inline with the terminology on the reserve market where offering to reduce power demand is on par with increasing the output of a power generator. The aggregate power flex function is continuously increasing (or decreasing, if negative), using (continuous or discrete) inputs. Mathematically spoken, a set of power production strategies $S = \{S_1, ..., S_n\}$ and a set of production inputs

$I = \{I_1, ...I_m\}$ are used to produce the data center's aggregated power flexibility PF_{DC} based on power management technologies $y_{s,i}$ as:

$$PF_{DC} = PF(y_{s,i}) \text{ with } \; s = 1...n \text{ and } i = 1...m, \tag{4.10}$$

where $y_{s,i}$ is the power flexibility output of technology s at the input level i. It is continuously increasing or decreasing:

$$PF(y_{s,a}) \;\geq\; PF(y_{s,b}) \text{ if } \; i_a \geq i_b \; \forall PF \geq 0 \tag{4.11}$$

$$PF(y_{s,a}) \;\leq\; PF(y_{s,b}) \text{ if } \; i_a \leq i_b \; \forall PF \leq 0. \tag{4.12}$$

This general function just expresses the dependency of the service output on the inputs and the technology; in this generic version is does not determine the shape of the aggregate power flex function which depends on the underlying power management strategies and how they are interrelated. The technical strategies applied in order to generate the power flex function can relate to any architectural layer of the data center as explained in section 4.2.5. Combining all strategies s that can be implemented in a way that optimizes their technical power flexibility PF_{DC} without considering cost constitutes the technical potential of power flexibility for this data center.

As a concrete example be referred to the flexibility induced by workload shifting as introduced in section 5.2.5 and represented by equation (5.11) in the context of the simulation system Sim2Win-HPC. In the same way, CPU scaling can be used to offer power flexibilty; its power flex function in the simulation system can be expressed by equation (5.12).

A very simple version of the power flexibility achieved through the shifting strategy, under the assumption of identical jobs, would be:

$$\Delta P_{DC}^{shift} = \Delta J * APJ, \tag{4.13}$$

where ΔJ are the shifted jobs and APJ the average power consumption per job. The maximum capacity of this power flexibility is then expressed in terms of a constraint, e.g. in the case of the shifting power flex function as:

$$0 \leq |\Delta J| \leq \hat{J} - j_0 \text{ and } j_0 + \Delta J \geq 0, \tag{4.14}$$

where $\hat{J}$ is the maximum shiftable workload and j_0 the currently running number of jobs. The maximum shiftable workload is determined through technical or business model constraints, or even due to a general risk adversity. The independent variable of the shifting power flex function is the shifted workload ΔJ. Due to the assumption that jobs are identical this power flex function is linear, as can be seen in figure 4.11, which is based on average values of the considered German HPC data center. This data center on average runs 160 jobs with an average power consumption of 38kW; assuming that 12.5% cannot be touched, the capacity constraint is to shift a maximum of 140 jobs. In the case of the figure, ΔJ is the the unit of the lower x-axis belonging to shifting power flexibility PF_{shift}, the maximum capacity for this power strategey would be $\hat{J} = 140$. The potential power flexibility gained (in kW) is depicted on the y-axes. This is only a technical function, independent on cost or contracts.

Also the approximated frequency power flex function in this figure is based on data of the considered data center; the default frequency is at 2.7 GHz, and the frequency changes ΔF are depicted on the x-axes at the top. Here the capacity constraint is given by the technical range of possible frequencies. Of course, in reality, only distinct frequencies can be chosen; the curve is therefore created by interpolation. To read this figure, it is important to keep in mind, that the focus is on the offer that is made to the flex market by *changing* the current configuration in terms of workload and frequency: If 90 jobs are moved away from the current time window, the data center can offer 350kW to the market. If the data center changes the frequency of all nodes running on average, e.g. by increasing it from the default value of 2.3GHz to 2.7GHz (i.e. an input of +0.4GHz) it can offer a negative power flexibility of -315kW. This means, in case the electricity grid suffers from an oversupply, e.g. in the early afternoon

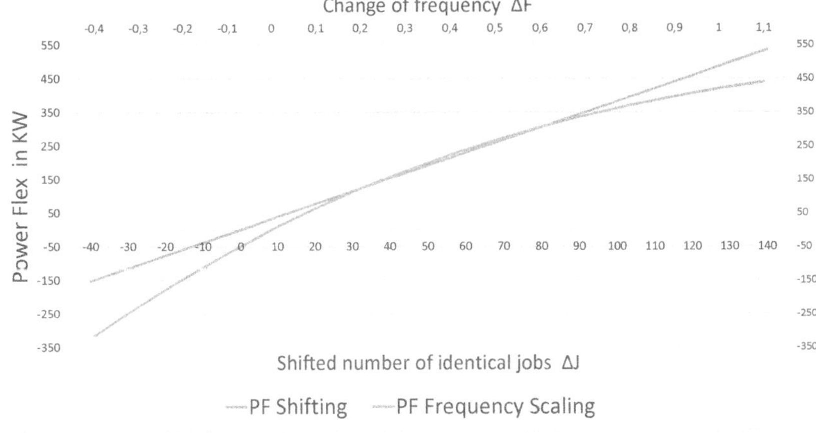

Figure 4.11.: Power flex functions of shifting and frequency scaling

of a sunny Sunday, the data center can consume additionally 315kW.

In order to aggregate the selected power flex functions from the different strategies into an aggregated power flex function that depends on all inputs and all applied power management strategies, inter-dependencies of the strategies need to be taken into account. For example, in the presented cases of shifting and frequency power flex functions, it is obvious, that frequency scaling can be applied only to the workload that has not been shifted away. This might seem rather obvious but combining more strategies will render these inter-dependencies very complex. So, sticking to the simple example, assuming identical jobs and calling the power flex functions of shifting and scaling ${\Delta P_{DC}}^{shift} = PF_{shift}$ and ${\Delta P_{DC}}^{scale} = PF_{scale}$ accordingly, the aggregated form of the power flex function is

$$PF_{DC}(PF_{shift}, PF_{scale}) = PF_{shift} + \frac{j_0 - \Delta J}{j_0} * PF_{scale} \tag{4.15}$$

This can be either positive (i.e. reducing power consumption) or negative (i.e. increasing power consumption), depending on the flexibility direction that the power markets demand.

Quality Impact of Power Flexibility

The overall objective of demand response is to move power load out of or into a certain time window. This means that power is mainly temporarily changed, and therefore under a demand response scheme the size of the workload measured in number of tasks, services or other non-energy related metrics system-wide remains constant. What might change, however, is the quality of service (QoS) related to the service creation, depending on the power management strategy applied. The QoS level might be increased, e.g. if jobs are pre-poned, or decreased, e.g. if they are postponed. The quality of service impact of a power management strategy can be generally expressed by a set of quality impact parameters $QI = \{QI_1, ..., QI_l\}$, each of them being subject to change, depending on the strategy s applied and the degree to which inputs i are employed:

$$QI_r = QI_r(y_{s,i}) \text{ with } \; s = 1...n; \; i = 1...m \; \text{ and } r = 1...R \tag{4.16}$$

with the same characteristics as the power flex function above:

$$QI_r(y_{s,a}) \geq QI(y_{s,b}) \text{ if } i_a \geq i_b \; \forall \; QI \geq 0 \tag{4.17}$$

$$QI_r(y_{s,a}) \leq QI(y_{s,b}) \text{ if } i_a \leq i_b \; \forall \; QI \leq 0 \tag{4.18}$$

Again, this quality impact function may be positive or negative and is continually increasing or decreasing accordingly in its determinants. A specific case of quality impact is delay, which is also the most frequently metri applied.

For the examples introduced above in the context of the Sim2Win-HPC simulation *delay* is the only QoS considered. The definition of delay is based on the physical extension of the time that the job is in the system, as 'delay' is a contractual term, contrary to 'runtime' or 'shifting time' which represent timing issues (see explanations in section 5.2.6) . In the case of shifting, the shifting time is just the difference between the originally planned starting time and the new starting time. It is determined by the desired shifting duration, which is obviously impacted by power market requirements. For the frequency scaling power flex function the change of the runtime can be calculated using the formula 5.15 in section 5.2.6.

As these examples show, even though the quality impact depends on the strategy employed, it needs not correlate directly with the shape of the power flex function. Similarly, the technical quality impact does not directly affect demand response transactions - this effect is mediated exclusively via the cost of power flexibility as will be explained in the next section.

Cost functions

As explained in section 4.2.6, analysing a data center from the viewpoint of demand response means to abstract from static cost as e.g. infrastructure related capacity investment cost, but focus on the cost elements that are impacted by power management strategies. The cost elements enumerated include energy and power cost, SLA and other cost. Mapping this to the suggested modeling framework for demand response with data centers leads to the following categories:

- the cost of quality impact C_{QI}, which ultimately depends on the technical characteristics of the power management strategies in combination with the SLA contracts,
- fixed cost of each strategy $c_{fix}(s)$, where applicable, e.g. the cooling manipulation might require human intervention
- and changed power cost C_{PC} as by increasing or reducing power, the power

charge part of a bill might be changed[5].

Additionally, for each power management technology, the QI cost element can be weighted with a *subjective risk adversity index* RI (aggregated or per strategy). This allows to calculate two instances of the cost function, an objective and a subjective one. The optimization or simulation can then be carried out in parallel for both instances and the results compared. In the current evaluation of the suggested modeling framework, this option is not further explored, i.e. the risk factor RI is set to 1.

The QoS impact cost is ultimately dependent on the power flex function via the quality impact function and therefore represented by

$$C_{QI} = \sum_{r=1}^{R} C_{QIr}(y_{s,i}) \text{ with } \; s = 1...n; \; i = 1...m, \text{and } r = 1...R \; , \tag{4.19}$$

with the same characteristics as the equations for the power flex and the quality reduction functions 4.4.3 and 4.16. As mentioned, the QoS change per se does not impact cost; this is always mediated via SLA. Even a high QoS impact QI does not lead to cost as long it is not part of an SLA breach.

As to fixed cost, they are reflected by the term

$$C_{fix} = \sum c_{fix,s} * b_s, \tag{4.20}$$

where $c_{fix,s}$ are each strategy's fixed cost and b_s is the corresponding boolean.

By the nature of power flexibility strategies, they change the power used by a data centre. Depending on the tariff of the data center, this does not lead to a modification of the power charge unless the peak power in the affected billing cycle is changed. In that case however, e.g. when the power flex function is negative and the power demand of the data center increased, the potential

[5]When time aspects are added to the picture, additionally change of energy cost must be accounted for.

changed power charge must be integrated as a constraint:

$$C_{PC} \geq pc * (P_0 + PF - \hat{P}) \; and \; C_{PC} \geq 0, \tag{4.21}$$

where C_{PC} denotes the cost of the power charge change, pc the power charge per kW, P_0 the current and $\hat{P}$ the maximum power of the considered billing period. The additional constraint $C_{PC} \geq 0$ makes sure that this applies only if the peak power $\hat{P}$ is surpassed. In the unlikely case that the tariff does not have a power charge based on a threshold, the constraint can be simply omitted. In the same way energy cost can be included in a time-depended instantiation of the model, if the tariff is per kWh.

The cost effectiveness of different combinations of SLA and quality impact is illustrated in figure 4.12: In some cases (lower left quadrant) there will be no quality impact as long as the power flex strategy is implemented within a technically determined, unthreatening scope, e.g. cooling set-point manipulation within ASHRAE boundaries [223]. In other cases (upper left quadrant) the QoS impact might be monitored but it is either not ruled in the SLA or within flexible boundaries of e.g. GreenSLA [27, 98] so that it is equally not cost-effective. Alternatively (lower right quadrant), cost may be generated, but they are not linked to QI, as for example fixed cost of applying a power management strategy. And finally (upper right quadrant), there are SLA based cost for delay or other QoS criteria which enter directly into the cost function.

All these options are captured in the modeling framework due to the generality of the approach. The total cost C_{DC} is then just an aggregation of the cost elements:

$$C_{DC} = C_{QI_{DC}} * RI + C_{fix} + C_{PC} \tag{4.22}$$

Connecting again to the example illustrating the simulation based approach in this thesis, the cost $C_{QI_{DC}}$ would be given by equation (5.20).

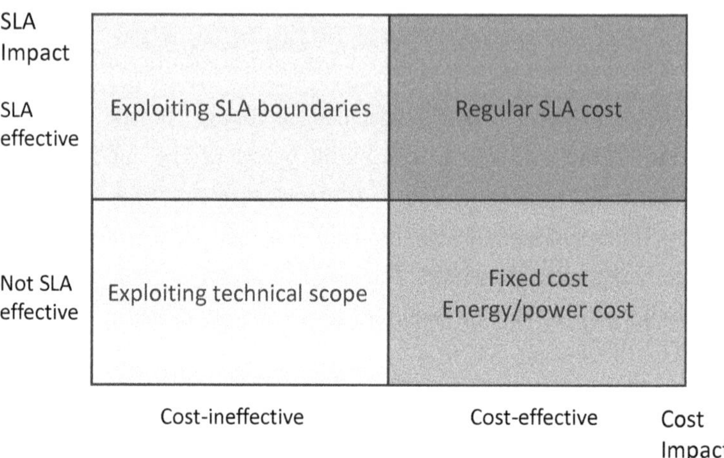

Figure 4.12.: Cost effectiveness of different contractual situations

4.4.4. The Market Side

The market side of the modeling framework is represented by the 'turnover' and associated cost that the data center can achieve via engaging on power flex markets. Here, the point of view of realizing a benefit from power flexibility is stressed. This implies that both types of power flex markets, explicit and implicit ones, are addressed in a similar way, although with regards to financial accounting one is attributed an income whereas the other, implicit demand response, just reduces the energy bill.

Power flex markets are modeled based on the respective pricing components and the constraints typical for these markets. From the point of view of the optimization there is no big difference between explicit and implicit power flex markets, as they typically carry similar constraints and as the bidding process into explicit markets *precedes* the optimization so that the prices are given for both market types. The reasons for this is that bidding rules are highly heterogeneous around Europe. Integrating this in the modeling framework would reduce the clarity of the approach *and* increase the computational weight. The same applies to the different contractual weights of the explicit versus implicit power flex markets: implicit power flex markets are comparable to an offer that the demand response candidate at each point in time can accept or ignore, whereas explicit power flex markets bind the market participants once the bid has been accepted. This contractual situation of different strengths of binding is not specified in the presented approach. It can be modeled on a more concrete level.

For implicit demand response, therefore, the remuneration for power flexibility is modeled via the difference between the baseline power price and the dynamic power price Δp exactly as it is explained for the case of the simulation system Sim2Win-HPC (section 5.2.7). For explicit power flex markets, there a different options: Some offer rewards for each kW adapted, which is then simply expressed as reward re. Others, like the French capacity market, offer to buy power certificates, that relate to a specific amount of power to be reduced (in kW), which are then reimbursed in terms of the number of certificates traded. This can be modeled through a variable z which is the number of certificates of size Z offered $z = \frac{PF^e}{Z}$ for the power flexibility PF^e sold to market e[6]. As a constraint, this number of certificates must then be a natural $z \in \mathbf{N}$.

The turnover function containing the revenues from all accessed markets $e = 1...k$ is then derived by adding up the different market revenues:

$$T = \sum T^e = \sum (p_Z^e * z^e + re^e * PF^e + \Delta p^e * PF^e) \text{ with } \ e = 1...k, \qquad (4.23)$$

where T^e is the turnover on market e, p_Z^e the price per power flex certificate z, re^e the reward per unit power offered on market e, PF^e the power flexibility sold on market e and Δp^e the difference between the baseline power price and the power price on the implicit power flex market e. In this equation the first term is for trading certificates on an explicit power flex market, the second

[6]In order to maintain a better overview which variables or parameters are 'market related' vs. 'data center related', the index for the markets is kept as a superscript instead of a lower script.

models power based explicit markets as reserve markets, and the third term represents implicit power flex markets. The following constraints that capture requirements from the specific power flex markets relate to the revenue function:

$$PF^e \geq \check{M}^e * b^e \tag{4.24}$$

$$C_{markets} = \sum (c^e * b^e + f^e * PF^e) \tag{4.25}$$

$$bigM * (1 - b^e_s) + D_s \geq D^e \ \forall \ s = 1...n, e = 1...k \tag{4.26}$$

$$\hat{M}^e * b^e_s \geq PF^e \geq \check{M}^e * b^e_s. \tag{4.27}$$

The first constraint is typical for both explicit and implicit demand response power markets and ensures that the data center's offer equals or surpasses the minimum power $\check{M}^e$ that can be traded on the respective market e. PF^e is again the power offered to market e, $\check{M}^e$ the minimum required offer and b^e the corresponding boolean (activated for the case of engagement in this market). This is a typical market entrance barrier that can be found on all types of power flex markets. Using a boolean, fixed market entrance costs c^e are formulated in the same way as fixed costs in the second constraint of the cost function 4.20. Total market cost are derived by adding the fees that are composed of a rate for a fee f^e which is proportional to the market turnover PF^e (constraint 4.25).

In explicit demand response power markets like ancillary services markets the market operator offers a reward for power adaptation PF^e which is defined through notification time, frequency of change, adaptation size, [158] and the required adaptation duration D^e for market e. This means that if some part of the flexibility created by strategy s is offered in market e, then the corresponding delay D_s must be greater than the adaptation duration required by the market D^e. This is expressed in constraint (4.26), where the boolean b^e_s signifies the 'engagement' of strategy s in market e, activated by the $bigM$ parameter. The behaviour of the boolean is defined in the last constraint (4.27): As soon as a strategy s delivers power flexibility to market e, the total power flexibility PF^e must be within the minimum requirement $\check{M}^e$ and the maximum requirement $\hat{M}^e$ of the considered market e.

As an example, the markets modeled in section 5.2.7 can be used: the optimized EPEX day-ahead prices are represented by the price delta, and the rewards on the secondary reserve market are the ones that were determined via the access to post-market data and the construction of artifical bids. Both markets have minimum offer requirements $M^{epex} = 100kW$ and $M^{res} = 5MW$[7]; specifically the secondary reserve market has high market entrance cost that can be modeled as annuities and thus as fixed cost c^{res}.

4.4.5. Optimization Objectives

The optimization framework can utilize any objective that uses the variables defined in the model. The most obvious optimization objective is the net benefit of the data center, expressed by:

$$max \ \ (\sum T^e - \sum C^e - C_{DC}) \tag{4.28}$$

under the constraints explained in the preceding sections above.

However, in some cases, other issues than maximizing the economic benefit might be accounted for. Here are some examples that illustrate that even though this is not yet covered by the presented modeling framework, it can be amended accordingly:

- It might be possible that the data center's objective for demand reponse is to be a 'good citizen'; this is what a survey of some 20 publicly owned data centers unearthed as guiding principle for the interaction with their grid operators [165]. In order to reflect this in the modeling framework, the economic benefit of the data center might be turned into a constraint, requiring that benefit needs to be at least e.g. non-negative. The optimization goal might then for example be to minimize the difference between an exogenous power parameter (vector) determined by the grid operator and the overall power (as $P_0 + PF_{DC}$) as suggested in the general demand response framework of [26].

[7]This was the limitation in 2014; meanwhile this threshold has been reduced to 1MW.

- Other possible optimization objectives might be the maximization of the utility of the data center or of the overall eco-system of data center and power flex markets. This would entail creating a new utility function, which would build on the current cost and revenue definitions; in case additional variables were to be introduced, this would then also require an additional set of constraints. An example might be a utility function that not only contains the data center benefit but also a 'good citizen' component that extends the economic optimization criterion through a technical part.

The optimization criterion pursued in this thesis, however, is benefit maximization. The result of this optimization is then the economic demand response potential of the data center.

5. Evaluation: Simulating Demand Response with Data Centers

The 5th step of the DSRM, after problem identification, objectives' definition, design and demonstration phases, is dedicated to *evaluating* the artifact created.

> *'IT artifacts can be evaluated in terms of functionality, completeness, consistency, accuracy, performance, reliability, usability, fit with the organization, and other relevant quality attributes.' [102, p.85]*

Evaluating a model means to confront it with real data and behaviour. Evaluating a modeling framework as the one presented in section 4.4 cannot be directly carried through in this way, as the mathematical formulation is too abstract. Instead, as explained in section 4.1.2 a hierarchical evaluation was designed that first creates a simulation framework on a slightly lower level of abstraction as the modeling framework, which is in a second step instantiated through a concrete simulation system. The latter can then be evaluated through real data and behaviour.

In the context of a model, *correctness* is often tested as 'Validation and Verification' (mostly called V&V [212]) which are defined in the following way:

> 'Verification *deals with the assessment of transformational accuracy of the artifact and addresses the question of "Are we creating the* ***artifact right?****"*
>
> Validation *deals with the assessment of behavioral or representational accuracy of the* ***artifact*** *and addresses the question of "Are we creating the* ***right artifact****?"* ' *[22, p.150]*

This implies that the instance created needs to undergo V&V in order to understand if the model is internally consistent ('creating the artifact right') and if it considers the functional requirements, i.e. in terms of 'creating the right artifact'. This terminology was coined in the Software Engineering discipline (foundations in e.g. [197, 212]).

When thus the *correctness* of the system in terms of V&V has been established, the responsibility of the *Software Engineering* discipline ends as system requirements have been fulfilled. The responsibility of the *Information Systems* discipline stretches further and additionally demands an evaluation in terms of *usefulness*.

In order to conform to the evaluation process illustrated above the simulation architectural framework *Sim2Win* was created that follows the general model as laid out in section 4.4. This was then instantiated into an implemented simulation system *Sim2Win-HPC* using the data of a German HPC data center and German power markets. The latter can be evaluated in terms of V&V, and then its usefulness can be tested.

The first section of the current chapter therefore introduces the general simulation architecture Sim2Win, and the second presents the simulation instance Sim2Win-HPC in detail. The last section of this chapter *validates* this instantiation against the original data (without demand response).

5.1. The Architecture of the Simulation Framework: Sim2Win

A generic simulation architecture that matches the framework for demand response with data centers as introduced in 4.4 needs to fulfil the following set of requirements which are in line with the requirements for the modeling framework presented in section 4.4.1.

5.1.1. Requirements

- **R1:** In order to be enabled to represent any data center the framework must offer starting points for all types of workload, generally being differentiated into batch and interactive workload, being provided via physical servers or VMs.
- **R2:** For the same reason, all infrastructure layers of the data center architecture (see section 4.2.2) need to be represented by offering power models for each of them (cooling, server, VMs, other power consumers like network and power distribution).
- **R3:** In order to allow for various types of power management strategies, the simulation framework must offer starting points for manipulating the power profile also at all layers of the data center architecture: Infrastructure and software layers.
- **R4:** To satisfy the claim that the simulation framework comprehensively implements demand response with data centers it needs to be enabled to simulate several different power management strategies at a time. Additionally, it needs to be sufficiently flexible to integrate more than one strategy and to allow for the later addition of new, yet un-identified power management strategies.
- **R5:** The economics of demand response with data centers require that in the simulation the applied power management strategies impact the cost of the data center, focusing on operational cost as laid down in section 4.2.6. This is mediated via components that influence these cost, i.e. SLA and energy/power cost.
- **R6:** To represent the reaction of the data center to explicit demand response requests, the simulation framework has to provide an event-based component that handles such requests, initiating power management accordingly.

- **R7:** In order to simulate the reaction of the data center to implicit demand response, the simulation framework must be enabled to continuously adapt to dynamic electricity prices.

5.1.2. Architecture

To address the above presented requirements, the generic architectural framework *Sim2Win* was developed. It builds on a CloudSim-based simulation framework created in the context of the EU project DC4Cities [63]. This basis was an event-based simulator aimed at simulating the reaction of a virtualized data center for interactive workloads to adaptation requests from explicit demand response markets. In order to become a *generic* solution for supporting demand response with data centers within the demand response with data centers framework, it needed to be redesigned. The main feature of this original simulator that was used to fulfill the requirements specified above, specifically requirements **R1-R4**, is the *modular principle* as illustrated in figure 5.1.

The architecture of Sim2Win follows a tree-like structure that has its root at the *SimulationController* component. It is structured into two parts: the **Facade** and the **Simulation Core**. The *SimulationController* component, the only component in the **Facade** part, is designed to provide functionality for the control of a simulation. Through its connection to a database, the *SimulationController* is able to conveniently monitor and store simulation data. All the other design components are located in the **Simulation Core** part. By modeling data center demand response through this architecture the data center takes center stage; the demand response scenario, especially the requirements from the power flex markets, are represented from the viewpoint of the data center. The reason for this is the general aim of this thesis, that wants to understand and promote the economic potential of demand response with data centers, rather than the effectiveness and the interaction of data centers with the smart grid in the context of demand response.

The **DC component** represents a complete data center within the simulation framework. And as shown in figure 5.1, all other design components in the

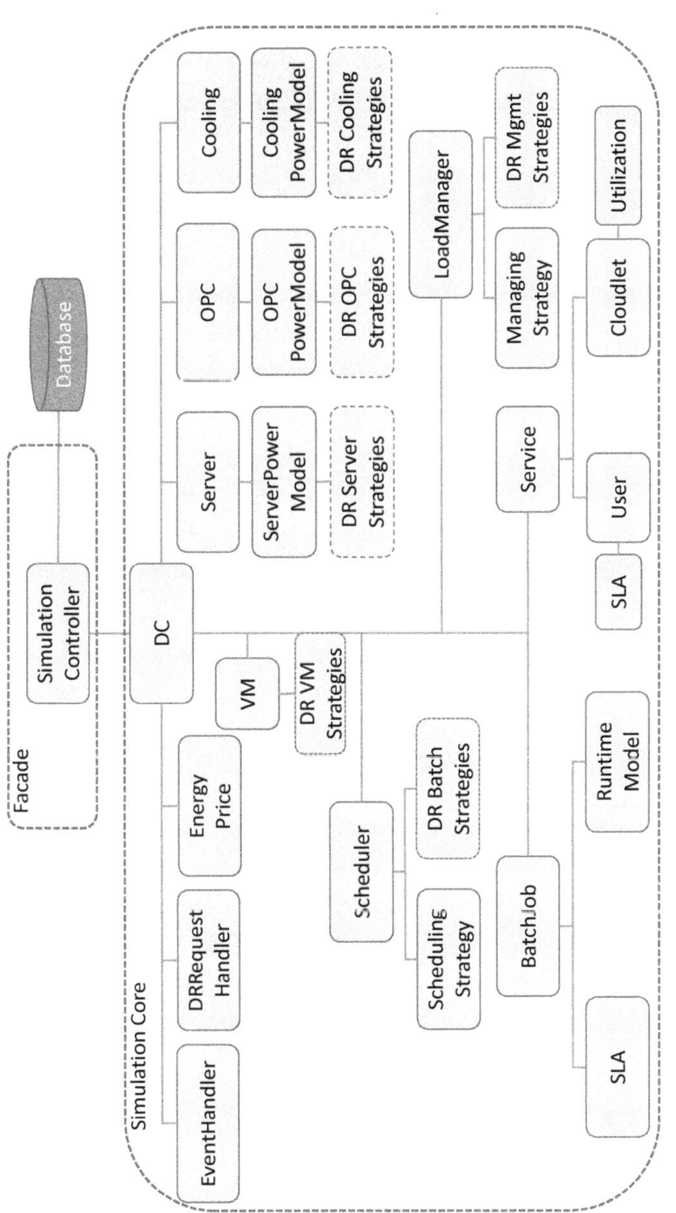

Figure 5.1.: Overview of Sim2Win's architecture

Simulation Core part are subcomponents of the **DC** component ensuring that the framework properly simulates the effects of the data center's power flexibility onto energy consumption and data center cost:

Hardware: There are three main hardware components, that represent the physical infrastructure layer of the data center architectural model (see section 4.2.2). These are the servers and the cooling infrastructure, and other power consumers (OPC) as e.g. network components. One single server is modeled by a distinct instantiation of the *Server* component. The *Cooling* and the OPC components represent the entire Non-IT infrastructure. All three components have a *PowerModel* as a subcomponent which models the power consumption of its respective parent. The power model of each component might reflect the interdependence of the subcomponents, which is most obvious for the modeling of server and cooling power. In case a power model of one of the components enables power management strategies, the respective *DR[X]Strategies* component, which is a subcomponent of the power model, is activated. Some of these strategies, e.g. reducing CPU frequency, form one part of a combined demand response strategy of the *DRBatchStrategies* component. The structure of the *Hardware* component satisfies the requirements **2** and **3**.

Scheduler: The *Scheduler* component is responsible for the execution of batch workload. It contains at least two direct subcomponents: one *SchedulingStrategy* and one or several *DRBatchStrategies*. The *SchedulingStrategy* component defines the regular execution schedule for a data center's batch workload. In case a demand response event is called, during this event the basic scheduler is replaced by a *DRBatchStrategies* component which changes the way that the workload is executed e.g. by shifting it in time or space. All possibly implemented *DRBatchStrategy* components define strategies to use several different techniques like re-scheduling or migrating jobs in order to to provide power demand flexibility. These components address the requirements **R3** and **R4**.

BatchJob: The *BatchJob* component represents a single batch job. As shown in figure 5.1 *BatchJob* is a direct subcomponent of *DC*. It has two subcomponents, the *SLAModel* and the *RuntimeModel*. *SLAModel* models the SLA specifications for each batch job separately. The same applies to the *RuntimeModel* which represents the amount of time a batch job needs for execution. Of course applying a demand response strategy, e.g. on the level of the scheduler or the server, may have an impact on the runtime of a job. These components are constructed in a way to fulfill the requirements **R4** and **R1**.

LoadManager: For the case of interactive workload, the *LoadManager* component takes care of workload management by specifying for each point in time, which services the data center currently offers and how many servers are allocated to each offered service. Thus, it has similar responsibilities as the *Scheduler* component for the batch workload and its basic design is the same: It has two subcomponents, one for regular workload management and one for demand response events: The first is the *ManagementStrategy* and the second the *DRMgmtStrategies* component. Here all possibly implemented *DRMgmtStrategies* components define demand response strategies relating to interactive workload in response to incoming demand response events as e.g. reducing the CPU frequency. Also application specific demand response strategies like the partial execution of web crawling search services [99] can be subsumed here. These components address the requirement **R3** and **R4**.

Service: Usually, a dynamic or interactive workload consists of services (e.g., web service) that are offered by a data center and that can be used by the customers via a network connection. The *Service* component models such a service and acts thus as the counterpart of the *BatchJob* component. Similar to the latter the *Service* component is a direct subcomponent of the *DC* component, which indicates that also each service instance is allocated to a distinct data center; this setup satisfies requirement **R1**. The

Service component has two subcomponents, which are namely the *User* and *Cloudlet* components. The *User* component is designed to model one distinct user of a service. This is done, to enable the possibility to model single SLA contract for each distinct user, thus fulfilling requirement **R5**. This implies that the *SLA* component is a subcomponent of the *User* component. The *SLA* component can also take the form of a GreenSLA and thus model the support of the customer for demand response activities of the data center. An instance of the *Cloudlet* component, the second service subcomponent, represents only a part of a complete service. Thus a service can be split into several parts that run on different hardware devices. Thereby, each *Cloudlet* instance can have a different utilization of the hardware device it runs on, which is represented by the *Utilization* component.

VM: The *VM* component represents a single virtual machine running on the server hardware of a virtualized data center. It is a direct subcomponent of the *DC* component and not of the *Server* component, although a virtual machine is executed on a physical server. The reason is that a VM can be interrupted in its execution. When this happens, the current state of the VM is stored on the storage hardware of the data center. At a later point in time the stored state can be used to assign the VM to another server and restart its execution. Therefore, a VM is not necessarily linked to the same server during the entire execution process. The subcomponent associated to an intentional activity as the one described above is the *DRVMStrategy*. When the modeled data center uses a virtualized execution environment, both, the individual batch jobs and the services can be executed on virtual machines, so that requirement **R1** is accounted for.

EventHandler: The Sim2Win framework uses an event based internal communication mechanism. Events in the Sim2Win framework are defined as anything that changes the current state of the data center (with the exception of a demand response request), for example a new job waiting to be scheduled, so that requirement **R6** is addressed. This set-up requires a component that handles the events that occur during a simulation. This task is taken care of by the *EventHandler* component. In addition, this component is responsible for allocating the data center's hardware resources to the current workload.

DRRequestHandler: As the name suggests, the *DRRequestHandler* component handles any request that is related to a data center's provision of power demand flexibility in the context of explicit demand response. This component satisfies requirement **R6**.

EnergyPrice: The*EnergyPrice* component finally represents the amount of money a data center has to pay for one electricity unit consumed. Depending on the implementation, this price might be static or dynamic over time. In the case of dynamic prices, using the corresponding scheduler this leads to implicit demand response adaptation. This component satisfies requirements **R5** and **R7**.

This setup stresses the overall aim of the simulation framework approach to place the operative decisions of the data center in the center of attention. This implies that data center infrastructure is a given and the simulation framework does not deal with capacity planning challenges.

5.2. The Simulating System: Sim2Win-HPC

In a second step, as explained at the beginning of this chapter, the architectural framework is instantiated into a concrete simulation system representing a specific data center and specific power flex markets. The main challenge of this endeavor is to identify appropriate power models that offer activators for the desired power management strategies *and* match the power models with the available data. Because, as will be explained in the subsequent sections, there is not only a trade-off between goodness-of-fit of a model and the amount and granularity of data needed, but more than that, data availability is a major constraint of modeling. This is the groundwork set up that needs to be validated before the core task of the simulator, implementing demand response as a concretization of the suggested optimization modeling framework can be enacted. In the presented thesis, an instance of the simulation framework Sim2Win was created using a set of data traces from a German HPC data center for 2014 and of two local power flex markets that the data center could potentially have accessed in 2014.

These data traces comprise the power related job data of each job of the available data center in 2014 including start and ending times and the maximum frequency. Also available are monitoring data from the IT room, which in addition to the server data contain other power consumers like network and power distribution. And finally, a dynamic PUE trace was provided, relating the total IT power consumption to the cooling power consumption. In order to represent the power flex market side, it was decided to represent one explicit and one implicit German power market that the data center could have accessed in 2014: the EPEX day ahead markets and the secondary reserve market. More information on the scenario is given in section 6.1.

It would have been desirable to compare this simulation instance against a second simulation of a data center with a different business model and therefore a different set of power management strategies. As such data were not available this comparison is left for future work.

Figure 5.2 illustrates which part of the simulation framework is implemented as a real simulation by greying out the components that are not used here. This pre-selection of components to be modeled illustrates clearly how dependent on the data center set-up both the technical and the economic potential of data center demand response are:

As can be seen, the components relating to interactive workload are not needed in this case; also the VM part is not applied. The reason for this is that the data center at hand does not use virtualization but its scheduling strategy

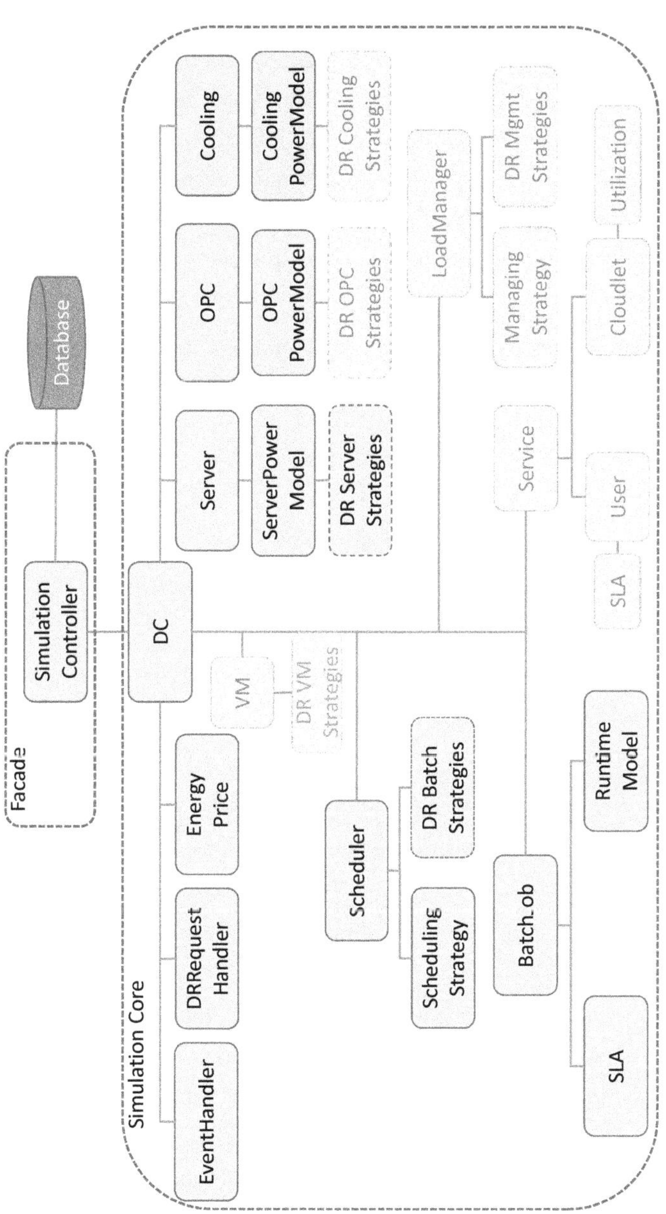

Figure 5.2.: Overview of Sim2Win-HPC implementation

assigns physical resources, i.e. more than 9.000 identical compute nodes. Based on data availability, two demand response strategies could be implemented using the *DRBatchStrategies* as well as the *DR[X]Strategies* component: a time-based workload shifting approach and the manipulation of the CPU frequency. Again, due to data availability, neither a cooling demand response strategy (*DRCoolingStrategies* greyed out) nor any OPC demand response strategy (*DROPC-Strategies* greyed out) could be applied. The simulator Sim2Win-HPC is coded in Java.

The subsequent sections will explain the models instantiating the components of the Sim2Win-HPC architecture for the available data traces and the interactions among these components.

Assumptions

The following assumptions reflect the situation in the considered data center scenario and the granularity of data available.

- **A1:** There is no virtualization layer in the HPC data center considered. Therefore jobs cannot be stopped and continued at a retained execution status.
- **A2:** Once started, a job has to be completed. This is connected to assumption **A1**, but an additional constraint: Due the data center's policy, jobs that are running must not be stopped prematurely. The strategy applied by [5], i.e. evicting of started jobs, albeit technically feasible cannot be implemented.
- **A3:** In the case of shifting workload, it is assumed that the earliest possible time for a job-start is the first timestep after the end of the considered demand response event window.
- **A4:** The data center does not use predictors for price or workload changes. This implies that there is no knowledge about the workload development for scheduling.

- **A5:** Once the information of explicit or implicit demand response events is received, the data center can implement frequency changes in real time.
- **A6:** In the case of shifting workload, neither the execution time of a job is changed nor does the rescheduling involve a further delay overhead.
- **A7:** The degree of parallelization of a job does not impact its energy consumption; i.e. a job running on a few servers consumes more time and less average power but the same energy as if the same job were running on many servers consuming less time and more average power.
- **A8:** The servers are homogeneous, i.e. nodes are deemed identical.
- **A9:** Idle servers are not shut down, but kept running at all times.
- **A10:** There are no upfront cost for implementing power management strategies, e.g. no investment cost. This means that the cost function of the power management strategies does not include a 'fixed cost' element.

5.2.1. The HPC Workload

Data center activity begins with a workload being injected into servers in order to transform this workload into results. Modeling the HPC workload consists of two issues: in general the available data set needs to be modeled in a way that is can be matched to a suitable server power model. 'Suitable' in this context means that it offers the possibility to manipulate the CPU frequency, as this is one of the power management strategies to be modeled. Once this has been set up, the workload needs to be scheduled first in accordance with the original schedule, but second in a way that allows to shift workload, as this is the second power management strategy to be modeled.

Applied Workload Model

The HPC data trace available for the current implementation of the simulation framework contains amongst others a job data trace for the whole year of 2014. For each job there is information about the start and end times, the average power consumption, the calculated energy consumption, and the maximum allowed frequency. After data cleaning the data set is made up of around 400.000 entries. The data trace and data treatment to make it available for power modeling will be described in more detail in section 6.1.1, that introduces the scenario in detail.

In order to be able to analyse the sensitivity of results towards the composition of the workload, it was decided to pursue the generative modeling approach using the method of clustering jobs into job classes. The most meaningful criterion was deemed to cluster into application types that have similar runtimes. However, information about application types was not available.

The challenge was therefore to determine how to model the workload composition based on the *available* information of job characteristics. The chosen approach enhances the external validity of this simulation that needs no additional data than what is available via regular monitoring equipment.

In order to link the workload data with a server power model that allows power manipulation, the key information apart from the job duration and average power consumption per job is its maximum allowed frequency. With this piece of information a server power model based on the frequency could be chosen. This lead to the conclusion to cluster the job data into a suitable number of classes based on the maximum allowed frequency, the average power consumption and job duration. Thus, the records grouped in one cluster have similar power consumption statistics, so that the average node power consumption can be modeled; however, they are not records of the same application type, even though the ratio between memory and computing effort within one class is comparable.

The records were clustered using the k-Means implementation of the WEKA framework. The k-means clustering algorithm is non-hierarchical, simply minimizing the squared Euclidean distance within a cluster, i.e. between each data point and its assigned cluster centroid. The 'k' represents the number of spher-

Table 5.1.: Average job characteristics of selected clusters. FR is the maximum frequency, AP the average power per node, JD the job duration, n the number of nodes, E the energy consumption, OC the occurrence of entries in this class

	No.	FR(GHz)	AP(W)	JD(hours)	n	E(kWh)	OC
High	7	2.52	378	16.33	6.1	2,658	2,061
	9	2.51	349	12.13	5.9	2,452	6,317
AP	20	2.43	320	11.58	5.3	2,249	3,448
Low	10	2.36	23	0.02	310.8	159	1,296
	21	2.36	44	0.07	121.3	307	8,612
AP	16	2.32	49	0.16	10.4	343	29,835
High	17	2.49	149	43.14	1,389.4	1,044	184
	0	2.50	183	38.29	441.0	1,286	932
JD	7	2.52	378	16.33	6.1	2,658	2,061
Low	10	2.36	23	0.02	310.8	159	1,296
	14	2.66	132	0.06	6,782.5	929	211
JD	21	2.34	44	0.07	121.3	307	8,612

ical clusters. Information about the k-means algorithm can be found in e.g. [46, 117].

The challenge of the k-means algorithm is to settle on a number of desired classes. This setting decides the trade-off between goodness-of-fit and modeling complexity.

So, for the available data set, different 'k's (3, 5, 10, 20, 30, 40, 50,100) were utilized. The resulting clusters were then used to evaluate the goodness-of-fit with the selected power model after the implementation of some other fitting steps (see section 5.2.3). In the end it turned out that beyond clustering into 10 classes the increase in the goodness-of-fit declined quickly, and that beyond using 30 cluster there was no real added value. Therefore, the workload model finally used consists of 30 clusters.

Table 5.1 shows the main characteristics of each cluster and the number of entries for the 9 clusters with the highest and the lowest power consumption.

As can be seen from table 5.1, the clusters mirror the high heterogeneity of the underlying job data. The assigned job class is then amended to the job data set so that it can be used to compute the average node power in the simulation model. For the sensitivity simulation runs, a subset of these clusters can be selected to evaluate the impact of different workload compositions on the simulation results.

The job data, however, are 'horizontal' data; that means that the data trace contains information per job: In order to be able to create the link between the workload model and the server (=node) model, the job data had to be transformed into time-series data for average node power consumption. That means that at each point in time, the following information needed to be aggregated per node: node activity (idle/not idle), ID of jobs running on each node (that includes the number of nodes a job consumes), average power consumption of this job. Figure 5.3 illustrates this procedure: each row signifies a node, each column as time slot. The nodes can be run at different utilization levels, i.e. CPU frequencies, so that e.g. job 1 consumed 100W and job 3 just 80 W. Also a job can occupy more than one node. Aggregating the job level information transformed in node level information for each time slot leads to a power profile as shown in the lower part of the image.

5.2.2. Scheduling Alternatives

In the current implementation of the simulation framework, five schedulers are used, which are regularly applied to the job-based workload, but for sensitivity analysis can also be applied to a subset of the job classes. The schedulers, which will be described later in this section, need to use the `SchedulingStrategy` interface within the scheduling package. This ensures that the scheduling strategies implemented can be easily exchanged.

1. the *HPC redesign (HPC-RE) scheduler*; it schedules the workload in a way that the original time series of the job data is fully retraced. The results of this scheduler are used as the baseline simulation run. In the architecture framework this is the concrete model for the 'scheduler' component.

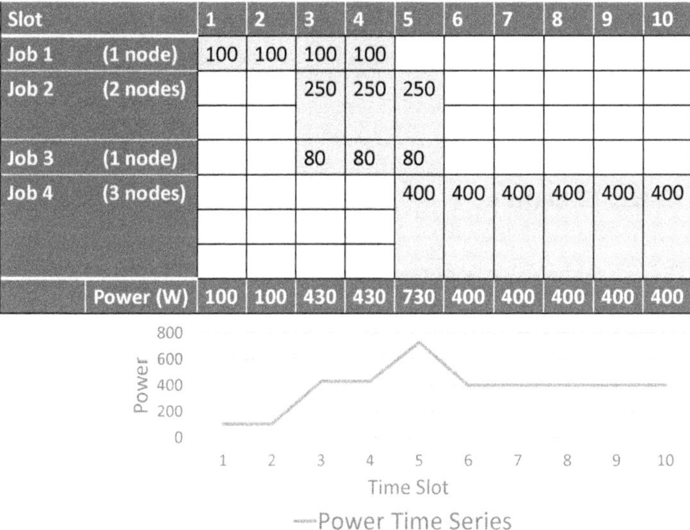

Slot		1	2	3	4	5	6	7	8	9	10
Job 1	(1 node)	100	100	100	100						
Job 2	(2 nodes)			250	250	250					
Job 3	(1 node)			80	80	80					
Job 4	(3 nodes)					400	400	400	400	400	400
	Power (W)	100	100	430	430	730	400	400	400	400	400

Figure 5.3.: Schematic representation of creating the link between job data and server power (interpolated data points)

2. the `shortest time to deadline first (STDF) scheduler`; it sorts all jobs according to the imminence of the pending deadline and schedules those first whose risk is highest to cause a delay and thus SLA cost. This scheduler is the default in the case of a demand response event and is comparable to *threshold time* approach from [82], but extended through an additional cost saving optimization.

3. the `longest time to deadline first (LTDF) scheduler`; it sorts all jobs vice versa to the imminence of the pending deadline and shifts those first whose risk is highest to cause a delay and thus SLA cost. This scheduler is enacted after the end of a demand response event in case workload was shifted.

4. the `continuous adaptation (CAS) scheduler`; it optimizes the benefit of implicit demand response by evaluating all possible adaptation options.

5. the `first in first out (FIFO) scheduler`; it sorts jobs according to submission time. It is used to analyse the sensitivity of results to SLA cost.

The HPC-RE Scheduler

The HPC-RE Scheduler is activated in case that there is no explicit demand response event: During normal operation jobs are read from the workload file and then take a status of 'submitted' so that they can be scheduled. As long as there is no demand response event, to schedule with the HPC-RE scheduler the information from the input file including job ID, planned frequency and number of nodes, start time and end time of the job are employed, and the starting times are used as scheduling information in order to retrace the original workload. This scheduler is switched on as a default. When a demand response event is finished, the HPC-RE scheduler is resumed as soon as possible, i.e. when the original workload curve and the new curve meet again. It then tries to schedule all the jobs that were not started at their original starting time. In case this is not possible the jobs are added to a waiting list and the scheduler uses backfilling.

The STDF Scheduler

The STDF scheduler is activated at the beginning of an adaptation (demand response) window and implemented as `DemandFlexibilitySchedulingStrategy` component that concretises the `DR Batch Strategies` component in the case of a demand response event. A demand response request is defined by adjustment height, direction (in terms of positive or negative reserve power), and duration. It takes basically the same information as the original HPC-RE scheduler, however without the start and end times. Additionally it needs the information about the job class as created through workload modeling.

The STDF scheduler uses the auxiliary job parameter $\Theta_{STDF}(x)$ which is defined as

$$\Theta_{STDF}(x) = \frac{t_{SLADeadline}(x) - t_{estEnd}(x)}{n(x)}, \tag{5.1}$$

where x is a batch job, $t_{SLADeadline}(x)$ the SLA deadline of x, $t_{estEnd}(x)$ the estimated end time of x, and $n(x)$ indicates the number of nodes that x utilizes. The jobs are then organized according to the ascending values of $\Theta_{STDF}(x)$.

The workload remaining in the event window is smoothed through a linear optimization approach which for the case of a positive power flex offer is formalized by:

$$\begin{aligned} \text{minimize} \quad & z \\ \text{subject to} \quad & -z + \sum_{j=1}^{J} x_{ji} * APJ_j \leq \alpha_i,\ 1 \leq i \leq T \\ & -y_j + \sum_{i=1}^{T} b_{ji} = 0,\ 1 \leq j \leq J, \end{aligned} \tag{5.2}$$

where z is the minimum power consumption sum in all timesteps within the optimized demand response event window, T is the total amount of simulation time steps in this event window, J is the total number of jobs that run at least partially therein, y_j is the number of simulation timesteps a job j is supposed to run within the concerned window, p_j is the average power consumption of job j, α_i is the total power consumption of all jobs that are not shiftable at timestep i, and b_{ji} is a boolean that indicates whether job j runs at the ith timestep of the demand response event window or not. A 'simulation time step' is defined as the combination of a simulation period and the number of nodes a job uses in order to differentiate different job sizes. The first constraint makes sure that the objective being minimized is actually the maximum power consumption sum out of all power consumption sums within the corresponding event window. The second constraint ensures that each job in the optimized schedule uses the same number of timesteps as in the original schedule in order to replicate correctly the job size. Additional constraints enforce that jobs are completely executed (due to assumption **A1** that there is no virtualization layer) and that the number of occupied nodes does not exceed the capacity at any point in time. As this linear optimization problem can get very complex depending on the setting, a timeout prevents obstructive computing times, reverting to a local minimum of this problem. To solve the linear optimization problems the java API of the *lp_solve* framework [34] is used, which is an open source linear programming system.

The LTDF Scheduler

Jobs delayed due to shifting are rescheduled using the *shortest time to deadline (STDF) heuristic* in a reverse order as *longest time to deadline* version. It uses the auxiliary job parameter $\Theta_{STDF}(x)$ as a basis but this time ordering the jobs according to descending values of $\Theta_{STDF}(x)$. This makes sure that the shifted jobs by having larger Θ_{STDF} values are executed after the non-shifted jobs in order to minimize the total delay cost by not adding extra delays to non-affected workload. The earliest restart-time after the shift is the first period after the event has ended. This means that there is no backfilling during the requested adjustment duration.

The CAS Scheduler

The CAS is aimed at minimizing the energy- and SLA cost of a job, which can be both shifted and scaled down through CPU frequency scaling. As a basis for the energy cost calculation it uses the estimated end time of a job $t_{estEnd}(x)$, which obviously is impacted by both frequency change and shifting the job in time. Therefore, for each job, the optimization procedure calculates the energy and delay cost for each potential combination of frequency and start times of this job for the next set of simulation periods. The resulting values are compared and the one is picked which offers the highest benefit compared to the baseline situation. If a start at the optimal timestep is not possible e.g.

due to the heterogeneity of the workload, CAS chooses a local optimum. If a job cannot be scheduled at once, the scheduling process waits in order to ensure that large jobs will be scheduled eventually. As in this process backfilling is not implemented and large jobs may not be able to be scheduled this scheduler in some cases is not able to schedule the total load.

The FIFO Scheduler

The FIFO is a standard scheduler often used as a baseline scheduler (e.g. [5, 151]. It takes the submission time information provided by the job data trace and sorts the jobs accordingly. This scheduler is used often in the absence of SLA constraints, and this is the reason why it is implemented here: in the sensitivity runs that evaluate the influence of SLA cost on the demand response results it replaces the STDF and LTDF schedulers at the time of the demand response event.

Interplay of HPC-RE, STDF, and LTDF Schedulers

Figure 5.4 illustrates the application of the schedulers for the case of an explicit demand response event where SLA cost are to be tracked and minimized. During normal operation, the HPC-RE scheduler is applied. When a demand response event is issued, in the figure signified by the green lines, that requests from the data center to reduce their load between time slots t_1 and t_2, the SDTF scheduler is applied, scheduling first the jobs with imminent deadlines, minimizing the remaining load. Thus the SLA cost inside the event are minimized. Once the event is finished the LTDF scheduler manages the workload until the originally planned baseline is reached again, ensuring that no extra SLA cost are imposed on the non-affected workload. Once the two instances of the job power curve meet again, the HPC-RE scheduler resumes the scheduling.

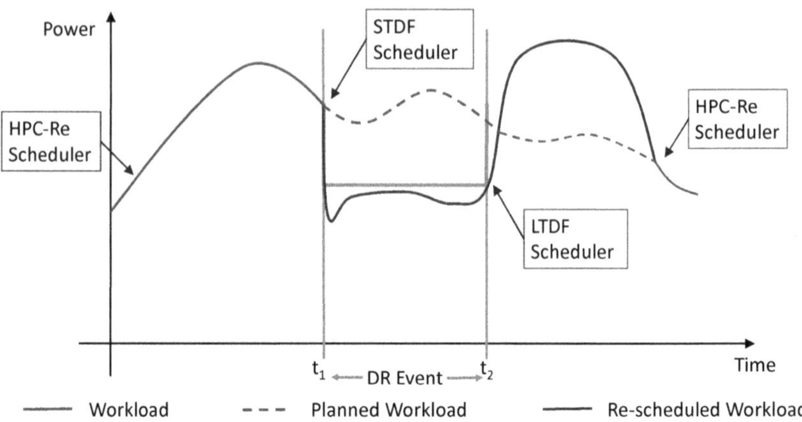

Figure 5.4.: Application of HPC-RE, STDF and LTDF schedulers during a demand response event

5.2.3. Server Power Modeling

As explained in section 5.2.1 the workload model needs to be logically connected with the server and network activity of the considered IT system as the 'real' power consumers. How this task is solved in Sim2Win-HPC is documented in the following sections.

Conceptual Basis for Server Power Modeling

Dayarathna et al. [61] provide a well structured overview of the most frequently used power models in data centers, differentiating mainly into additive and utilization based models. As the current version of the simulation framework is based on data that allow to manipulate the CPU frequency and to time-shift workload, a utilization based model that accounts for CPU frequency is needed.

A suitable model by *Elnozahy et al.* [66] is equation (4.2), introduced in chapter 4.2.4. It is defined as $P_{serv}(f) = Af^3 + P_{idle}$, where A is a server specific constant and f is the CPU frequency of the server. Based on this model, other, more fine-grained server power models were developed, e.g. differentiating between parallelization (represented the used numbers of node n as a proxy) and frequency dependency parts of applications [186]. However, the requirements for a model to be consistently applicable in a concrete setup is that

1. the necessary model inputs (variables and parameters) are available in the required granularity in the provided data trace and

2. that the model is suitable for the phenomenon it should represent in the current physical setting i.e. it can be fitted with the available data (model validation). For instance, a model targeted at a very specific server type will not render good fitting results with a different server even if the data needed are available.

Therefore a slightly different version of the equation (4.2), is used which was validated by *Shoukourian et al.* for the Sandy Bridge servers and specific applications in the SuperMUC system [186]: The version of [186] is adapted further as the number of utilized nodes of the application is not a necessary parameter for the presented model version. The reason is that the number of nodes is not to be manipulated through a power management strategy Also the static parameters of the idle and the dynamic part of the server power are merged. This implies the assumption that the power consumption of the server is independent of the number of nodes an application uses, i.e. of the parallelization of the application. Thus a model very similar to [66] is derived with the main difference that the parameters of [66] become fitting parameters.

$$P_{serv}(f^3) = k_1 f^3 + k_2, \tag{5.3}$$

where k_1 and k_2 are application and server specific fitting parameters and f^3 is the variable. Using this quite simple, but very well validated approach promised to have an adequate computational load for the total simulation system.

Fitting the Server Power Model

Fitting the selected power model with the provided data center traces was carried through with the help of the regression algorithms in the WEKA data mining framework, an open source java-based tool [96]. As a metric to evaluate the fit of the equation (5.5) with the measured average power/node values the Pearson correlation coefficient was calculated which is suitable for measuring the correlation between two linearly connected variable x and y:

$$\rho_{x,y} = \frac{cov(x,y)}{\sigma_x \sigma_y}, \tag{5.4}$$

where $cov(x,y)$ is the covariance between variables x and y, σ_x is the mean of variable x, and σ_y is the mean of variable y.

Deriving k_2 looked straightforward at first, as the idle power of 'identical' nodes even though not being truly identical (see [218]) is at least very similar. In the current set-up, the average value was 49W. The main issue, therefore, seemed to be the assessment of k_1. In the original formulation of *Elnozahy et al.* [66] the dynamic part of the server power $P_{serv_{dyn}}$ was decomposed into:

$$P_{serv_{dyn}} = A * C * V^2 * f \tag{5.5}$$

with A being an activity factor accounting for the frequency of gate switching, C the capacitance of the gate outputs and thus dependent on the physical architecture of the utilized server, V processor voltage and f frequency. As voltage follows frequency, in later research the variables V^2 and f were condensed into f^3; and as for one specific application on one specific server A and C are constants, they could be merged, too (see [66]). However, if applied *not* to a single application, but to an application mix (as in the case of a whole data center), the product of the parameters A and C is not constant. Therefore, using this model directly by fitting the parameters k_1 and k_2 for the 2014 data trace with the help of the WEKA framework achieved, not unexpectedly, a Pearson correlation of a mere 0.3311. The result implies that the applications run as batch jobs in the data center at hand are heterogeneous not only with regards to workload statistics, but also with regards to CPU activity.

Unfortunately, no further data containing information about the application or even an application type were available. The decision to cluster the workload into 30 classes with comparable application statistics and behaviour, taken to allow sensitivity analyses of the workload composition (see 5.2.1), therefore proved beneficial also for the case of fitting the power model: using the power model on job classes instead of individual jobs improved the goodness of fit drastically.

Before fitting could be implemented, however, the next obstacle was the assignment of frequencies to the applications by the IBM loadLeveler, used in the corresponding HPC data center. The values of frequencies inside the 30 job classes did not differ greatly, so that there were not enough data points (in terms of different values of the variable f^3) for a good fitting procedure. This issue could be mitigated by capitalizing on the results of a study determining the behaviour of the typical set of applications run in an HPC data center under different frequencies (see figure 5.5, created from data in [17]). As can be seen, 2.7 GHz were used as nominal frequency and the power consumption of the typical HPC application portfolio was normalized to be 100% for 2.7 GHz. Interestingly, the power consumption is about halved (47,7%) with respect to the norm at a frequency of 1.2GHz and is around 63.1% at the so-called 'sweet-spot' of the configuration, 1.8 GHz, where the application's energy consumption is minimized. Below this frequency, even though power is reduced - which is the objective of demand response programs - the applications run so slowly (runtime extended by 40%) that in the end the energy consumption is even increased compared to the most efficient configuration.

Thus, before fitting equation (5.5) within a job class, all job records within this class were scaled using the data from [17] so that after this scaling procedure, the data set used to create the fit for a job class contained 16 records for

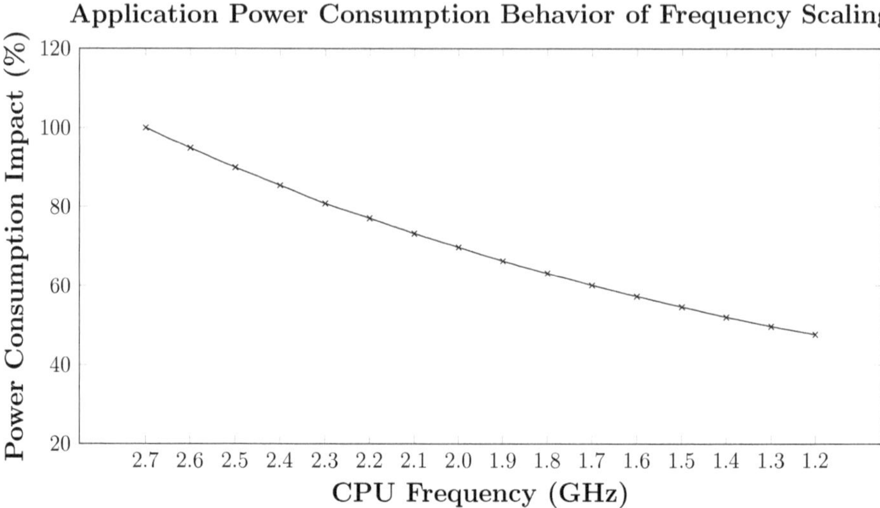

Figure 5.5.: Power consumption behaviour of an HPC application portfolio under frequency scaling (data from [17])

each original record (one for each frequency as illustrated in Figure 5.5).

Using this approach the correlation of the original average power/node values and the predicted average power/node values finally achieved a Pearson correlation of 0.98, which is a sufficient fit for the targets of the simulation. Therefore, strictly speaking, the derived power model is an abstraction of the original frequency based power model as the values for the 'static' part can be significantly below the measured idle value of 49W. This idle value is used whenever a node is not executing workload.

As mentioned, this power model is just one option of modeling server power within the simulation framework. Also the current simulator version allows an easy exchange of power models through the `PowerModelSelector` class that calls the `getServerPower-method`. The status of the server can be OCCUPIED, IDLE, and OFF. In Sim2Win the 'OFF' status remains unused due to the data center's policy of not turning off servers (see [91] and assumption **A9**).

5.2.4. Other Infrastructure Components

Other infrastructure components that need to be modeled in order to determine a data center wide offer of power flexibility can be differentiated into cooling power, as a major power consumer, and other power consumers (OPC) that all together typically use less than 20% of total data center power (see section 4.2.4).

As explained in section 4.2.4, there are a lot of different *cooling models* ranging from physical white box to empirical black box models. The more detailed the modeling of physical interactions, air flows and hot spots is, i.e. the more 'white-boxed' the modeling, unfortunately, the more data is needed. This is the bottleneck in many modeling approaches, so that when no detailed data is available often a rather coarse empirical model is chosen: the consumed power of the cooling equipment is monitored and put into relation to the IT infrastructure consumption, thus leading to the definition of a 'partial' PUE that abstracts from power of other non-IT power consumers as e.g. the PDU (4.2.4). Due to the lack of deep data availability and thus the impossibility to apply white box modeling, for the implementation of the cooling component in the HPC instance of the simulation framework Sim2Win the following simple cooling power model, already introduced in 4.2.4 was applied:

$$P_{cool} = P_{IT} * (PUE - 1) \tag{5.6}$$

Even though the data trace that the current model is built on contains minute-based monitoring results, thus increasing correctness of the calculated cooling power, unfortunately, this approach does not offer any starting point to execute a cooling-based power management strategy. Therefore the subcomponent `DRCoolingStrategies` of the subcomponent `CoolingPowerModel` is greyed out in the Sim2Win-HPC generic architecture version.

The same applies for OPC subsuming *all other IT room power consumers* apart from the servers, mostly the communication network, the power distribution infrastructure and storage. In this case the lack of data is less of a problem: as studies show on the one hand the share of other power consumers at the total power demand of a data center is small and on the other hand, the biggest part of it, which is network power consumption, is largely static power consumption. Therefore, to apply a simple rule of thumb in this case can be justified. As explained in 4.2.4 the simplest model that can be applied is a static approach which is modeled in the following way:

$$OPC = n * P_{serv} * frac_{OPC}, \tag{5.7}$$

where $frac_{OPC} = \frac{P_{IT} - n * P_{serv}}{n * P_{serv}}$ with P_{serv} as server power consumption and P_{IT} the IT power consumption, i.e., data that were taken from the monitoring system in the server room. $frac_{OPC}$ can be estimated via a regression analysis.

In the simulation model, this fraction is used to calculate an estimated total IT power consumption from the server power consumption. This calculated IT power consumption is then multiplied with the real PUE to derive cooling and thereby total facility power P_{DC}:

$$\begin{aligned} P_{DC} &= P_{IT} + P_{cool} && (5.8) \\ &= n * P_{serv} + OPC + P_{cool} && (5.9) \\ &= n * P_{serv} * (frac_{OPC} + PUE) && (5.10) \end{aligned}$$

5.2.5. Modeling Demand Response Strategies

The preceding sections provided the foundation for modeling two different demand response strategies:

- Temporal shifting of workload, as the workload modeled can be managed by different scheduling alternatives which allow to shift the workload;
- Frequency scaling, as the server power model allows to manipulate frequency. These power management strategies can be applied both for explicit and implicit demand response schemes.

For explicit demand response, whenever a `issueDemand-ResponseRequest` is called by a subcomponent of the `EventHandler` due to a `DRRequestHandler` activation, a check is carried through to determine if the event size is above the *maximum achievable adjustment size* at the very moment. This is a technical feasibility constraint, defined by shifting the entire affected workload out of the demand response event time window and scaling the non-shiftable remains to minimum frequency. Even though this check must be done before offering the demand response bid, a double-check is necessary to avoid the infeasibility of solutions.

For the case of implicit demand response, the original scheduler is replaced by the CAS scheduler for the total evaluation time, thus producing independent results. Comparing the results of these two schedulers therefore displays continuous differences as one takes prices into account and the other does not.

In the presented simulation system Sim2Win-HPC the power management strategies *temporal workload shifting* and *frequency scaling* form a configuration which is represented as a tuple of percentage of shiftable workload (in terms of the number of nodes and the execution time) as well as desired frequency for the remaining workload. An optimization procedure evaluates the combination of each possible number of shifted jobs with all possible CPU frequencies thereby determining the least costly combination that just fulfills the power flex market requirements.

The cost for the demand response adaptations are calculated by running two copied instances of the simulation: one using the original scheduling and CPU scaling parameters, and the second using the optimized demand response results. These instances are maintained until they are both again in the same state. The additional cost that are caused by the adaptation are then calculated as the difference between the energy- and SLA cost of the two simulation instances.

Temporal Workload Shifting

Temporal workload shifting means that workload is post- or preponed, contrary to geographical shifting where workload is shifted to a different data center site. This is implemented in a way that in the workload trace for an affected job the starting point is replaced by a new starting point given by first the STDF algorithm and then the LTDF algorithm in the case of postponing workload and by the STDF algorithm in the case of pre-poning jobs (see section 5.2.2 for details on the scheduling algorithms). The average power consumption remains untouched, the end time is adapted accordingly. As the HPC data center at hand does not use virtualization, only a complete job can be shifted out of the affected time window. Depending on the workload structure this means that the response to the event cannot be met exactly; it might be overfulfilled slightly.

The impact of the shifting strategy on the power consumption of the data center at one particular time period is given by

$$\Delta P_{DC}^{shift} = \sum_{j=1}^{\Delta J} AP_j * n_j * (frac_{OPC} + PUE), \tag{5.11}$$

where AP_j is the average node power consumption of the j-th shifted job, n_j the number of nodes of job j, and ΔJ the number of shifted jobs.

It is assumed that there is no timing overhead of rescheduling the jobs so that the time-based requirements from the power flex markets can be fulfilled. Thus the shifting activity only impacts the part of the workload that is already in the queue, but has not been scheduled. The 'ratio workload shifting' (RWL) metric monitored in the documentation of the results is the share of the shifted jobs compared to all shiftable jobs, i.e. the ones in the queue that have not been scheduled yet. It is used as an indicator for the degree to which shifting is applied. The delay of enacting shifting involves the time spent on receiving the request, computing the adaptation request and exchanging the scheduler. Also *Cupelli et al.* rely on rescheduling; they even assume real-time reaction [60].

Considering this context the power impact of such a strategy, which uses only the small share of jobs that are queued but not started is questionable. Also, depending on the variance of the workload execution time there is some delay until a workload-driven reduction of power takes its full effect. This was empirically tested in [88]: After scheduling was stopped and the jobs were allowed to finish it took up to 72 hours until the server power consumption in the Lawrencium cluster at LBNL was in idling mode. As the current composition of the workload is always a snapshot of jobs with different execution times, this statement is corroborated through analyses of the utilized workload trace: with execution times between 52 hours and a couple of seconds, the ability of rescheduling is highly dependent on the chosen time slot. These are the reasons, why the decision was taken not to rely on temporal shifting alone, but to combine scheduling and frequency opportunities, which is a solution also favoured by *Bates et al.* [31].

CPU Frequency Scaling

As shortly mentioned in the sections 5.2.6 and 5.2.3, contrary to temporarily shifting workload, manipulating the CPU frequency impacts both the average power of a job and its execution time. The start time, however, remains untouched. The implemented version of the frequency scaling strategy switches the frequency of *all* active jobs to the desired average frequency. After the requested power adaptation time window, all jobs are scaled back to their originally specified, individual CPU frequency.

The impact of manipulating the frequency of the data center workload on the overall power consumption at one particular time period is given by

$$\Delta P_{DC}^{scale} = \sum_{j=1}^{m} \Delta AP_j * n_j * (frac_{OPC} + PUE), \tag{5.12}$$

where ΔAP_j is change of the average node power consumption of the j-th shifted job, n_j the number of nodes of job j, and m the total number of active jobs. The power consumption change ΔAP_j is calculated according to the server power model for the respective job class in equation (5.5) in section 5.2.3. It is again assumed that there is no timing overhead for reasons of compliance with the requirements from the power flex markets.

That this assumption is realistic is corroborated by *Bhattacharya et al.* [37]. They executed empirical tests with three different servers in order to understand the total delay composed of network latency, system latency, and power change delay. The network latency in the observed case was less than a millisecond so that the authors concluded it to be negligible. The system latency which includes the time for executing the threads for reading and manipulating the frequency ranged between 10 and 50ms on different servers. The power change delay due to the capacitance of the servers and the time used in the power circuits was between 100 and 300ms using the frequencies that are furthest apart. So all in all, the reaction time can be reckoned to be well below a second, which is a lot faster than required even by the most demanding German power reserve market: The primary reserve market requires the offered power adjustment to be activated completely within at maximum 30 seconds[1].

5.2.6. The Cost of Power Management

In the current instance Sim2Win-HPC of the Sim2Win architectural framework the cost of power management inside a data center to enact the two selected power management strategies is represented by SLA and energy cost. Fixed power cost are not included (assumption **A10**): any upfront investment for implementing the power management would relate to both power management strategies in the same way and would thus not shift the weight of either strategy; also compared to market entrance cost of the modeled explicit demand response market due to automation options the cost are deemed negligible (see section 5.2.7).

[1] https://www.regelleistung.net/ext/static/technical, accessed May 1st 2020

The two cost items of power management inside the data center are therefore SLA cost and energy cost. In order to calculate SLA cost, in the current instance of Sim2Win, the `BatchCost` subcomponent of the `Batchjob` component interacts with the other subcomponents `SLA` and `RuntimeModel`. Energy and power cost are calculated using the `Batchjob` component and the `EnergyPrice` component.

Energy cost are based on the energy price vector - in the case of the baseline run, this is the average industry price of 2014 is used [42]. It contains an average value for the power cost of a medium sized industry. It is not necessary to calculate a power cost impact, as the technical capacity constraint of the data center in terms of the maximum number of nodes coincides with the peak power value of 2014. This cannot be surpassed in any case.

SLA cost are dependent on SLA parameters and how they are being affected by the power management strategies as well as on the price tag of breaking an SLA. As no information about SLA terms and price tags are available for the data center at hand, these need to be modeled based on realistic assumptions for the modeled scenario.

SLA specifications are obviously dependent on the workload that they are applied to (see e.g.[3]). In the case of interactive workload, SLA are often related to broad network accessibility, response times, or information losses aka packet loss ratio (PLR). In the context of batch workload the main SLA parameter modeled is regularly based on execution time (e.g. [214, 138, 21]). The SLA parameter used in the current work is generally defined as *delay* in terms of a *surpassed deadline*, which then induces the payment of penalty cost. The cost model for SLA consequently comprises the definition of the delay which is based on an assessment of a job's runtime and the calculation of the cost based on this delay.

Batch Job Runtime Model

As explained for performance and energy consumption (see section 5.2.1), the execution time[2] of a job depends on

- job characteristics as cycles per instruction (CPI) and I/O activities,
- the IT infrastructure as server and network characteristics but also their architecture,
- and run-time settings as the CPU frequency.

In order to model the cost of implementing a power management strategy the focus of this work is on run-time settings, because these are manipulated through the selected power management strategies.

For the case of workload shifting, it is assumed that the runtime of the job is not changed. This assumption does not fully reflect reality in HPC computing as even nodes marked as identical through the server brand name have slight differences [218]. Therefore computing a batch job at another point in time on a different (set of) server(s) might lead to slightly differing runtimes. However, as in the current scenario (homogeneous servers, see assumption **A8**) these differences are negligible and as the strategies applied do not capitalize on workload consolidation, the execution time (not the end time!) of workload shifting is deemed constant.

In order to estimate the impact of the demand response reaction of the data center on the QoS through frequency scaling two approaches are possible: either starting from modeling the execution time and comparing it before and after manipulating frequency or modeling directly the change of frequency.

An example for the first approach is given by *Shoukourian et al.* in [186]. The model is defined as

$$TtS(n,f) = \frac{t_1}{f} + \frac{t_2}{n} + \frac{t_3}{nf} + t_4 n + t_5 \frac{n}{f} + t_6, \tag{5.13}$$

[2]'Runtime' and 'execution time' are used as synonyms.

where TtS is a job's execution time, f is the execution frequency, n is the number of nodes the job utilizes, and t_1 through t_6 are constant fitting parameters that depend on the application type of the job. However, as the jobs within the workload trace cannot be assigned to an application type and as this model requires six application dependent fitting parameters, this approach is not possible in the current scenario.

On the other hand, the utilized workload trace gives information about the measured runtime of a job and its configuration in terms of frequency and the execution number of nodes. This information allows the application of the second modeling approach which matches well with the impact-based point of view of the micro-econmics based modeling framework. Yet, the information basis limits the choice of applicable models: For instance the model introduced in [17] builds on information about the cycles per instruction and the memory transactions per instruction - again a granularity of information that is not available. A way out is given by a very simple consideration about the impact of frequency of the computation part of a job. *Rountree et al.* [179] discovered that scaling frequency scales execution time reciprocally proportionally, which can be expressed as:

$$T(f) = \frac{f_0}{f_n} * T(f_0), \tag{5.14}$$

where $T(f)$ is the execution time of a job at frequency f, f_0 is the original frequency, f_n the new frequency and $T(f_0)$ the original execution time.

This simple relationship, however, only applies to the execution time of computation; when the memory is accessed, this happens independently of the frequency. In reality, however, jobs are never fully compute bound, but they always have proportion of work that is memory bound. This is also true in the case of the available data trace.

As memory access times are not sensitive to CPU frequency, the impact of a frequency adjustment onto the runtime of a job is limited by the degree of *memory boundedness* of the job [180, 179]. This lead to the introduction of a parameter β as a ratio between 0 and 1 which expresses the ratio of *compute boundedness* of a job. Only this part of an application can be influenced by frequency scaling [111]. Later, the compute boundedness β was incorporated into an enhanced runtime model by *Etinski et al.* [67], which is defined as follows:

$$\frac{T(f)}{T(f_{max})} = \beta(\frac{f_{max}}{f} - 1) + 1, \tag{5.15}$$

where $T(f)$ is the job's runtime at frequency f, $T(f_{max})$ its runtime at a nominal frequency f_{max}, and β the fitting parameter that depends on the degree of compute boundedness of a job. Decomposing the total execution time T of a job into computation time T_{CPU} and memory access time T_{MEM}, which is insensitive to frequency changes, β can also be expressed as [67]:

$$\beta = \frac{T_{CPU}(f_{max})}{T_{CPU}(f_{max}) + T_{MEM}}. \tag{5.16}$$

It is generally possible that the parameter β varies for different (f_{max}, f) pairs of one application. However, according to *Etinski et al.* [67] in most cases it is reasonable to assume that these variations are negligible so that one β value can be used per application.

In 2014, *Auweter et al.* [17] analyzed this relation for a typical set of applications that are executed in an HPC data center using 2.3 GHz as default frequency and comparable to the considered data center. They show how the runtime scales for more than 300 typical applications when the default frequency is manipulated. The IBM LoadLeveler predicts the parameters needed to assess β, so that by measuring themselves, *Auweter et al.* could verify the model by comparing the LoadLeveler predictions with their own measurement.

In case the parameters are not available - as for the current data trace - this model has to be applied vice versa: The deviation from proportionality indicates the influence of β. With the average values handed over by the authors, it was thus possible to fit the model from Equation (5.15) to the known runtime behavior for each (f_{max}, f) pair. As a result, for the fifteen different frequency pairs, 15 different β values were obtained (one for each (f_{max}, f) tuple) although according to equation (5.16) the β value should be constant for all frequency pairs. The average value of β is 0.79; the maximum deviation from this is 4.5%. As the maximum acceptable deviation according to *Etinski et al.* [67] is 5%, it was decided to use this average as a basis for the runtime calculation (see figure 5.6) in the Sim2Win-HPC simulation.

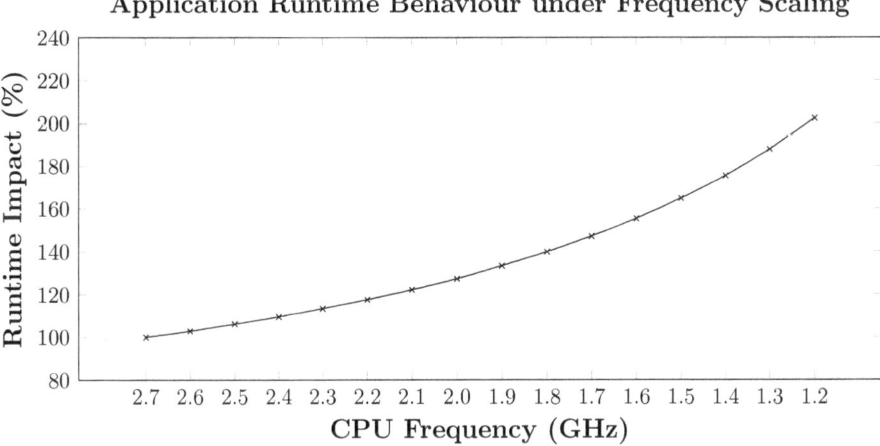

Figure 5.6.: Average application runtime behavior under frequency scaling (data from [17])

SLA Cost Model

An SLA cost model consists of the definition of the cost unit, the price per unit, and the way that these are connected to generate a penalty sum. For the case of delay cost that means that as a first step 'delay' needs to be defined. As unfortunately there are no data concerning an SLA cost model for the considered data center, the delay is defined based on the runtime calculation, as explained in the section above, and on an artificially constructed deadline. *Garg et al.*

have supplied the following deadline model which is reusable in the present case [82]:

$$t_{SLAdl}(x) = t_{jobStart}(x) + ExeTime(x) + (ExeTime(x) * uniform(0,2)), \quad (5.17)$$

where $t_{SLAdl}(x)$ is the point in time of the batch job's deadline, $t_{jobStart}(x)$ is the point in time where the job starts, $ExeTime(x)$ is the time that the job needs under optimal execution conditions, and $uniform(0,2)$ is a sample from a uniform distribution in the interval between 0 and 2. Other research papers use the 4-fold time of the expected execution time [145], determine that jobs should not wait longer than 4 days [151], or they simply do not state the origin of the deadlines used [173, 54]. *Jiang et al.* [119] determine deadlines with up to 50 times the job runtime. As the uniform distribution reflects the heterogeneity of job importance, be it due to monetary values or other attributes this model was considered a sensible solution and therefore chosen for the current implementation. Obviously, the value of 2 is a random choice, applied by *Garg et al.* that determines the spread of deadlines between the default execution time $ExeTime(x)$ and thrice the default execution time. Both the randomization value of 2 and the weight of the default runtime can be used for manipulating the flexibility in simulation runs. Due to the high heterogeneity of the jobs in the considered job data trace, the original version of the model lead to very hard deadlines. As the spread of deadline definition in literature is extremely high the default deadline was finally defined as:

$$t_{SLAdl}(x) = t_{jobStart}(x) + ExeTime(x) + 2 * (ExeTime(x) * uniform(0,2)) \quad (5.18)$$

The original definition of *Garg et al.* was used as a 'hard SLA' version for sensitivity simulation runs. Via information of the start- and the end-time the job data trace the runtime is available. So, the artificial deadline could be computed once for the entire cleaned job data trace and added as an additional job parameter.

Regarding the second step of a cost model, i.e. linking the deadline and a price for surpassing this deadline in order to calculate a penalty, for a batch workload *Garg et al.* suggest an approach depending merely on the computed delay and the penalty rate [82]. This implies that as soon as the deadline is surpassed, cost are attributed proportionally, and that there are no penalty cost if job finishes before the deadline. The penalty Pe is calculated according to the equation introduced in 4.2.6

$$Pe = y * db, \tag{5.19}$$

where y is a fixed penalty rate, and db is the delay calculated as the absolute difference between the deadline and the termination. However, this cost model cannot differentiate between jobs of different sizes and weights in terms of number of nodes used. Also the delay is absolute, which effectively privileges jobs with an extremely high runtime compared to shorter running jobs.

For the current scenario, the penalty should depend both on the weight of the job and the job's time in the system. As no realistic data for SLA cost were to be found, the baseline price was determined based on the node usage price in a comparable data center. Therefore the model for SLA cost C_{SLA} was adjusted to meet those requirements:

$$C_{SLA} = uP * rD, \tag{5.20}$$

where uP is the usage price (in €) of a job, and rD is a relative delay. This usage price is calculated on the basis of the number of nodes that a job utilizes and the expected runtime. The relative delay ($rD \geq 0$) is calculated as

$$rD = \begin{cases} \frac{(t_{EndTime}(x) - t_{SLAdl}(x))}{ExeTime(x)} \; \forall \; t_{EndTime}(x) \geq t_{SLAdl}(x) \\ 0 \; \forall \; t_{EndTime}(x) < t_{SLAdl}(x), \end{cases} \tag{5.21}$$

where $t_{EndTime}(x)$ is the job termination time which might be modified, e.g due to being shifted or processed at a lower processor speed. $rD = 0$ when the job is not delayed.

5.2.7. Modeling Accessed Power Flex Markets

On the part of the data center simulation framework Sim2Win and the implemented instantiation Sim2Win-HPC, the reaction to incentives by the power flex markets is handled via the `DRRequestHandler`-component (for explicit demand response) and the `EnergyPrice`-component (for implicit demand response) in cooperation with the `EventHandler`-component.

In order for the simulator to receive power market incentives these have to be modeled according to the specified interfaces. The Sim2Win-HPC modeling solution is explained in the subsequent sections.

Explicit Power Flex Markets

A explained in section 2.2.2 the European system of reserve power is made up of basically three reserve markets that are called subsequently once the frequency in the transmission system goes beyond the allowed band around 50Hz. The primary reserve control takes over unexpected shortfalls of supply and demand until the resources of the secondary reserve control are up and running. The latter bridges the time until the tertiary reserve takes over. The activation of these reserves is beyond a market based control; it needs to happen in a predetermined process. However, in order to enter into the list of reserve control suppliers, market participants need to undergo a prequalification process that is cost effective. In many EU member states the reserve suppliers need to bid into the respective control power market. This bid corresponds to entering into a contract; having concluded it, the supply of the offered power and energy is mandatory. In case that during the considered week the TSO needs the contracted power, it is merely activated e.g. via a direct manipulation by the TSO, via a phone call or email or triggered by IT based communication. The compensation can relate to the supplied power, to the supplied energy, or to both.

For the simulation based in Germany the secondary reserve market was chosen as on the one hand it is more profitable than the tertiary market and the requirement for activation time (full provision after 5 minutes) can be fulfilled by the two applied power management strategies. The primary reserve needs to be fully activated within 30 seconds; even though the technical implementation of the two applied power management strategies within 30 seconds might be possible, adding the communication overhead makes this requirement critical. Primary reserve, on the other hand, will always be controlled by the grid operator or aggregator, whereas for the secondary reserve it can be assumed that in future the enactment within the regulation power service provider can be executed self-controlled.

In order to include the secondary reserve market in Sim2Win-HPC, artificial bids are created and the data center collaboration is activated according to the real counterparts of these bids through the activation data of the TSO for 2014. This process is explained in detail in section 6.1.2, as it precedes the simulation.

Interfacing with the simulator, a demand response event from the real activation data trace is then described in terms of provision type (positive or negative), adjustment height, starting time, duration and compensation and read by the `DRRequestHandler`. The size of the bid must be consistent with a pre-bidding test about the maximum technically achievable adjustment height as explained in 5.2.5. This should be carried through in a conservative way in order to ensure that an activation is possible when called. Otherwise high penalties from the TSO are due, additionally to being removed from the list of potential control power providers. The pre-bidding test can be carried through by the Sim2Win-HPC simulator on the predicted workload, maintaining a safety margin.

Dynamic EPEX Prices as an Example of Implicit Power Flex Markets

Contrary to explicit demand response, the contractual binding of implicit demand response is much lower: for a pre-specified product the participant can buy electricity at a pre-determined, dynamic price. There are many options for implicit demand response one of which is the stock market for electricity. The main stock market for electric power in Europe is the European Power Exchange (EPEX) (see section 2.2.2).

Interfacing with the Sim2Win-HPC simulator, the EPEX market is represented as a vector with different prices (pay-as-clear prices) at each time of the day for the whole year of 2014. Again, the way that this vector is constructed is modeled outside the simulating system.

When the EPEX market is activated in the simulation, the CAS scheduler (see section 5.2.2) optimizes the cost for sourcing the electricity.

5.3. Validation of Sim2Win-HPC

The result of applying the validation & verification procedure to a system can be internal and external validity (e.g. [139]). This distinction is mostly used in experimental research; however, simulation with real data can be interpreted as a method of experimentation [159], so that it is applicable in the current research process: *Internal validity* signifies, that the validated system is behaving correctly in the studied scenario. *External validity*, on the other hand, deals with the question to which extent the validated system can be applied to other than the originally intended scenarios.

In this section, the internal validity is being tested by comparing simulated results of the behaviour of the Sim2Win-HCP simulation system in the absence of any demand response schemes with all available real data traces from 2014.

The technical configuration of the validation run was a Windows 10 Pro machine with an Intel i7-7600U CPU with 2 physical cores at 2.8GHz and a 16GB RAM. As the data traces relate to all 2014, also the validation ran from 01/01/2014 until 06/01/2015 in order to allow for all processes to finish. As the provided workload trace is on seconds basis, a simulation step length of one real time second was used. The scheduling interval length was set to one simulation step.

Table 5.2 contains the validation statistics for the year 2014. The decreasing values of both correlation and Pearson coefficient from job power (0.985 vs. 0.97) over IT power (0.812 vs. 0.659) to facility power (0.808 vs. 0.654) can be explained with the increasing knowledge gap with regards to the power components. The most important parameter is the job power time series, as the job power is the central power model where power management strategies are to be applied. The other power curves are used to construct the total facility power which is necessary to calculate remunerations. The job power time series' statistics have high values of correlation and Pearson Coefficient, and low error rates which implies that the solution of using job classes for workload modeling resulted in very accurate predictions of the power consumption.

With the validation parameters being sufficiently high, this validation run will be used as the ground truth for the evaluation baseline run, that also contains cost elements. Figures 5.7 and 5.8 show the validation runs and the differences between the original and the simulated time series data.

Table 5.2.: Statistics of the comparison between original data traces and simulated data traces

	Correlation	R^2	MAE	MAPE
Job Power	0.985	0.97	51.2	4.37%
IT Power	0.812	0.659	165.764	10.11%
Cooling Power	0.896	0.803	21.508	10.11%
Total Facility Power	0.808	0.654	187.269	10.11%
Active Nodes	0.999	0.999	1.329	0.03%
Running Jobs	0.999	0.999	0.007	0.02%

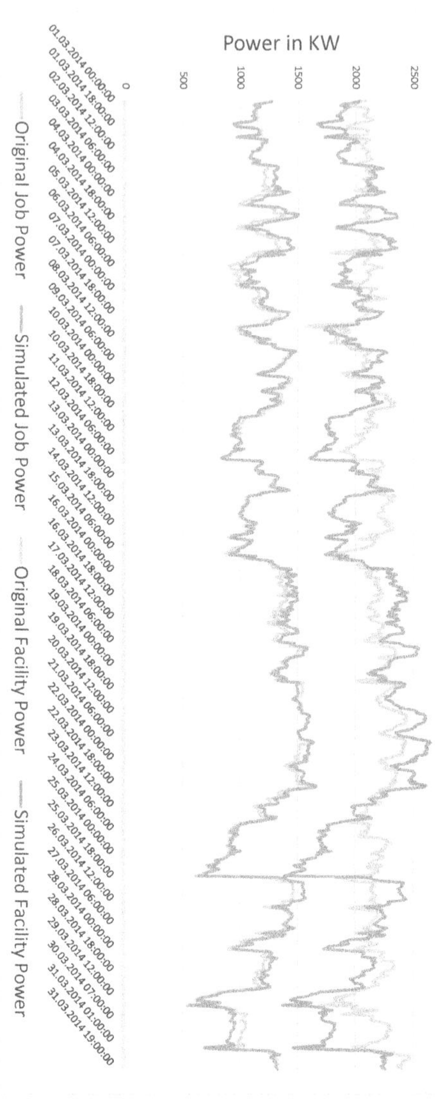

Figure 5.7.: Sim2Win-HPC job and facility power validation

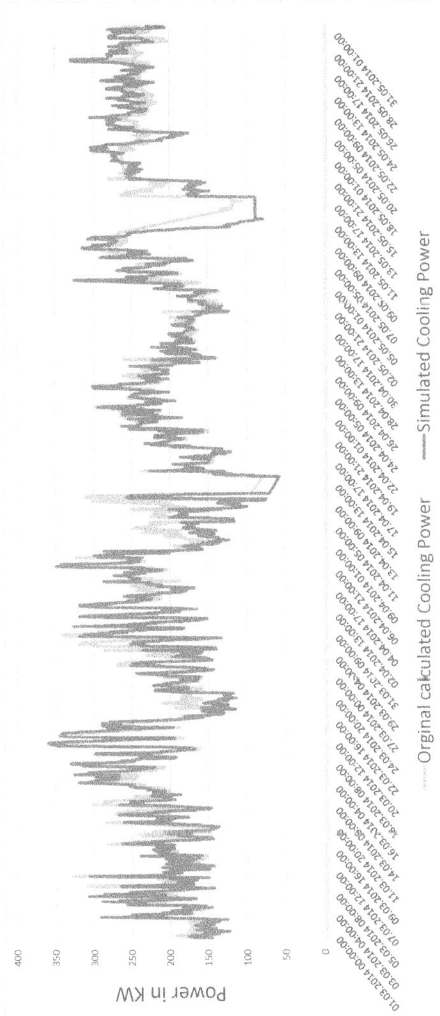

Figure 5.8.: Sim2Win-HPC cooling validation

6. Simulation Runs and Results

6.1. Scenario and Data

6.1.1. Data Center

Both the simulation and the optimization framework for demand response with data centers are evaluated using data traces from a large scale HPC system in Germany. This implies that contrary to many other works, the data traces are not combined from various different sources so that they are internally consistent with regards to workload, server power, power demand of cooling, and of OPC.

The traces are derived from a homogeneous (in terms of installed system software stack and system hardware) HPC system with more than 9000 compute nodes. Each node contains two Intel Sandy Bridge-EP Xeon [113] E5-2680 8C octa-core processors that each have a thermal design power of 130 W[1] and a maximum CPU frequency of 2.7GHz. The default operating frequency is set to 2.3 GHz, but other frequencies may be employed. The frequency setting policy is based on efficiency: Applications assessed to experience a runtime degradation of at least 5% if computed at the 2.5GHz instead of at the default 2.3GHz, will be executed using 2.5GHz. Applications are only executed at 2.7GHz instead of 2.3GHz if they would incur a runtime degredation of 12%; this policy accounts for the overproportional increase of power consumption. The physical resources, i.e. blade servers, are managed using the IBM LoadLeveler[2] (no virtualization). The workload consists nearly exclusively of scientific batch processing with an

[1]The thermal design power quantifies the power value that an electric component must not exceed during operation.

[2]https://www.ibm.com/support/knowledgecenter/en/SSFJTW_5.1.0/com.ibm.cluster.loadl.v5r1.load100.doc/am2ug_ch1.htm, accessed 08/06/2020

Table 6.1.: Example of entry in job data trace

Job ID	**Submission Time**	**Start Time**	**End Time**
abc.297906	01.01.2014 00:09:40	01.01.2014 00:10:32	01.01.2014 00:56:50
CPU_Freq	**#Nodes**	**Energy (kWh)**	**Power (W)**
2.3	2	0.256636	332.573642

algorithmic and computational background of a high complexity. In 2014, the total energy consumption of considered data center was roughly 20000MWh; its theoretical peak power is near 4MW. Efficiency measured as computational power versus consumed electrical power is 0.85GFLOPS/W. For cooling purposes the considered data center employs hot water cooling, classified into the ASHRAE W4 [16]. The default inlet temperature is set to 40°C in summer and 30°C in winter, and it is not adapted to the IT load. The inlet temperature is measured at the point where the water enters into the nodes. Data provided were acquired via a realtime monitoring toolset for the year 2014.

The downside of using real data from a real operating environment is that the origin of the data cannot be disclosed[3].

Job Data

The *job data trace* contains information for every job that was executed in the HPC system at hand in 2014. This information consists mainly of job ID, submission-, start-, and end-time, allowed maximum frequency, energy and average power consumption. Table 6.1 shows an example with a small selection of entry fields (the real job ID has been replaced by abc).

As explained in section 5.2.1 the data trace of the workload is used for the creation of a workload model that fits with the power model. This means that the original data trace is slightly changed before being fed into the simulator: parts of the real data trace, namely IDs, beginning times and normed job sizes are maintained, the workload cluster number is added, and the average node

[3]Upon personal request data access might be mediated.

power consumption is calculated using the workload cluster attribution. After data cleaning, the job data trace contains almost 400,000 job records. The jobs are very heterogeneous with regards to both runtime and nodes used. The median of the runtime is only 3% of the average; its maximum in 2014 being more than 2 days. The same tendency can be seen in nodes used: on average, jobs run on 32 nodes, the mean, however is only 2 nodes. The frequency data does not relate to the executed frequency, but to the maximum allowed frequency. As the default frequency setting is 2.3GHz, it is not surprising that the average maximum frequency is at 2.38GHz.

The procedure of data cleaning is explained in more detail in the appendix (A). The *Job Power* time series generated from the available job data for March 2014 can be seen in figure 6.1.

PUE and IT Power Time Series

Contrary to the job data trace, the two other available data traces are time series data: *IT power trac*e and *PUE trace*.

The *IT power trace* is the power in kW measured hourly at the main power lines that supply the room which contains servers, storage, network, internal cooling pumps, and PDUs. The average IT power consumption in 2014 was 1,892kW with a standard deviation of 312kW. It does not contain the external cooling power, i.e. the roof-top cooling towers' power consumption. It includes the power of the server cluster which was provided indirectly as *job data trace* and computed as *job power*. As there is no information about the composition and behaviours of other power consumers OPC data were calculated as a proportion, see section 5.2.4. Therefore it is not surprising that at 0.83 the correlation between job power and the IT power trace is not very high.

The *PUE data trace* contains hourly values of the (dynamic) PUE for the complete year of 2014[4]. It is however, not calculated according to the origi-

[4]Some rare missing values were estimated by linear interpolation.

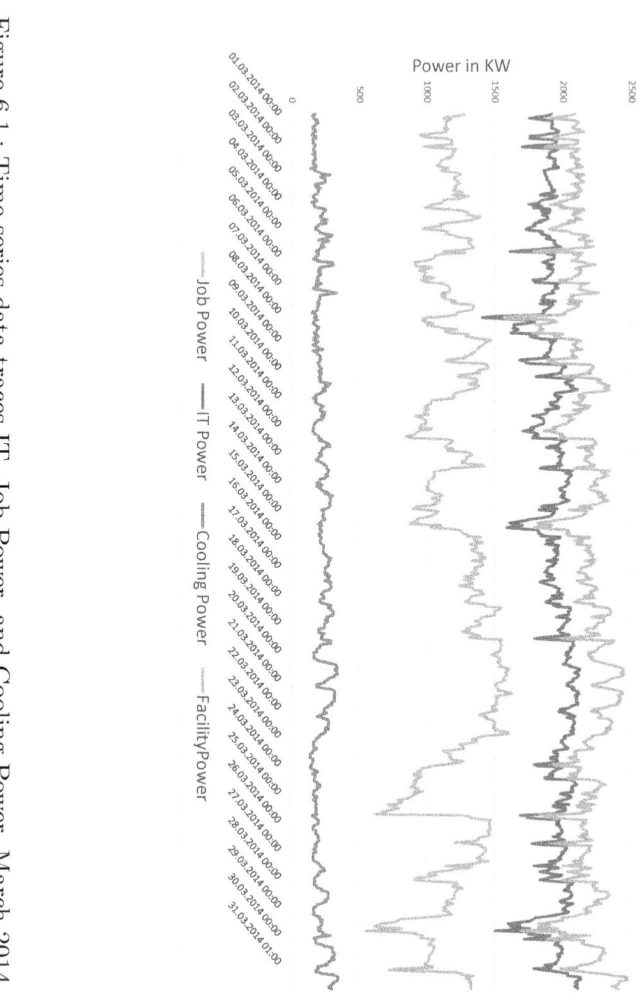

Figure 6.1.: Time series data traces IT, Job Power, and Cooling Power, March 2014

nal PUE definition [174], but based on the difference between IT power and $SystemCoolingPower$, i.e. the external cooling power:

$$PUE = \frac{ITPower + SystemCoolingPower}{ITPower} \tag{6.1}$$

It has a range between 1.06 and 1.35, with a standard deviation of 0.3. The latter is rather high, but as both a correlation and a regression analysis showed, this is more due to the influence of the weather (correlation with wetbulb temperature[5] is 0.7) than due to the impact of the workload: the correlation between the measured PUE and the measured IT power traces is a mere -0.4. This is inline with general policies in the HPC data center community to operate cooling equipment in a mostly static way, based on the maximum heat removal necessary [47],[219] and not scaling it with the dynamics of the workload.

The PUE data trace was used to calculate the cooling power (figure 6.1) and the total facility power, using equation (6.1). This means that figure 6.1 is a combination of measured curves (*IT power trace*) and calculated curves (cooling power and job power), so that even if there were a causal power model to model the OPC curve (the difference between IT power and job power), the components would not add up to the 'real' facility power. Therefore, in order to achieve a consistent system, an artificial facility power curve was generated out of the job power, the cooling power and the OPC power data.

Cost

For running the simulations, according to the model set-up in section 5.2.6 two cost items are needed, the electricity cost and the SLA cost.

In order to calculate baseline electricity cost that is used to calculate the benefit from investing into power flex services, the information about the energy cost for 2014 is needed. In Germany, industry or big commercial consumers

[5] This is the temperature taken from a sensor embedded in moist material and therefore also dependent on humidity.

typically have a component-based electricity tariff [165] where the power charge (per kW) depends on the peak power needed during a year. The second component is the price per consumed energy unit (per kWh); for smaller premises the kWh-price is static, but for big consumers, there is often a two-period (weekdays between 8-18h and other times) or three-period (including peak times) time-of-use tariff. Unfortunately this information was not disclosed. As for big customers both pricing components are highly dependent on individual contracts with the electricity power provider the published average industry price for 2014 of 0.1532€/kWh was used for the calculation [43]. It contains both the power and the energy pricing components.

SLA cost is calculated according to formula (5.20) in section 5.2.6which needs the input of a usage price uP of a compute node hour. Also this information was not publicly available for the considered HPC data center. So the compute node price of 0.16€/nodehour of a comparable data center, the HLRS in Stuttgart, was used instead [110].

6.1.2. Power Markets

The Secondary Reserve Market in Germany

As explained in section 2.2.2 the European system of reserve power is made up of generally three reserve markets that amend each other. For the simulation within Sim2Win-HPC the secondary control reserve (SCR) market in Germany was chosen as explicit demand response market. The SCR market is auction based; in 2014 auctions were carried out weekly. There are four separate auctions, one for each combination of the provision times (main vs. secondary) and reserve types (positive vs. negative)[57]. A bid consists of the offered reserve power (in MW), a power price (PP) (€/MW) offering, and an energy compensation price (EP) (€/MWh).

From these bids two so-called *'merit-order lists'* (MOL) are created, one that sorts the offers for PP in an ascending order, and a second one that sorts the

EP offers in an ascending order. The TSO then estimates the power needed for the next week and accepts the bids of the PP MOL in an ascending order until the necessary power supply is reached. Those bids are accepted until the last supplier is reached and compensated contrary to the wholesale market pay-as-bid (i.e. with the price of the original offer, not with an equilibrium price), thus in total offering the least costly regulation service. When during the affected week an activation is necessary, the TSO activates the suppliers' load using the EP MOL to make sure that again the least costly energy supply is chosen first. The participant is then compensated through two processes: one relates to the power of the offered load. This is paid independently of the activation for each unit of the offered power (in kW). The other relates to the activated energy and is paid for each energy unit adapted (in kWh).

For 2014 the results of these biddings were obviously generated without the data center at hand having taken part in the process. However, as the aim of this simulator is to simulate realistic results of a participation of the said HPC data center in the SCR market, the real MOLs are to be utilized instead of modeled MOLs. Therefore artificial bids were created reflecting the situation *as if* the data center had been participating in the SCR market. The real activations of this artificial bid were then isolated from the activation data of the TSO; and thus an activation data trace for this specific artificial bid was generated using the data traces from the transparency pages of the German transmission operators[6].

As the minimum bid size (5MW[7]) is much larger than the power consumption of the considered data center, it is assumed that the data center participates in the SCR market via an aggregator who in return is estimated to keep 30% of the returns [8].

[6]`https://www.regelleistung.net/ext/tender/`, accessed 08/06/2020
[7]Meanwhile, this has been reduced to 1MW
[8]This is an educated guess based on discussions with stakeholders.

EPEX Spot Market

For the EPEX Day Ahead Market, which is the example of implicit demand response chosen for the implementation in Sim2Win-HPC, the integration is less complex than for the SCR. The only challenge is to determine a price vector with an hourly price for the year of 2014.

EPEX consists of several sub-markets: Day-ahead-auction, Intraday Continuous, Intraday-auction markets and the capacity market. For Germany in 2014 only the day-ahead auction and the intraday-auction market are relevant, as the intraday continuous was introduced only 2015, and the capacity market is a French specialty created in 2016. Both intraday and day-ahead market trade a set of different 'products' with different timing specifications: for each hour of the next day, a bidder can bid for a price of 100kWh, so that both volume and price may differ from one hour to the next. The traded products can be hourly products, but they are also bundled into blocks of several hours and at specific times of the day (baseline vs. peak). For the current implementation, assuming that the data center optimizes their electricity sourcing decisions, the minimum of the available products is calculated for each hour of the year 2014. The price vector was calculated using the EPEX website[9] where trading prices and corresponding volumes are published.

6.2. Simulation Runs

The simulation tool Sim2Win-HPC as an instance of the created modeling framework for demand response with data centers will be evaluated using a set of different simulation runs. The baseline run, against which all other simulation runs are compared, is created by simulating the data center activity for the whole year of 2014 without offering any kind of power flex services, using the data center's original workload and the measured dynamic PUE and IT data

[9] http://www.epexspot.com/en/market-data/dayaheadauction/chart/auction-chart

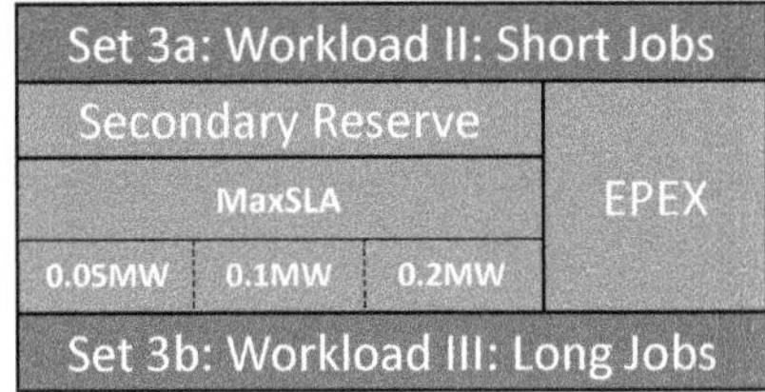

Figure 6.2.: Set up of simulation runs to evaluate the usefulness of the provided approach

traces (for more information please be referred to appendix A.2). The first set of additional simulation runs evaluates the engagement of the considered data center in the German SCR market and alternatively in the EPEX day-ahead wholesale electricity market based on a parameter setting which is deemed realistic. The second set of simulation runs simulates the impact of harder SLA cost parameters than originally assumed based on the model of Garg et al. [82], both on the SCR market and on the EPEX market. In order to furthermore understand the influence of the workload composition, in the third set of simulation runs the workload itself is manipulated extracting in one case particularly long running and in a second case particularly short running jobs. The simulation set up is illustrated in figure 6.2.

The metrics that are used to evaluate the impact of the manipulated sets of simulation parameters are presented in table B.1 in the appendix. Some metrics relate to power characterstics, some signify how the characteristics of the workload changes, and finally some metrics calculate the economic benefit or loss of said strategies.

6.2.1. Baseline Simulation

The week chosen for the simulation is the first week of March from Monday 03/03/2014 to Sunday 09/03/2014. The choice was made based on the combination of characteristics both in the data center and on the SCR market: In these

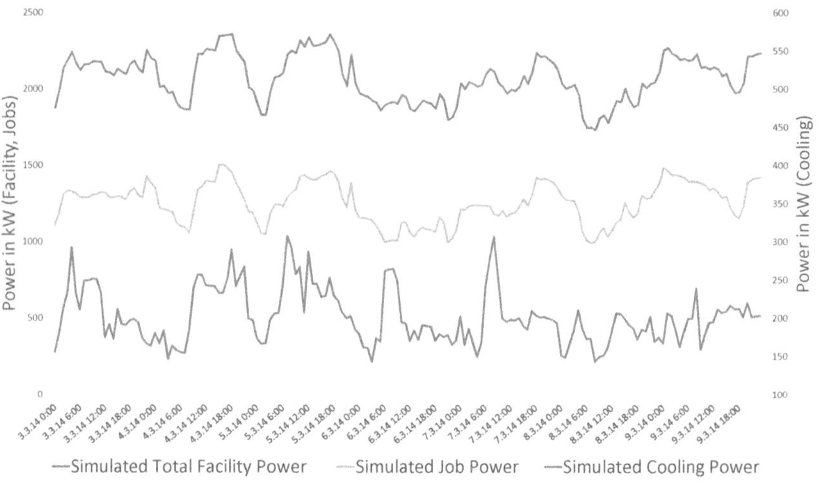

Figure 6.3.: Baseline (BL) simulation run: Simulated data traces of facility power, job power, and cooling power, 03/03/2014-09/03/2014

two cases that week was 'normal' in terms of the absence of unusual demand patterns. Regarding the data center, for example, the mean of the total facility power of the affected week was only 3.6% below the overall mean of the facility power in all 2014. Figure 6.3 shows the simulated values for the simulation week of the job power, the facility power, the cooling power, and the reported PUE. As the PUE of the considered data center is very low (in this week between 1.08 and 1.17), the influence of the cooling power on the total facility power is small. It can be seen, however, that the cooling power (depicted on a second axis) is influenced to a great degree not by the workload but by other parameters as e.g. the outside temperature.

The data traces delivered by this baseline simulation are used as 'groundtruth' against which the various sets of demand response scenarios are compared.

6.2.2. Simulation Set-Up

This section explains in more detail how the parameters of the baseline simulation are manipulated in the different simulation runs.

Set 1: Monetizing the Flexibility of the Original Data Center Set-Up

The first set of alternative simulation scenarios is based on the original workload model. As the left side of figure 6.2 displays, it consists of four simulations runs: three that evaluate different options to bid into the SCR market and a fourth that is dedicated to implicit demand response via the EPEX day-ahead market. Consistent with the available data center traces, also for the SCR market 2014 data of the considered week was used.

As explained in section 6.1.2, on the German SCR market pricing and activation order is determined via individual biddings of market participants, so that artificial bids had to be generated for the data center at hand. It is assumed that of the four available SCR products, the data center participated in the auction for *main time positive reserve power* provision from Monday, 03/03/2014, to Friday, 07/03/2014.

All successful bids in terms of the amount of electricity offered, corresponding PPs (Power Price) and EPs (Energy Price) are published on *regelleistung.net*[10]. As the data of the mentioned platform also include how often regulative power was activated for which (anonymous) participant, it was possible to generate data traces containing the activation data of the artificial bids of the data center. The data about successful bids in the considered week were used to create two sets of artificial bids that reflect two extreme situations in order to evaluated the range of benefits (or losses) of the data center: the *MaxBid* scenarios and the *MinBid* scenarios.

The MaxBid scenario consists of the maximum accepted PP and the energy price EP that generated the highest income, i.e. the participant who originally

[10] `https://www.regelleistung.net/ext/tender/`, accessed 08/06/2020

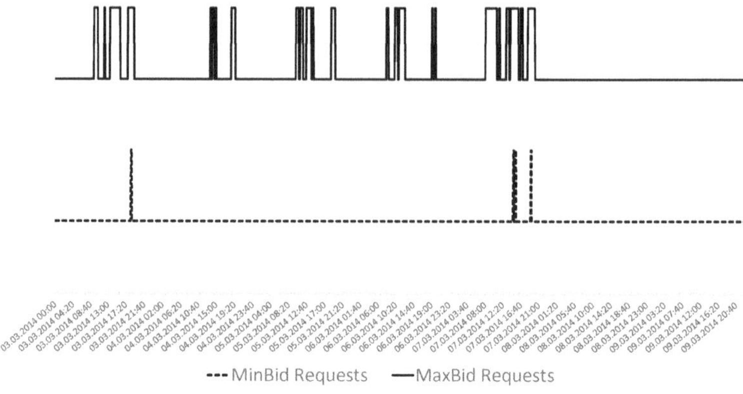

Figure 6.4.: The demand response activations in MaxBid and MinBid scenarios, 03/03/2014-09/03/2014

gave the bid gambled in a way that this bid was the most expensive just accepted for the MOL. Contrarily, the MinBid scenario combines the lowest PP, that consequently was the first to be accepted to the MOL with the EP that generated the lowest positive income. For the considered week the MaxBid PP was 382€/MW and the corresponding EP 63.1€/MWh whereas the MinBid PP was 271€/MW and the corresponding EP 64.1€/MWh. It is conspicuous that the MinBid EP is higher than the MaxBid EP. The reason for this is that reserve power providers who offer low PP values regularly bet on being activated, so that they require comparatively high EPs in order to benefit from frequent activation. Constructing the data traces it turned out that as the activation from the MOL list calls the lowest EPs first, the MinBid provider would have been activated only in 4 15-minute-intervals, much less than the MaxBid provider with 90 activation time slots. The SCR power activation data trace created from this information is shown in figure 6.4.

According to the reserve power regulations, a provider must offer the same product for the entire week. This implies that the adjustment height and provision type are equal for all entries in the activation data trace. As it is assumed that the adjustment duration for each activation is the maximum activation duration (15 min) as set by the regulation guidelines, for each entry all parameters are fixed. The adjustment height, however, needs to be determined before entering into bidding process, and it is mandatory that this adjustment be carried in case of activation. In order to do this, before the SCR simulation runs, pre-tests were carried through with the original workload in steps of 100kW. It turned out that adjustments beyond 600kW are technically infeasible[11], so that for each scenario alternative offers between 0.1MW and 0.6MW were simulated. The focus of the documentation lies on the results of the four runs 0.2, 0.4., 0.5, and 0.6. These runs include the SLA model introduced in section 5.2.6 defining delay as the original execution time (according to the job data trace) being surpassed by up to four times, including a random element for different job values. The SLA cost then increases proportionally to the size of the job in terms of nodes and to the length of the delay[12]. These runs are called MaxSLA0.2, MaxSLA0.4, MaxSLA0.5, and MaxSLA0.6. Additionally, separate simulation runs without SLA limitations were carried through accounting for the fact that the real SLA costs are not known. In this run, scheduling was done in 'first in- first out' order combined with backfilling; the decision was based on default scheduling algorithms in other HPC environments withoug SLA cost ([151, 5]). These runs are documented as Max0.2, and so forth.

The reward remuneration of each simulation run is calculated by adding up the revenue streams, i.e. the turnover of the offered power (T_{PP}^{SCR}) and the turnover of the activated energy (T_{EP}^{SCR}):

$$T_{PP}^{SCR} = PF_{DC} * PP \tag{6.2}$$

$$T_{EP}^{SCR} = \#Events * PF_{DC} * EP * 0.25 \tag{6.3}$$

For the case of the *power offered*, the flexibility of the data center (PF_{DC}) is multiplied with the offered power price PP, whereas for the case of the *activated*

[11]Infeasible means that at least one event cannot be complied to

[12]for more information on the cost model see section 5.2.6

Figure 6.5.: EPEX Day Ahead Prices used for the simulation, 03/03/2014-09/03/2014

energy, in order to turn power values (kW) into energy values (kWh), the power flexibility of the data center is multiplied with 0.25. Based on the assumption of full activation for the whole duration, this reward is granted for the *number* of 15-minute activations (*#Events*).

The final simulation run of the first set of simulations is the data center's participation in the EPEX day ahead market instead of using a static electricity price for the same week. As explained before, contrary to reacting to demand response events, here the data center generally exchanges the original scheduling approach by a scheduler (see section 5.2.2) that constantly adjusts to the dynamic EPEX spot energy prices. The volatility of the hourly prices on the EPEX day-ahead market for the considered week is shown in figure 6.5.

Set 2: Simulating the Impact of Hard SLA

The second set of simulation runs serves as a sensitivity analysis to the assumed cost model for delay cost (SLA cost) accruing in the data center due to the impact of the applied power management strategies on the jobs' completion time. This can be delayed due to waiting times in the case of temporary workload shifting or due to extended execution times due to the manipulation of the frequency.

The applied deadline model 5.17 which determines the definition of delay is based on [82] and was introduced in section 5.2.6. Comparing the outcome of this model with other assumptions in other papers [151, 119, 145], the deadline construction of Garg et al. seemed a rather hard constraint, even though the modeling approach is convincing. Therefore for the baseline execution the deadline model was softened. However, in order to test the impact of a different slack in jobs' deadlines the second set of simulation runs uses the original parameters of Garg et al. (see equation (5.17)).

In the corresponding result section (section 6.3.2) the versions are called 'SoftSLA' and 'HardSLA'.

Set 3: Manipulating the Composition of the Data Center Workload

The final set of simulation runs is dedicated to understanding the sensitivity of results to the workload composition. To this end, as shown on the right hand side of figure 6.2, the workload was analysed with regards to the original job runtime and two extracts were constructed that exhibit a similar shape of the job power curve as the original workload, but contain only either *'short'* or *'long'* jobs. Short jobs are defined as jobs belonging to job classes with average job runtimes of up to 6 hours. Long jobs are defined as jobs belonging to job classes that last between 7 hours and 16 hours. Thus, the outliers with an execution time of up to several days are excluded from this artificial workloads. Tables 6.2 and 6.3 display the median and the average values of the artifically

Table 6.2.: *Median values* of the artificial workload traces, Jan.-March 2014

Median	**Energy (kWh)**	**Power (kW)**	**Runtime (minutes)**	**Frequency (MHz)**	**Nodes (number)**
Short Jobs	0.01	0.97	0.67	2.3	8
Long Jobs	1.97	0.80	79.63	2.3	4

Table 6.3.: *Average values* of the artificial workload traces, Jan.-March 2014

Average	**Energy (kWh)**	**Power (kW)**	**Runtime (minutes)**	**Frequency**	**Number of Nodes**
Short Jobs	16.32	4.38	172.53	2.42	42.4
Long Jobs	38.75	4.15	566.95	2.43	22.2

created workload traces with either 'short' jobs or 'long' jobs.

Figure 6.6 shows the curves of the three different workloads: the original workload and the artificial 'short jobs' and 'long jobs' workloads. As shown in the simulation set-up figure 6.2 the size of the explicit demand response simulation runs in this simulation set differs from the original sizes. The reason is that the total facility power of the 'short job' and 'long job' subsets of the workload is too small compared to the total workload: the overall energy consumption in the considered week, for instance, is 37% lower in the case of the short job workload compared the original workload; for the case of the long job workload this ratio is even -44%. Pretests showed that a reduction beyond 0.2MW was infeasible in all partial workloads.

6.3. Results

Even though the demand response activation week ran from 03/03/2014 to 09/03/2014, the simulation covered the whole period of 01/01/2014 - 15/05/2014. Representative for the various simulation runs, the execution time of the MaxBid 0.5MW simulation run was recorded which lasted 1,373 sec (approx. 22.9 min). This section documents the results of the three sets of simulation runs.

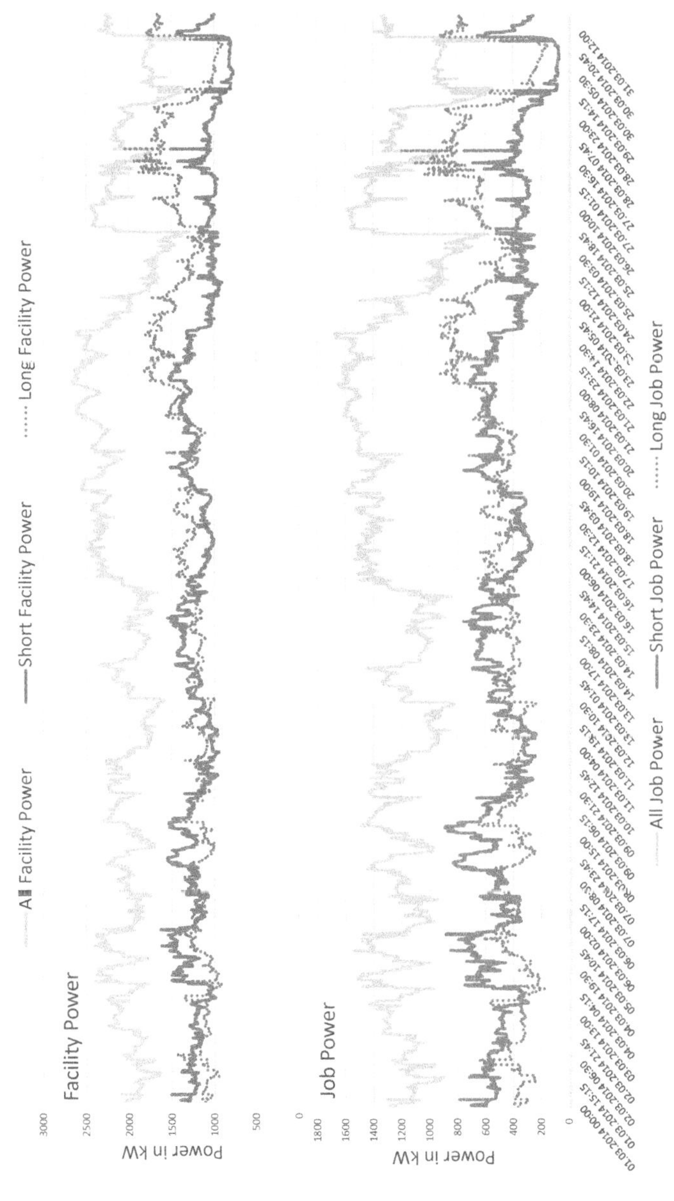

Figure 6.6.: Comparison of job power and number of jobs for the baseline and the two alternative workload compositions, 01/03/2014-31/03/2014

6.3.1. Set 1: Monetizing the Flexibility of the Original Data Center Set-Up

The simulation result of the first set of simulations as defined in section 6.2 are presented in the same order as introduced there: first the MaxBid scenarios MaxSLA0.2 - MaxSLA0.6, then scenarios without SLAs (Max0.2-Max0.6), the MinBid scenarios with SLAs (MinSLA0.2 - MinSLA0.6), and finally the EPEX day ahead scenario. At the end of this section the results of these first runs are compared against each other.

MaxBid scenarios: High Price Bids into the Secondary Reserve Market

The results of the MaxBid scenarios, i.e. the results of 'high' bids into the SCR, are shown in figures 6.7, 6.8, 6.9, and 6.10, and a summary of the KPIs is given in tables 6.4 and 6.5.

Figure 6.7 depicts the total facility power in green and the job power in orange colours. The curves belonging to the baseline run are shown in light colors, the MaxSLA0.2 run, i.e. reducing the power in the event window by at least 200kW, with dotted lines, and the curves of the MaxSLA0.6 run are represented by dark lines. This image shows not only the week of the SCR activations, but it adds a couple of days, in order to illustrate how effects linger some time after the initial impulse has subsided. The general impression of the image is that facility power and job power are more or less aligned, and that the two reaction curves behave more or less similarly (the dotted lines of the 200kW run in both curves seem to be between the baseline run and the MaxSLA0.6 run). The most conspicuous observation is the discrepancy of the three different curves on the early morning of the 11th of March, more than three days after the last activation request. For a deeper analysis more detailed views are needed.

Figure 6.8 gives a first impression about the development of the job power and the number of jobs for the baseline and the MaxSLA0.5 simulation run for the

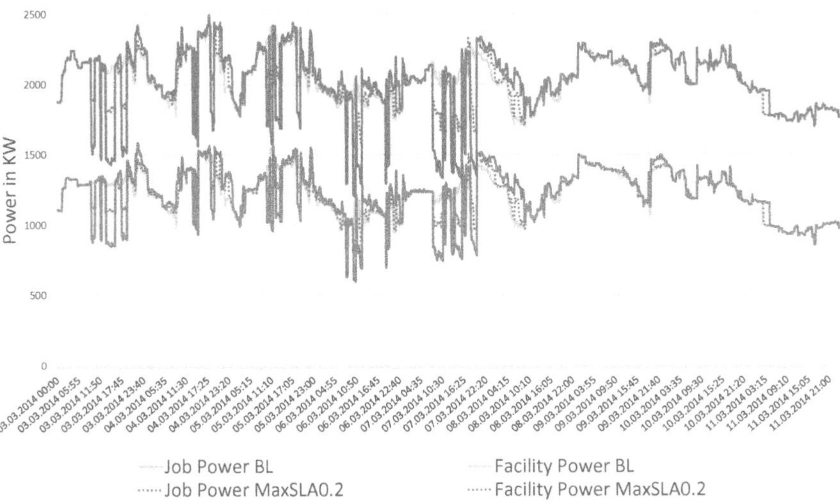

Figure 6.7.: Comparison of facility power and job power between BL and MaxSLA demand response events, 03/03/2014-11/03/2014

whole simulation week. It shows that the number of jobs does not necessarily correlate with the job power which is supported by the original job statistics that reveal a correlation coefficient of 0.75. This behaviour is even more extreme in the case of demand response, especially for the illustrated case of MaxSLA0.5. The power decreases due to SCR events, e.g. on the afternoons of the 3rd and the 5th March, are obviously not implemented primarily through workload shifting as the number of jobs tends to increase instead of decrease. However, it has to be kept in mind that the SLA cost incurred due to waiting and extended execution times are accounted for, and that the STDF scheduler that takes over in the case of an SCR activation event resorts the jobs, obviously scheduling first some shorter jobs. In the whole period of 03/03/-09/03 to which the statistics in table 6.4 relate, in each timeslot an average 3.9% of the shiftable jobs were actually shifted and the number of jobs increased by 2.3%. The average runtime, on the contrary, impacted by frequency scaling, increased by nearly 23% (see

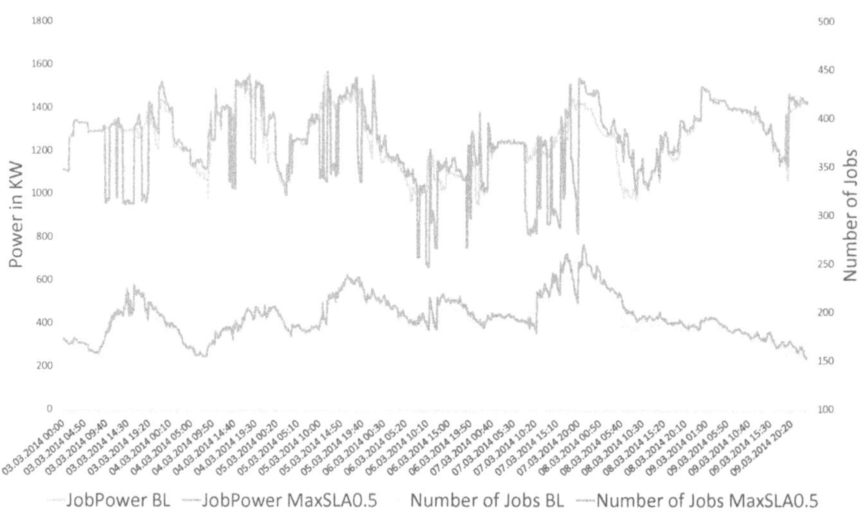

Figure 6.8.: Relationship between job power and number of jobs for baseline and MaxSLA0.5, 03/03/2014-09/03/2014

table 6.4). This short analysis gives a first hint that in general frequency scaling seems to be preferred to job shifting. However, again in order to understand the underlying activities, it is necessary to zoom in.

As shown in figure 6.4, the demand response events are quite unevenly distributed over the considered simulation week - a peak number of events took place on the 7th of March, which is why this day is analysed in detail (see figure 6.9). It traces the job power, the number of active nodes, and the number of jobs for the MaxSLA0.2, MaxSLA0.5, and MaxSLA0.6 scenarios, and it illustrates how in each scenario the current composition of workload and the results of previous events lead to different adaptation activities. The dotted lines represent the MaxSLA0.5 run which was expected to exhibit a behaviour between the extremes MaxSLA0.2 (lighter line) and MaxSLA0.6 (darker line).

The image focuses on two major demand response events, one in the morning from 8:00-10:45h and the other in the late afternoon from 18:15-20:00h. In the

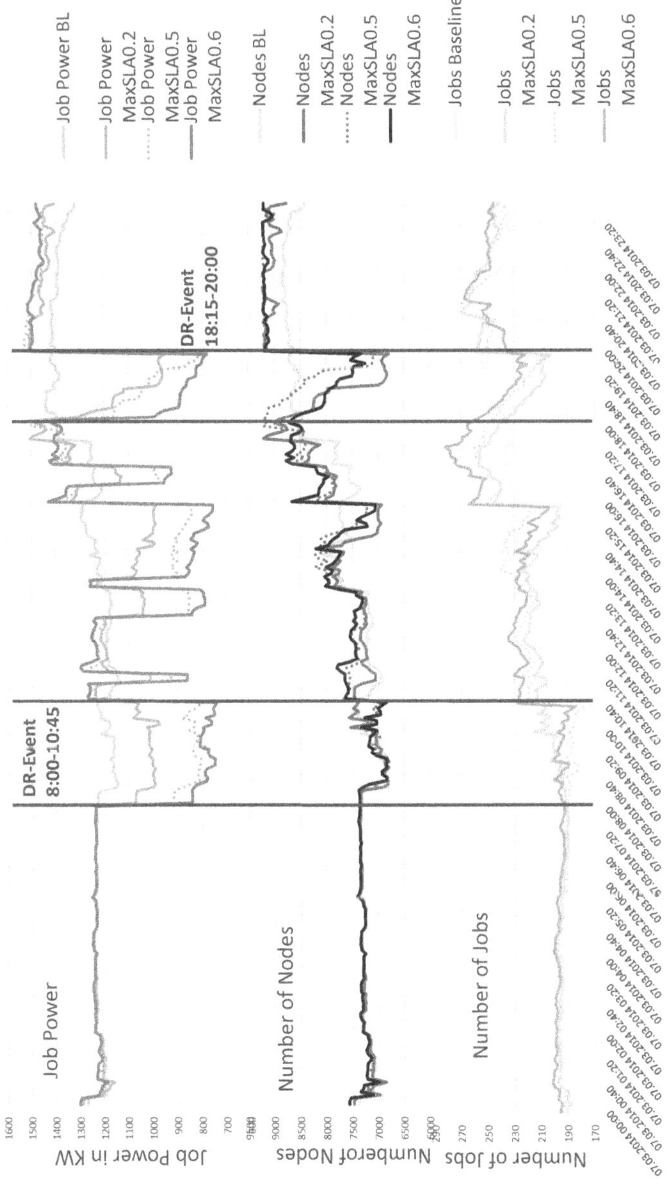

Figure 6.9.: Comparison between BL and MaxSLA demand response simulations, March 7th

morning, power reduction starts instantly with the request to reduce power. As neither the number of nodes nor the number of jobs change at first, this reaction is obviously exclusively incited by frequency reduction. In the case of MaxSLA0.2 the number of jobs remains close to the baseline run; but for the MaxSLA0.5 and MaxSLA0.6 runs the lower two curves show that, after a short hesitant phase, jobs are shifted. As the analysis of job data shows, some jobs with a low energy consumption are even preponed, and a few jobs shifted away from the demand response window. This is because during the event the job schedule is optimized to keep the load as steadily reduced as possible. At the end of the event, as often described (e.g.[162]), there is a tiny peak, also called *'rebound effect'*, where the modified power curves exceed the baseline curve in order to partially recapture the big (in terms of number of nodes) shifted jobs.

There are four more demand response events during the day, where the data center needs to comply to the contractually bound power reduction requests. The final event of the day lasts from 18:15 to 20:00h (see again figure 6.9). Here the different adaptation activities seem more disruptive, even though the demand response window is a little shorter than in the morning. The reason for that is that during the day more and more adaptation processes started without the impact of the previous having been fully compensated. What adds to this is a sharp increase in the baseline power demand right before the activation period. Therefore, in the different simulation runs the reactions are quite disparate. The most striking observations are that both the number of nodes and the number of jobs of the MaxSLA0.2 run are decreased more than for the cases where a higher adaptation is required. Analysing the statistics about the average frequency and the workload shifting ratio corroborates this observation; MaxSLA0.2 exhibits the highest value for the workload shifting ratio in this afternoon event: 88% vs. 59% (MaxSLA0.5) and 71% (MaxSLA0.6). This is due to the fact that MaxSLA0.2, only delivering 200kW, experienced less disruptions before the increase in baseline power demand and reacted to this request by additionally pre-poning jobs before the event and thus could deliver the requested power mostly through shifting. This power management

Table 6.4.: Impact of MaxSLA scenarios on power and job characteristics

	BL	MaxSLA0.2		MaxSLA0.4		MaxSLA0.5		MaxSLA0.6	
		absolute	% BL	absolute	% BL	absolute	% BL	absolute	% BL
Power									
TFE	347,804	344,390	-0.98%	342,429	-1.55%	341,848	-1.71%	341,565	-1.79%
ATFP	2,070	2,050	-0.98%	2,038	-1.55%	2,035	-1.71%	2,033	-1.79%
PTFP	2,408	2,423	0.63%	2,467	2.47%	2,486	3.24%	2,499	3.77%
JE	210,833	209,244	-0.75%	208,556	-1.08%	208,580	-1.07%	208,906	-0.91%
AJP	1,255	1,245	-0.75%	1,241	-1.08%	1,242	-1.07%	1,243	-0.91%
PJP	1,546	1,533	-0.85%	1,566	1.31%	1,566	1.31%	1,583	2.43%
Jobs									
ART	16,319	19,791	21.28%	19,897	21.93%	20,026	22.72%	20,127	23.34%
WL	190.9	192.5	0.86%	194.2	1.73%	195.3	2.34%	197.6	3.54%
RWL	0		3.24%		3.79%		3.90%		6.00%
AF	2.35	2.33	-0.92%	2.30	-2.14%	2.28	-2.81%	2.26	-3.73%

strategy has the advantage that it is more fine-granular and thus controls SLA cost better as it relates to individual jobs, whereas the average frequency is adapted in each timeslot for all active jobs.

Even though, thus, in general in this setting shifting is preferable to scaling, in reality only the small fraction of the workload that has been submitted but not yet started can be shifted. Whenever therefore a higher amount of power adaptation is requested the ratio of frequency scaling necessarily increases.

This is also reflected in the SLA cost as can be seen in Table 6.5, which for all scenarios sums up energy (EC) and SLA cost (SLA_C), the power and energy rewards (SCR_P and SCR_E) as well as the gross (GB) and the net (NB) benefit (the difference lies in the assumed aggregation fee of 30% of SCR remuneration) for the week of 03/03-09/03. The gross benefit is calculated as the sum of the difference between the baseline energy costs and the scenario energy and SLA costs, the EP and the PP benefit. The percentage value of the benefit relates to the original energy cost. Both cost and benefit values are evaluated with static electricity prices (marked by an 'S', so e.g. GBS) versus dynamic electricity prices (marked by a 'D'), reflecting the option of a data center of this size to not necessarily being subject to a flat price but to potentially engage at the wholesale market. The main comparison is with static prices though, as the considered data center does not source their electricity at the wholesale market. The second column of table 6.5 (column 'BL') shows a high difference between the energy cost based on the assumption that the data center uses the average industry price (ECS) of €53,284 and the energy cost the data center would pay if it purchased their electricity at the EPEX market without power management (€10,339). This means that *the data center would have been able to save nearly 80% of the energy bill by sourcing their electricity demand at the EPEX day ahead market without even changing the power profile*[13]. This means, of all changes possible, the by far most beneficial one is to turn to the wholesale market for electricity sourcing.

The most striking result in the cost and benefit table is the high amount of SLA cost in the MaxSLA0.4 scenario compared to the MaxSLA0.5 scenario which is the most profitable solution. The main reason of the high MaxSLA0.4 SLA cost lies in the fact that in order to reduce the necessary amount of power demand, in many cases in this particular run it is not sufficient to compute the workload with a comparably high frequency and add some workload shifting on top; rather in order to reduce power sufficiently, in many events the next higher level of frequency needs to be chosen thus accruing a high level of SLA cost. In order to understand this, it has to be kept in mind, that the simulator uses specific rules to implement reactions to incentives, it does not optimize!

The most beneficial SCR run, as can be seen, is therefore MaxSLA0.5 where, contrary to MaxSLA0.4 and MaxSLA0.6, the rewards are not compensated by SLA cost. In MaxSLA0.2, the energy cost savings of a reduced CPU frequency and the restructuring of workload according to deadlines dominate the benefit, whereas later the energy cost savings are lower compared to the SCR remuneration. Therefore also the impact of the aggregator fees of assumed 30% of the SCR reward gain importance, especially as SLA cost grow over-proportionally with the power offered. Looking at the net benefit results in table 6.5 reveals

[13]However, the real price/kWh may be considerably lower than the average industry price; this is not known to the author.

Table 6.5.: Cost and benefits of MaxSLA scenarios

	BL	MaxSLA0.2		MaxSLA0.4		MaxSLA0.5		MaxSLA0.6	
Cost		absolute	% BL	absolute	% BL	absolute	% BL	absolute	% BL
ECS	53,284	52,761	-0.98%	52,460	-1.55%	52,371	-1.71%	52,328	-1.79%
ECD	10,339	10,216	-1.20%	10,144	-1.89%	10,124	-2.09%	10,108	-2.24%
SLA_C	0	176	n.a	1,443	n.a	699	n.a	2,501	n.a
Benefit									
SCR_E	0	284	n.a	568	n.a	710	n.a	852	n.a
SCR_P	0	76	n.a	153	n.a	191	n.a	229	n.a
GBS	0	707	1.33%	102	0.19%	1,114	2.09%	-464	-0.87%
GBD	0	308	2.98%	-526	-5.09%	418	**4.04%**	-1,188	-11.49%
NBS	0	599	1.12%	-115	-0.22%	844	1.58%	-789	-1.48%
NBD	0	200	1.93%	-743	-7.18%	147	1.43%	-1,513	**-14.63%**

that with 1.12% the net benefit of MaxSLA0.2 is slightly smaller than for the most beneficial run MaxSLA0.5 (1.58%) where the offer of power flexibility is more than doubled.

In order to assess the general scope of SLA cost, especially for publicly owned data centers that often do not apply SLA cost, the same runs were executed without activating the SLA cost component. Without the need to avoid SLA cost, there is no incentive to apply the deadline-based STDF schedule (see section 5.2.2), so that for this set of simulation runs jobs were scheduled according to the widely used first-in-first out algorithm. The electricity and job related results do not change fundamentally, but as figure 6.10 shows for March 7th, there are slight differences as e.g. regarding the number of active nodes between the runs with (MaxSLA0.2 and MaxSLA0.6) and without SLA (Max0.2 and Max0.6).

The cost (see Table 6.6), however, do change substantially; and as expected, in this case the highest power reduction offer (Max0.6 scenario) is the most beneficial one, creating a net income which is worth 3.23% of the static energy cost and 9.53% related to the baseline dynamic electricity cost.

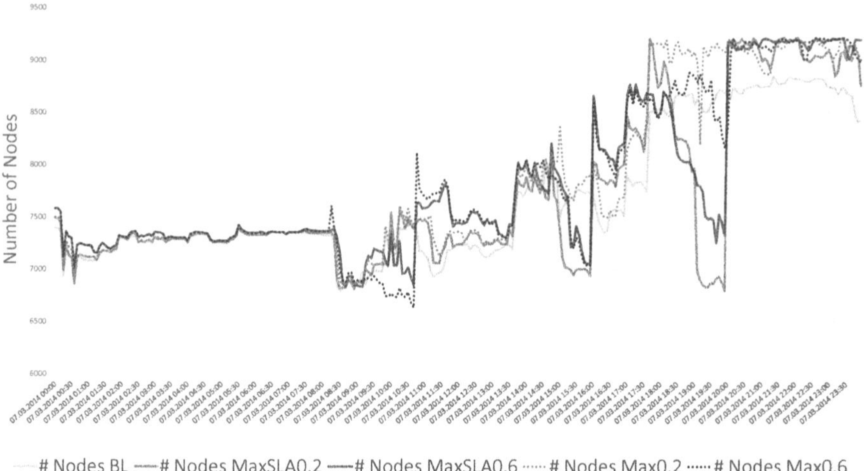

Figure 6.10.: Comparison of number of nodes between BL and MaxBid demand response scenarios with and without SLA, March 7th

Table 6.6.: Cost and benefits of the MaxBid scenarios without SLA

	BL	Max0.2		Max0.5		Max0.6	
		absolute	% BL	absolute	% BL	absolute	% BL
Cost							
ECS	53,284	52,470	-1.53%	52,304	-1.84%	52,321	-1.81%
ECD	10,339	10,151	-1.20%	10,114	-1.20%	10,111	-1.20%
SLA_C	0	0	n.a	0	n.a	0	n.a
Benefit							
SCR_E	0	284	n.a	710	n.a	852	n.a
SCR_P	0	76	n.a	191	n.a	229	n.a
GBS	0	1,174	2.20%	1,881	3.53%	2,044	3.84%
GBD	0	548	5.30%	1,126	10.89%	1,310	12.67%
NBS	0	1,066	2.00%	1,610	3.02%	1,720	3.23%
NBD	0	440	4.26%	856	8.28%	986	9.53%

MinBid scenarios: Low involvement on the secondary reserve market

As explained in section 6.2, additionally to the MaxBid scenarios with and without SLA, MinBid scenarios were created through the artificial bid of the combination of the lowest energy and power price offer in the SCR market which had just entered into the MOL in the considered week. Contrary to the MaxBid scenarios, the activation trace of the MinBid scenarios contains only four demand response events where the data center must respond, as shown in figure 6.4. Obviously, four events have a lower potential for a disruptive impact than 90 events. And obviously, this extends also to the benefit side. This hypothesis was confirmed by the simulation results.

Three of the four demand response events happened on the 7th of March (black activation curve at the bottom of figure 6.11), and the results for the job power and the number of jobs in each time slot are shown in figure 6.11. In order to contrast these curves with the disruptions in the MaxBid scenario, the MaxSLA0.6 curves are added to the picture. It can be seen that the job power consumption of the MinSLA scenarios equals the baseline power consumption until the event at 14:45. The reason for this is that there were no events since March 3rd, so that the data center could fully recover from this only other event. Similarly, after all three events on March 7th, there is much less difference between the baseline and the MinSLA curves than in the case of the MaxSLA scenario. Also the curves of MinSLA0.2 and MinSLA0.6 hardly differ except for the demand response events themselves; all adaptations nearly exclusively relate to the time-slots of the activations. All this can be explained by the extremely rare events of this SCR activation trace, as in this case no impacts build up over time.

Table 6.7 sums up the costs of these runs. Compared to the MaxSLA scenarios the benefits of the respective MinSLA scenarios are generally smaller by factors between 5 and 10! There are two main reasons for that: On the one hand the PP, which is paid independently of activation, is significantly lower. On the other

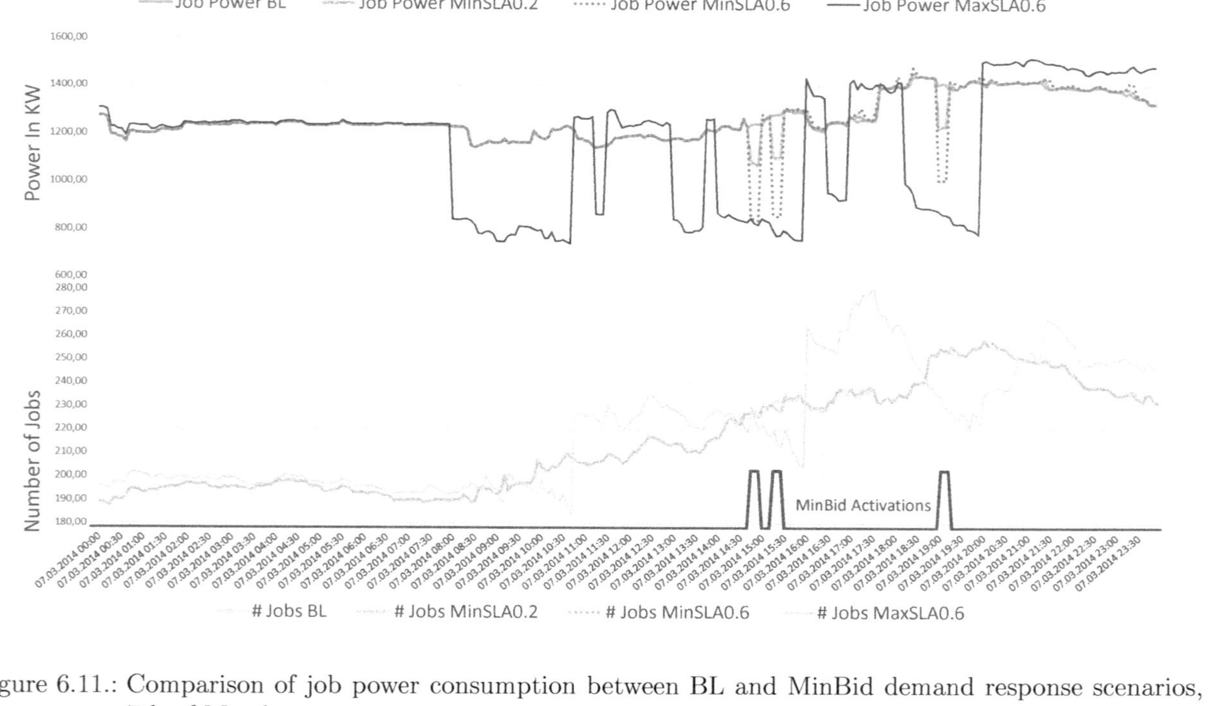

Figure 6.11.: Comparison of job power consumption between BL and MinBid demand response scenarios, 7th of March

Table 6.7.: Cost and benefits of the MinSLA scenarios

	BL	MinSLA0.2		MinSLA0.5		MinSLA0.6	
		absolute	% BL	absolute	% BL	absolute	% BL
Jobs							
AJL	16,319	19,591	20.05%	19,606	20.15%	19,614	20.20%
WL	190.9	190.9	0.04%	191.1	0.13%	191.2	0.16%
RWL	0		0.00%		0.02%		0.04%
F	2.35	2.35	-0.04%	2.35	-0.12%	2.35	-0.15%
Cost							
ECS	53,284	53,260	-0.04%	53,243	-0.08%	53,240	-0.08%
ECD	10,339	10,334	-1.20%	10,331	-1.20%	10,330	-1.20%
SLA_C	0	10	n.a	14	n.a	10	n.a
Benefit							
SCR_E	0	13	n.a	32	n.a	39	n.a
SCR_P	0	54	n.a	136	n.a	163	n.a
GBS	0	81	0.15%	194	0.36%	234	0.44%
GBD	0	62	0.60%	162	1.57%	200	1.93%
NBS	0	61	0.11%	144	0.27%	174	0.33%
NBD	0	42	0.41%	112	1.08%	140	1.35%

hand, even though the EP, i.e. the energy price, is higher, the associated income is lower due to the rare activation. Interestingly, here the MaxSLA0.6 scenario is the most profitable one, as obviously four events generate substantially less SLA cost than 90 events.

Implicit demand response: buying electricity on the wholesale market

The simulation run for the EPEX market started at the 01/01/2014 and ended at the 15/05/2014. However, due to the higher complexity of the CAS scheduling procedure it took 13.5 hours (48,629 seconds) to complete. Figure 6.12 shows the basesline and EPEX scenario for the total facility power (green colors) and the number of jobs (yellow colors) and contrasts it with the EPEX prices (black) for the same week. At first sight this image shows that contrary to explicit events, here the baseline and adaptive curves are extremely disparate.

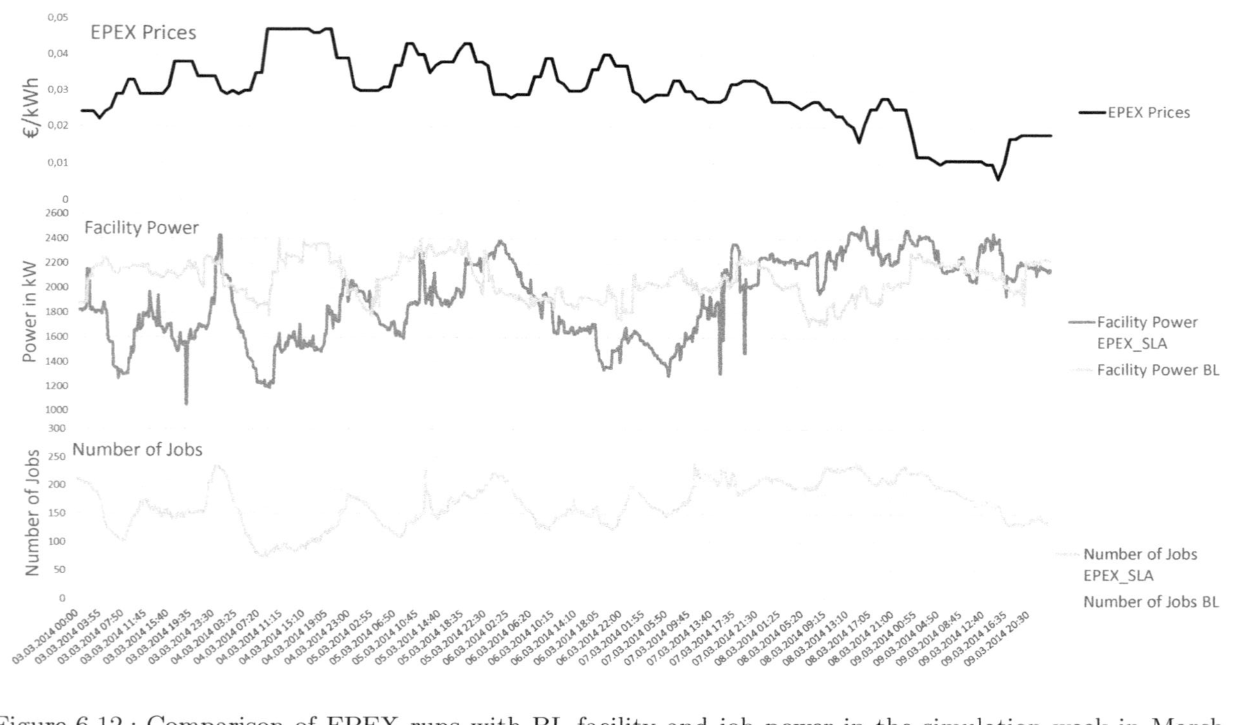

Figure 6.12.: Comparison of EPEX runs with BL facility and job power in the simulation week in March 2014

This is can be understood easily by noting that the EPEX scheduler replaces the original scheduler at all times trying to mirror the EPEX price curve to the utmost degree. The statistics in table 6.8 support the impression that the EPEX curves of Facility Power and Number of Jobs are on average below the baseline curves: the total facility energy consumption is reduced by 7.81% - contrary to MaxSLA0.5, that also sees a reduction, but only of 1.71%. This is eventually caused by a reduced utilization of the data center, as the workload, measured by the average active number of jobs in all timeslots, is reduced by nearly 12%. The reason lies in the fact that the EPEX scheduler is less efficient than the original scheduler as it does not use backfilling. So part of the cost savings can be attributed to a reduced data center utilization. Compared to the high overall net benefit of 5.77% this is still a very reasonable strategy. In the case of no SLA cost, contrary to the MaxSLA runs the scheduler is not exchanged, and the result would be increased to 7,8% net benefit.

The SLA cost are subject to sudden changes when the prices on the EPEX market exhibit spikes in either direction. An analysis of the total SLA cost of €1,082 in this week reveals that a high share of these, namely €721 were created on Saturday, where the EPEX prices dropped as they frequently do on the weekend thus spurring CAS to schedule a high number of jobs.

Summary of Simulation Set 1

Figures 6.13 and 6.14 summarize the effects of a general engagement in both the SCR and the EPEX market under different circumstances with regards to presence or absence of SLAs and higher or lower price bids in the SCR market auctions.

The complete statistics of all simulation runs can be found in appendix B; figure 6.13 only visualizes the most interesting ones. Overall, it is obvious that the demarcation line runs between the EPEX and the SCR simulations, mainly due to the different characteristics of the event-based vs. continuous adaptation. What is further interesting is that the total results are comparably unaffected by the various sizes of SCR offers, however, the minimum of the job power is

Table 6.8.: Comparison of the statistics of the MaxSLA0.5 and the EPEX scenarios

	BL	MaxSLA0.5		EPEX	
		absolute	% BL	absolute	% BL
Power					
TFE	347,804	341,848	-1.71%	320,657	**-7.81%**
ATFP	2,070	2,035	-1.71%	1,909	-7.81%
PTFP	2,408	2,486	3.24%	2,505	4.05%
JE	210,833	208,580	-1.07%	184,474	**-12.50%**
AJP	1,255	1,242	-1.07%	1,098	-12.50%
PJP	1,546	1,566	1.31%	1,621	4.87%
Jobs					
ART	16,319	20,026	22.72%	17,567	7.65%
WL	190.9	195.3	2.34%	168.2	**-11.88%**
RWL	0		3.90%		
AF	2.35	2.28	-2.81%		
Cost					
ECS	53,284	52,371	-1.71%	49,125	-7.81%
ECD	10,339	10,124	-2.09%	9,202	-11.00%
SLA_C	0	699	n.a	1,082	n.a
SCR_E	0	710	n.a	0	n.a
SCR_P	0	191	n.a	0	n.a
GBS	0	1,114	**2.09%**	3,077	5.77%
GBD	0	418	4.04%	56	0.54%
NBS	0	844	**1.58%**	3,077	**5.77%**
NBD	0	147	1.43%	56	**0.54%**

more volatile than the maximum, and especially the variance increases, although it not even doubles when the offered amount of power is tripled. Overall the workload, here represented by the number of jobs, is not changed a lot except for the EPEX simulation. The most noteworthy development is the the runtime of jobs, which for the MaxBid runs increases by 20-25% percent whereas for the EPEX run it is not half as much affected (+7.65%). This explains why the SLA cost in the EPEX run are low compared to the MaxBid runs.

This is also supported by figure 6.14 that compares the benefits of all simulation runs in the first set. It illustrates how the benefit ratios calculated on the basis of the dynamic electricity cost are in general more extreme as the basis is smaller. But it also shows impressively that this basis decides on the overall best

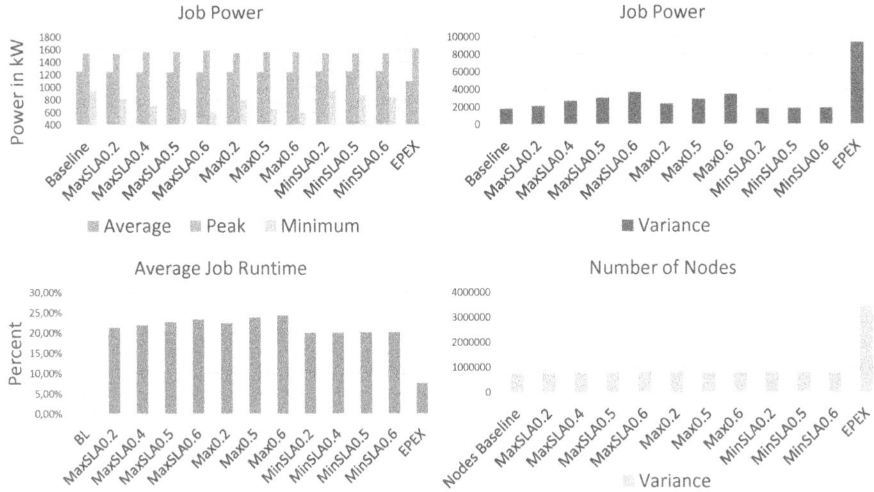

Figure 6.13.: Selected statistics on the first set of simulation runs, 03/03/2014-09/03/2014

solution: if the considered data center is subject to the average industry price, it would have gained a lot of budget by merely sourcing their electricity demand on the EPEX day ahead market. If, on the other hand, it had already taken to the option of buying electricity on the wholesale market without changing their planned power profile, they would have benefited additionally by investing into the SCR explicit demand response market.

6.3.2. Set 2: Simulating the Impact of Hard SLA

The second set of simulations is dedicated to the influence of alternative SLA parameters. This is different from the MaxBid runs without SLA insofar as the SLA component (and with it the STDF scheduler) is activated, however, as explained in section 6.2, the deadline assumptions in the SLAs are tightened to the version originally suggested by Garg et al. [82]. As the underlying workload trace is the same, the relative distance between the original deadlines

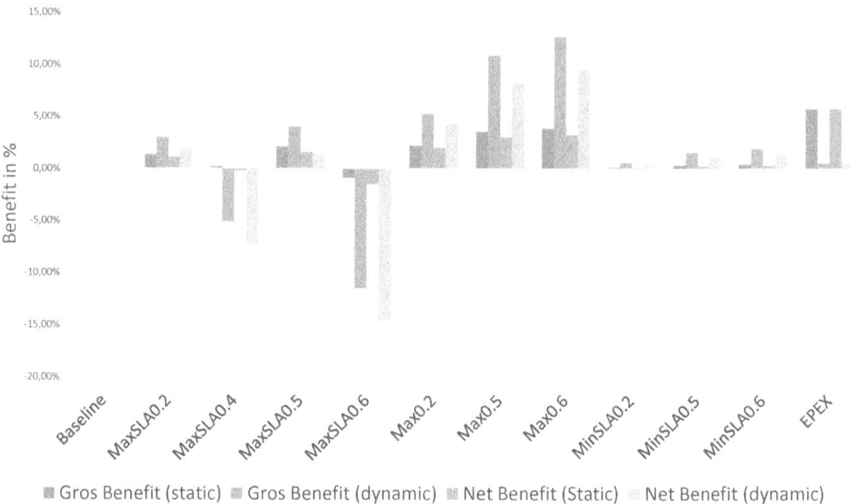

Figure 6.14.: Comparing the net benefit of the first set of simulation runs, 03/03/2014-09/03/2014

and the new, hard deadlines should not change much so that the STDF scheduler should yield similar results as for the simulation runs of the first simulation set. However, the deadline definition contains a randomization element, that was introduced in order to represent different economic weights of different jobs. This randomization element, that scales the addition to the original execution time is obviously computed again and accounts for the scheduling differences of the jobs with the new hard SLAs.

Figure 6.15 for the job power of the MaxSLA0.5 runs spans the part of the simulation week where demand response events in the positive - high time product of the SCR are happening, i.e. 03/03/2014 - 07/03/2014. Similarly to the first analysis, where it was shown that the impact of power reductions build up as more activations take place, here the deviations between the original, 'Soft-SLA' runs and the 'HardSLA' runs are also getting slightly higher during the

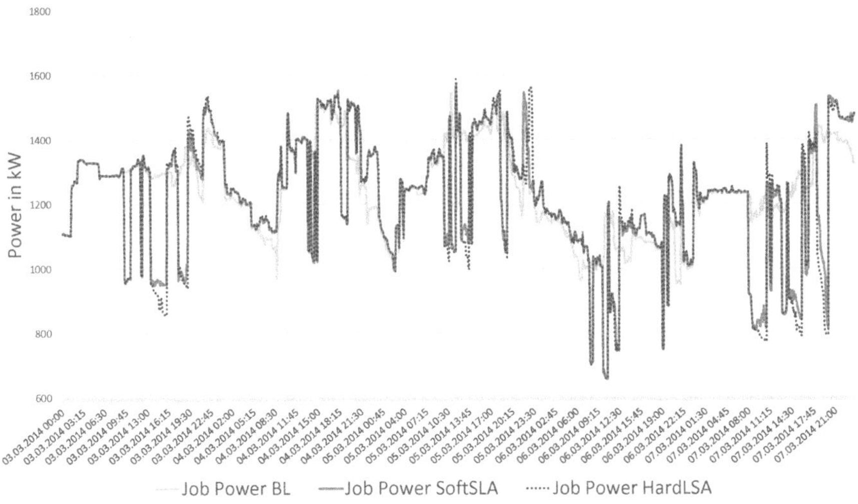

Figure 6.15.: Comparing Job Power between original and hard MaxSLA0.5 runs, 03/03/2014 - 07/03/2014

course of events, although the overall sums of energy and power consumption, of numbers of nodes and jobs do not change much (see table 6.9).

On the level of job statistics that are impacted by the power decreases, however, there are some small differences, which can be explained by looking more closely into the reaction to specific events, as displayed in figure 6.16. It shows in detail the impact of hard versus soft SLA definitions on the MaxSLA0.5 simulation run on March 7th, from 14:00h to 22:00h, two hours after the last event terminated.

Figure 6.16 presents the job power in the top and the number of nodes in the bottom part which together with the number of jobs represents the shifting of workload. This figure gives the impression that the reactions of the hard SLA simulation are a bit more extreme than the reactions of the soft SLA simulation. Not only is the job power slightly more reduced in the longer events, but also is this development mirrored in the number of nodes which implies that the

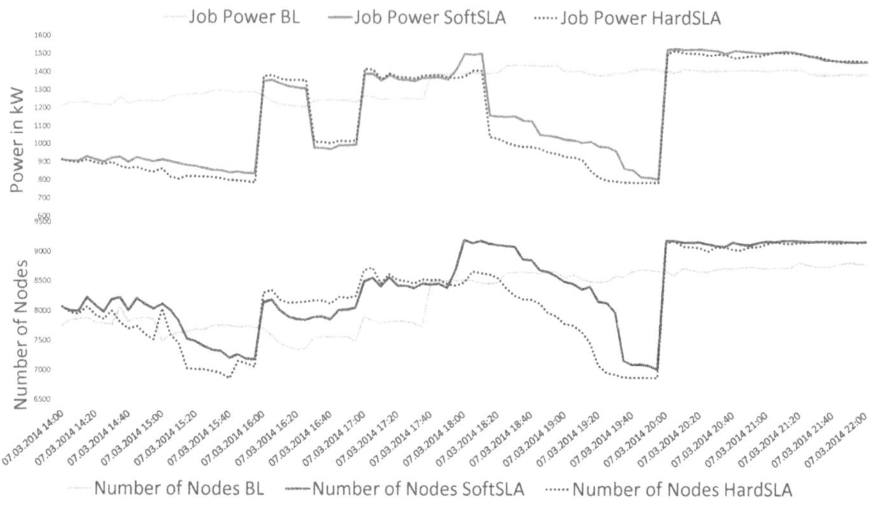

Figure 6.16.: Comparing Job Power between original and hard SLA runs, 7th of March

supply of control power in the case of hard SLA is more dominated by workload shifting than for the case of soft SLAs. This is corroborated by the statistics in table B.4, that for the MaxSLA runs give ratios for workload shifting of 3.9% for soft and 7.73% for hard SLA. The MaxSLA0.5 run is not an exception, the same applies for the other MaxSLA runs. Also, the average frequency on the whole is slighty reduced whereas the average runtime is slightly increased. This may look inconsistent at first sight but can be explained with the phenomenon that depending on the timeslots where the frequency is changed, more or less, smaller or bigger jobs and thus their runtimes are affected. Obviously, this effect grows over time when more jobs are shifted. Again, even though the physical differences are small, they build up during time.

The EPEX simulation with hard SLAs, however, exhibits a contrary behaviour: Here, as figure 6.17 shows for the three days 07/03-09/03/2014, the reactions of the hard SLA runs seem less extreme than for the soft SLA runs.

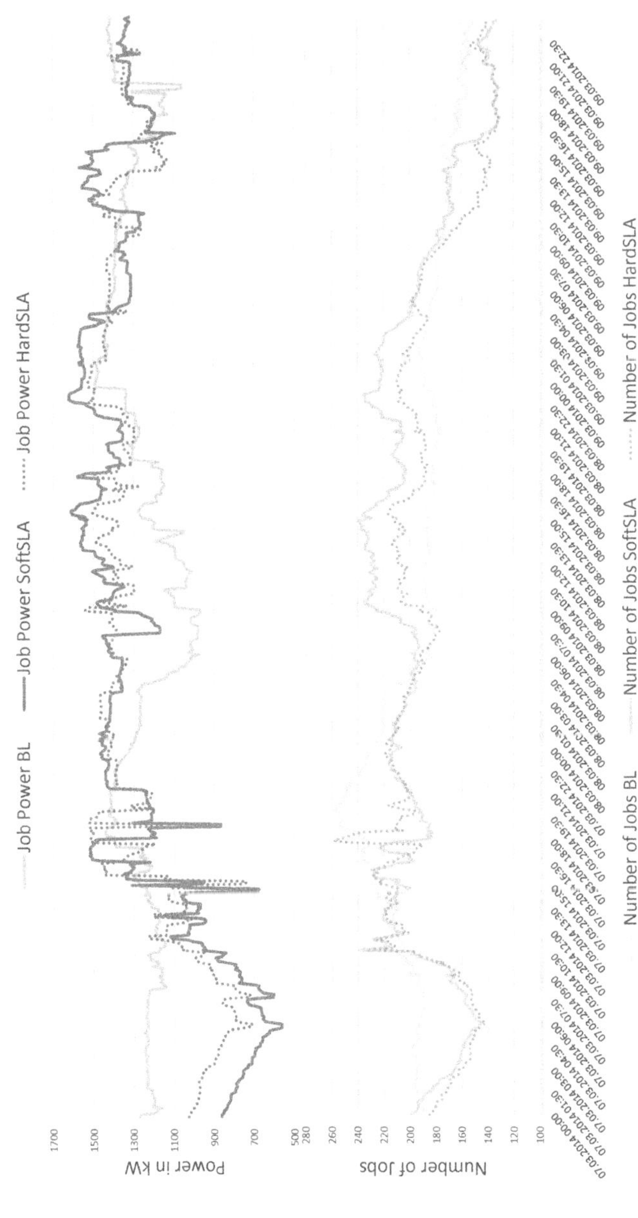

Figure 6.17.: The EPEX simulation under regular and hard SLAs on the weekend with comparably high EPEX price spreads

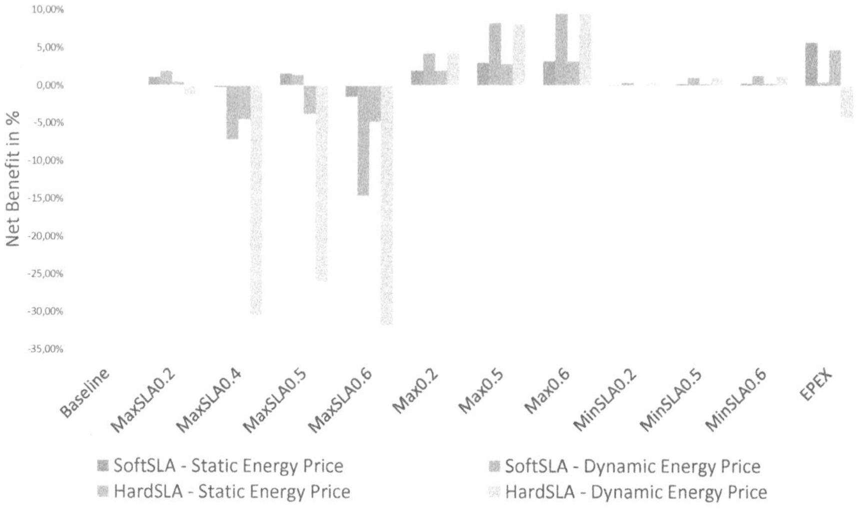

Figure 6.18.: Illustrating the impact of hard vs. regular SLA on the net benefit of set 2 simulations, 03/03/2014-09/03/2014

This is intuitive, because the less SLA constrain the adaptation to dynamic prices, the more elastic the power demand can be. This is why both the peak power consumptions (see table B.4) and the variance of the power consumptions are much higher for the case of soft SLAs. The job and node curves of hard SLA in figure 6.17 display less similarity than it was the case for the job and the node curves in the SCR market analysis. This means that the adaptations to the EPEX price vector are implemented to a lesser degree by the shifting of jobs, but rather by step-by-step frequency tuning.

However, in order to avoid excessive SLA cost, the 'Hard SLA' EPEX run is even less efficient than the 'Soft SLA' run, so that the reduction of workload processed is slightly higher. Despite of that endeavor, the SLA cost of the original EPEX run are only two-thirds from the 'Hard SLA' EPEX run. The

Table 6.9.: The statistics of the 'Soft' vs. the 'Hard' simulation set. Except the SLA cost, the table contains **percentages** that relate to the baseline

	MaxSLA0.2		**MaxSLA0.4**		**MaxSLA0.5**		**MaxSLA0.6**		**EPEX**	
	Soft	**Hard**	**Soft**	**Hard**	**Soft**	**Hard**	**Soft**	**Hard**	**Soft**	**Hard**
Power										
TFE	-0.98	-0.98	-1.55	-1.86	-1.71	-1.66	-1.79	-1.78	**-7.81**	**-9.99**
PTFP	0.63	0.63	2.47	2.72	3.24	2.70	3.77	2.79	4.05	-0.99
JE	-0.75	-0.75	**-1.08**	**-1.44**	-1.07	-1.01	-0.91	-0.91	**-12.50**	**-14.51**
PJP	-0.85	-0.85	1.31	1.29	1.31	2.71	2.43	3.08	4.87	-1.11
Jobs										
ART	21.28	21.04	21.93	22.68	22.72	22.55	23.34	23.86	7.65	7.49
WL	0.86	0.85	**1.73**	**0.92**	2.34	2.65	3.54	3.53	-11.88	-12.88
RWL	3.24	4.50	3.79	6.26	**3.90**	**6.73**	6.00	7.26		
AF	-0.92	-0.92	-2.14	-2.20	-2.81	-2.87	-3.73	-3.76		
Cost										
SLA_C	**176**	**501**	**1,443**	**3,881**	**699**	**3,532**	**2,501**	**4,270**	**1,082**	**1,518**

cost and benefit side of the 'Hard SLA' runs compared to the 'Soft SLA' runs are displayed for the whole simulation set 2 in the lower part of tables B.4 and B.5, and the net benefit is visualized in figure 6.18. The huge difference in the net benefits using dynamic cost somewhat hides the fact, that the difference of net benefits between the hard and the soft SLA using static electricity cost is also huge. The MaxSLA0.5 run, that originally was the most beneficial engagement in the SCR market, under hard SLA turns into an economic loss. The only SCR engagement that leads to a very small benefit (0.51% for the static net benefit NBS) is MaxSLA0.2. For the case of 'Hard SLA' there is no real option to earn an additional benefit by implementing demand response! Even sourcing power at the EPEX power market, if the baseline energy cost is already low due to the dynamic EPEX energy prices, leads to a loss of 4.22%. The reason is the surging SLA cost depending on the power reduction offered: SLA cost in all SCR cases outweigh the reward that can be gained on the SCR market; only in the MaxSLA0.2 case the energy cost savings are high enough to compensate for that loss.

6.3.3. Set 3: Manipulating the Composition of the Data Center Workload

The final simulation set explores the impact of a modified workload composition on the results of the HPC engaging in the SCR market or sourcing its electricity on the EPEX market in the first week of March 2014. The original workload was decomposed into jobs belonging to 'Long Job' job classes and 'Short Job' job classes. As therefore the size of the workload is considerably smaller than the original workload, in the case of explicit demand response, only reductions of 0.2, 0.1, 0.05MW are possible.

Figure 6.19 shows the case of a positive SCR bid of 0.2MW for both the new 'Long Job' (dark green, dotted line) and 'Short Job' (dark green) Facility Power trace compared with the original load (light green). The MaxBid activation trace in the upper part of the picture depicts where the data center *must react* to the activation; unfortunately, on March 4th, the 'Long Job' workload would not have been able to reduce its power consumption by 200kW due to a still high fix power block. As a result, of course it is paid neither the power nor the energy SCR reward. The contractual consequences are up to the aggregator. Apart from this effect, figure 6.19 gives a first impression, that the 'Short Job' trace is less agile than the 'Long Job' trace. This is not unexpected, considering that the 'Short Job' trace contains 4007 jobs, the 'Long Job' trace merely 1872 jobs, the energy load however of the 'Short Job' trace being 11% higher than of the 'Long Job' trace. This finding is supported by figure 6.20 that displays the results of March 7th for the Job Power, the Active Nodes and the number of Jobs of the MaxSLA0.1 run which was successful for both job traces.

As a matter of comparison, again the original curves for MaxSLA0.1 are presented. This illustrates how the reaction of the 'Short Jobs' is slightly more extreme but more or less retraces the original data trace which illuminates the fact that the original data trace for the considered week is dominated by short jobs. The most conspicuous results of this run are that the average active number of 'Long jobs' is rather constant, and that the corresponding active

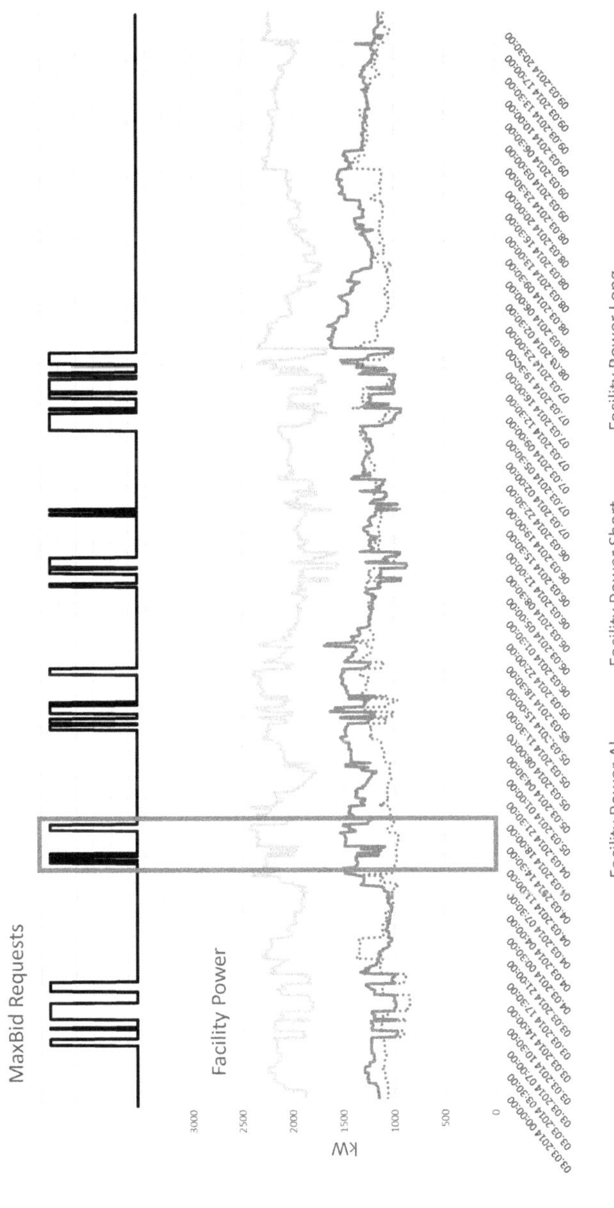

Figure 6.19.: The Facility Power data traces of the MaxSLA0.2 simulation of 'Short Jobs' vs. 'Long Jobs'; unsuccessful for Long Jobs

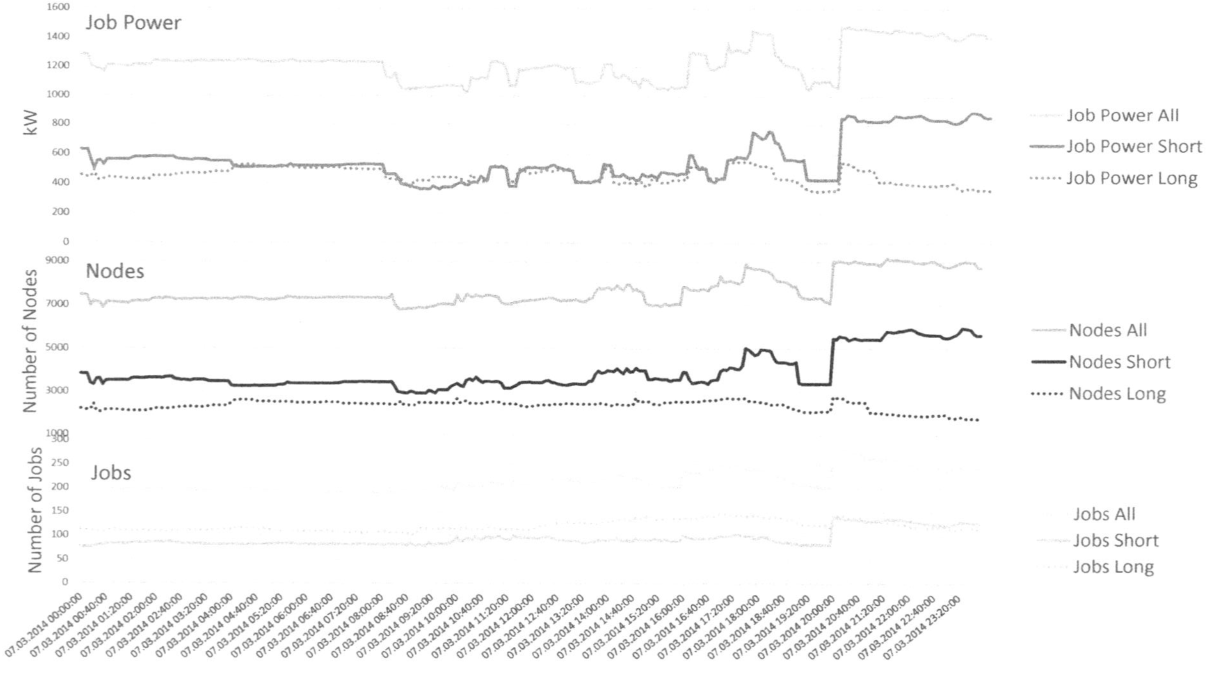

Figure 6.20.: Comparing the Job power, the Active Nodes and Jobs of the successful MaxSLA0.1 simulation of 'Short Jobs' vs. 'Long Jobs', 7th of March

number of nodes are even behaving counter-intuitively in the evening event which means that there is not much room for a 'rebound effect' after the event has finished as jobs that are lasting for hours cannot be moved.

The differences between the two sets of workload traces are even more conspicuous when simulating an engagement on the EPEX markets, which means exchanging the scheduling algorithms (original HPC-RE vs. CAS) during the whole simulation time. The numbered blue buttons on figure 6.21 highlight the difference in behaviour of the 'Short Jobs' and the 'Long Jobs', the corresponding arrows differentiate between price adaptations that worked out well (blue arrows) from those that could not be implemented in the intended direction (red arrows). The first blue button shows how both traces adapt to a price decrease by increasing their load. The second and the third blue button, however, point out that the facility power of the 'Long Jobs' could not increase in spite of a price dip (number 1) or even had to increase load (number 2) when unfortunately also the price level increased. These findings are reinforced by the curves of the number of active nodes and jobs in figure 6.22. Again opposing the two different workloads against the EXPEX day ahead price vector in this figure the number of Active Nodes of the 'Short Jobs' workload exhibits an extremely elastic behaviour compared both to the Job curve and the corresponding curves of the 'Long Jobs' workload. Analysing these curves, it needs to be taken into account that the active Number of Jobs contains snapshots of each time slot, so 'Long Jobs' linger much longer and therefore a spike as in the morning of the 5th of March implies that some new jobs started without old jobs being finished due to an increase in the baseline 'Long Job' workload. The old jobs are obviously terminated directly after this spike, so that the curve drops. For the case of the 'Short Jobs' the Number of Active Nodes reacts more sharply than the Number of Jobs. This can be explained with the fact that on average the 'Short Jobs' run on more nodes than the 'Long Jobs' (see also tables 6.10 and 6.11 that summarize the results) which also implies that the average power per job is not much different (not to be confounded 'Average Job Power' as a result of averaging the time series, see table 6.3) .

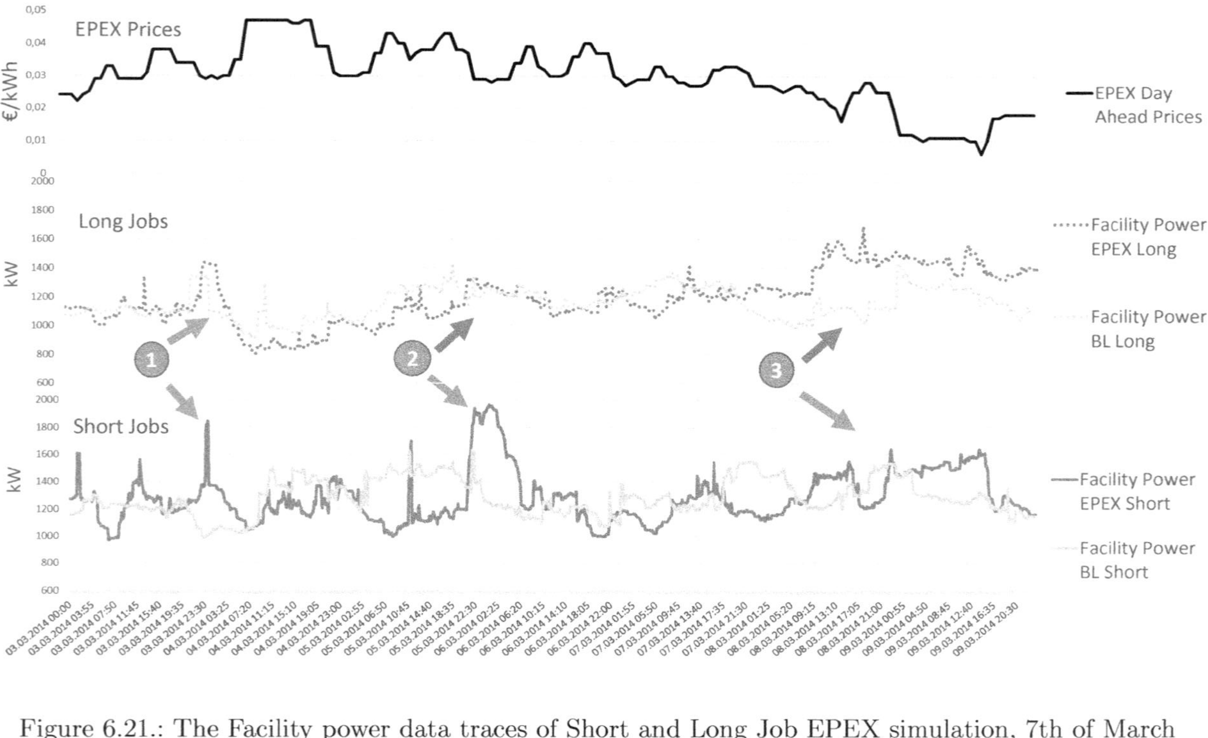

Figure 6.21.: The Facility power data traces of Short and Long Job EPEX simulation, 7th of March

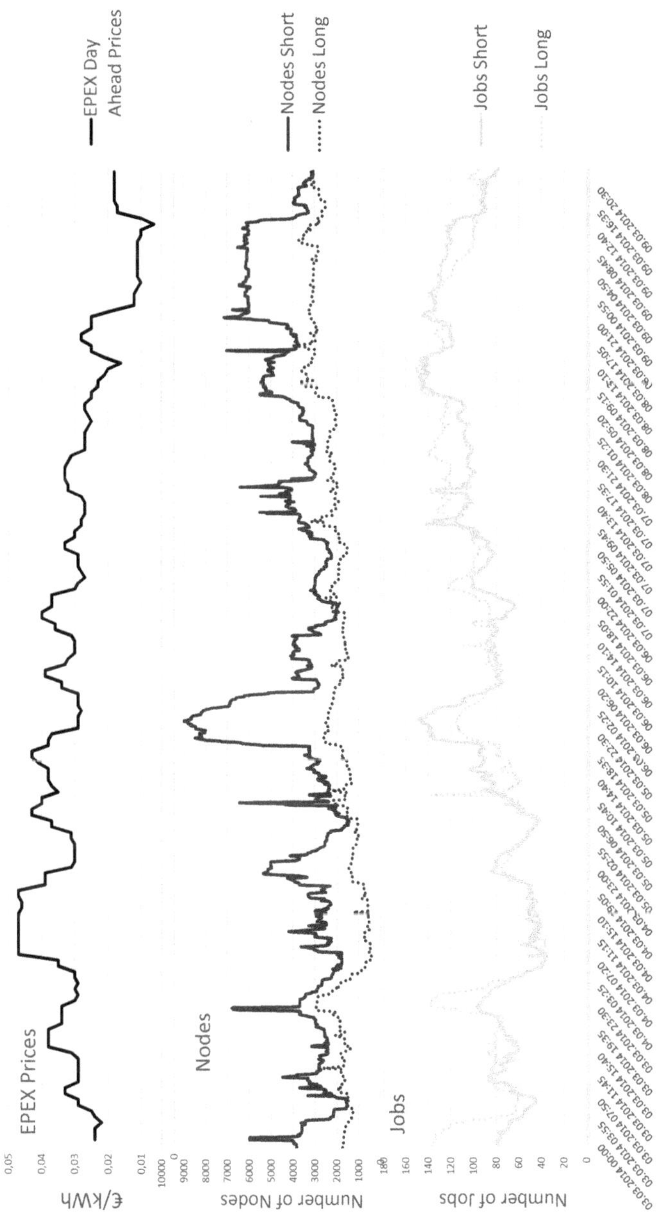

Figure 6.22.: The number of Active Nodes and Jobs data traces of Short and Long Job EPEX simulation

This difference in adaptivity to both the dynamic prices in the EPEX power flex market and the SCR events of the two data traces is also mirrored in the disparity of benefits as represented in figure 6.23. In case the data center had a flat tariff that equals the average industry price in 2014, represented by the 'static' benefit tags, for both workloads it is more beneficial to invest into the SCR market than to implement power management in order to adapt to the dynamic EPEX prices. Interestingly, the 'Long Job' workload is affected more extremely than the 'Short Job' workload, also with regards to benefits, which is an unexpected outcome. This is due to the high difference in SLA cost payable to the data center's customers (see tables B.6 and B.7 in the appendix): in the case of the 'Short Jobs' the level of SLA cost is considerably lower than for the 'Long Job' workload, even though they grow with a lower inclination. And regarding the MaxSLA0.2 run, which would have incurred surging SLA cost for the 'Long Job' workload, this had to be annulled as in one single event during the considered week the adaptation of the 'Long Job' workload was technically infeasible. In case the data center in 2014 purchased energy at the EPEX day ahead market without managing their power profile accordingly, the 'Short Job' workload would have benefited from additionally rescheduling and scaling their job workload in order to adapt to price differences: in that case the net benefit of such activity would have been an additional 2,8% rent based on their (dynamic) energy bill. Investing in the SCR market would have lead to a loss, contrary to the 'Long Jobs' workload driven data center, which would have benefited slightly from bidding into the SCR market (through an aggregator), whereas an EPEX engagement would have led to additional cost only, again due to the difference in SLA cost.

6.4. Discussion of Simulation Results

The high sensitivity of simulating results to the parameter settings shows that there is no one-fits-all strategy of data center demand response. In some

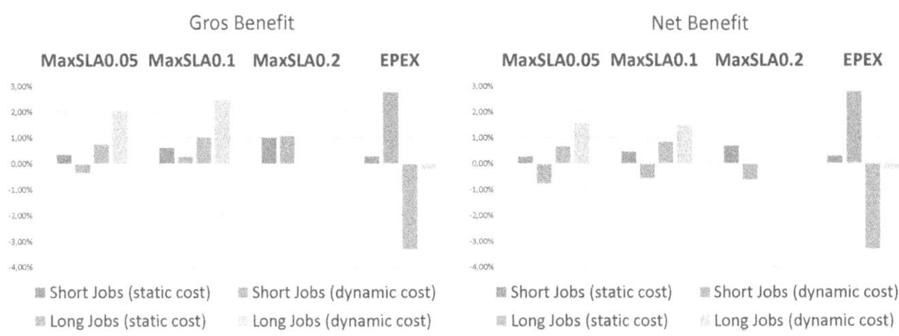

Figure 6.23.: Gross and net benefit of the third simulation set: Short versus Long Job traces

Table 6.10.: 'Short Jobs' statistics. Percentages relate to the Short Job BL, except for the Short Job BL relating to the original data trace

	BL Short		MaxSLA0.05 Short		MaxSLA0.1 Short		MaxSLA0.2 Short	
	absolute	% BL	absolute	% BL	absolute	% BL	absolute	% BL
Power								
TFE	216,340	-37.80%	215,148	-0.55%	214,735	-0.74%	214,058	-1.05%
PTFP	1,630	-32.29%	1,647	1.00%	1,649	1.12%	1,691	3.70%
AJP	566	-54.91%	563	-0.54%	562	-0.70%	562	-0.72%
Jobs								
ART	15,282		14,149	-7.41%	14,281	-6.55%	14,403	-5.75%
WL	93.2		93.8	0.65%	94.1	1.04%	95.5	**2.50%**
AF	2.42		2,33	-3.67%	2,32	-4.16%	2,28	**-5.73%**

cases as for instance, if there is a sharp increase of SLA cost, the outcome is as expected: The benefit of all versions of investing into demand response is reduced, benefits turned into losses (see B.4), and even power management in the EPEX market which under the originally assumed SLA cost resulted in a

Table 6.11.: 'Long Jobs' statistics. Percentages relate to the Long Job BL, except for the Long Job BL relating to the original data trace

	BL Long		**MaxSLA0.05L.**		**MaxSLA0.1L.**		**MaxSLA0.2L.**	
	absolute	% BL	absolute	% BL	absolute	% BL	absolute	% BL
Power								
TFE	194,406	-44.10%	193,494	-0.47%	193,000	-0.72%	192,591	-0.93%
PTFP	1,438	-40.29%	1,436	-0.12%	1,436	-0.11%	1,454	1.12%
AJP	386	-69.21%	384	-0.70%	382	-1.02%	382	-1.01%
Jobs								
ART	30,703		30,691	-0.04%	31,002	0.97%	31,294	1.92%
WL	94.9		95.4	0.47%	96.1	1.26%	97.9	3.09%
AF	2,43		2,34	-3.39%	2,32	-4.28%	2,25	-7.16%

profit of 5.8% is reduced by one percent point. This still means that the EPEX market at first glance is the most resilient investment.

Removing the SLA component all together (MaxBid runs without SLA), as expected leads to considerably higher benefits, for both explored implicit and explicit demand response markets. Thus in the absence of SLA cost, earning €1,720 in the considered week, representing 12.67% of the original static baseline power cost would have been a possibility for the considered data center offering 0.6MW to the SCR. This is not unrealistic taking into account that HPC data centers are often publicly owned and therefore do not charge SLA cost. At no cost, here the technical potential of demand response is analysed which leads to potential reductions in this considered week of up to 0.6MW of a peak power consumption of 2.4MW, due to high fixed block of server and cooling infrastructure which is independent of the workload computed. Also, the point in time when the SCR called plays an important role: the events calling for reduction on March 6th come at a time of a comparably low utilization of the data center, when the job power only just exceeds 1MW. With an average power consumption of 1.25MW of the job power, the activations might have happened at more but also at less suitable times.

This highlights not only the sensitivity of both technical and economic demand response potential to the power system conditions but also to the bidding strategy of the data center: the MinBid scenarios explored the low-risk investment which implied a lower activation frequency but also a lower remuneration for the provision of power. Comparing the gross economic results of SLA-based MinBid and MaxBid scenarios, e.g. a benefit of 0.44% of the original flat tariff electricity bill for MinSLA0.6 (table 6.7) versus a benefit of 2.09% for MaxSLA0.5 (table 6.5) renders the MaxBid scenarios on average superior (see tables B.2 and B.3 in the appendix). However, accounting for the higher risk involved (SLA cost of €699 vs. €10) a data center operator might decide on a lower involvement.

The overall strategy from these first two sets of simulation runs seems obvious: not to be bound by mandatory activations on the SCR market but instead turn to the EPEX day ahead market. Simply exchanging the static tariff for the dynamic electricity prices without manipulating the power profile reduces the energy bill by 80%, i.e. from €53,284 to €10,339 in the first week of March 2014. This ratio is even increased to 84% looking into the data from 03/03-30/03. Adding power management on top of this results only in a slight increase of additional €56 saved.

The same holds in principle for the two alternative workloads, the 'Long Jobs' and the 'Short Jobs' trace: By sourcing their power on the EPEX power market, without implementing power management, the data center management in March 2014 could have saved about 80% of their power bill (assuming the average industry price!).

However, in case the data center sticks to the flat energy tariff and considers investing into the SCR market or the EPEX market by managing their power profile according to the price differences, the situation is different: For both workload models, the 'Long Jobs' and the 'Short Jobs' in that case the engagement into the SCR market would prove more beneficial than into the EPEX market. The 'Short Job' workload would make a slightly higher profit offering 0.2MW to the SCR market than to invest into the EPEX market (1.09% vs. 0.29%), the 'Long Job' workload, unfortunately, in the latter case would lose

3.3%. This is a contradictory finding to the original workload where the EPEX market in all cases proved to be the best alternative.

7. Conclusion and Outlook

With the future energy system facing disruptions from intermittent REN power sources and an increase of electric vehicles, demand response becomes a necessary supplement to fast responding power sites in the endeavor to avoid gaps between power feed-in and power draw. Data centers can play a major role as participants in demand response schemes offering various starting points for temporary power management at all layers of a general architecture. This thesis evaluated this opportunity from a data center's point of view.

Conclusion

The focus of this work was put on the complexity of the potential variety of different power management strategies in a data center facing a variety of power flex markets. In order to deal with this complexity a modeling framework was presented that allows to understand the relevance of individual approaches in the context of an overarching framework. It comprises both a generic data center architecture that structures the different starting points for power management and a micro-economics based optimization modeling framework. As an example of applying this framework a generic simulation architecture was created which was instantiated into a concrete simulation system [132]. In order to produce meaningful results, this simulation system represents a specific data center that generates power flexibility by applying power management strategies on two different layers of the data center architectural framework, i.e. on the infrastructure layer and the software layer. Implementing these two strategies, frequency scaling and workload shifting, required to consistently link the provided 2014 workload data with the physical infrastructure data in a way that offers activators to manipulate the data center power profile. The simulation thus shows how the resulting flexibility could have been monetized on two real power flex markets that might have been accessed in 2014 by this concrete data center, namely the secondary reserve market and the EPEX day-ahead market in Germany.

The most striking result of this concrete evaluation through the simulation tool Sim2Win-HPC is the following: Assuming a baseline of billing electricity by applying the (flat) average industry price of €0.1532 results in a power bill of €53,284 in the simulated week. Compared to this baseline, the financially most attractive strategy would have been to just replace this price by the dynamic price vector of the EPEX market, thus saving 80% of the original electricity bill. This means, that under the market conditions of 2014 the largest financial efficiency gain for the considered data center would have been *not* to implement demand response, but to turn to a different pricing scheme. This statement also holds if the average industry price had been only half of the real one.

Entering into the explicit demand response market SCR for the best combination of bids in the considered week would have resulted in an activation trace of 24 distinct events, all together covering 90 15-minute timeslots. The data center would have been able to fulfill all these events offering up to 600kW. Under the assumption of no SLA cost, which is realistic for publicly owned HPC data centers, it would have been valuable for the data center to further invest into the SCR market, offering 600kW and therefore achieving another 12.7% gross and 9.5% net (substracting the aggregator fee) benefit based on the reduced power bill of €10,339. Applying the baseline SLA cost model which is relevant for most commercial data centers, the SLA cost of this offer would not have been compensated by the SCR remuneration. Here, the most beneficial offer would have been 500kW, resulting in an extra benefit of 4% on top of the dynamic EPEX price gain, assuming the data center had been able to access the market directly, still a net benefit of 1.4% under the more realistic assumption of accessing the market via an aggregator. If instead the data center, additionally to applying EPEX prices to the *original* power profile, had manipulated their power profile based on the EPEX prices and aiming at a cost optimization, they would have gained a meager extra savings of €56.

These results illustrate the large gap between the technical (i.e. power adaptation without SLA cost) and the economic potential of demand response in the presented case. However, these results, as the results in other works, are largely dependent on the parameters of the simulation. Simply halving the deadlines that entail penalties to be paid to the data center's customers, on the SCR reserve market turns the net benefit into a loss of -2%; on the EPEX market the data center would have lost even -2.2%. Also tuning the bid-sizes offered to reserve market (the MinBid scenarios) or changing the composition of the workload ('short jobs' vs. 'long jobs') impacts the outcome considerably. The same can be said for market conditions: A baseline flat price of €0.07 instead of €0.15 would for instance increase the gros benefit of MaxSLA0.5 from 2.1% to 2.5% related to the original flat priced electricity bill. But still, just using the dynamic EPEX price vector instead of the reduced baseline flat price would reduce electricty cost by 57%.

As a summary, the current power market conditions are not very attractive for data center demand response. If society wishes to activate the technical flexibility potential of data centers, the reimbursement should be increased.

This is where the greater picture created by the generic modeling framework comes into play: The presented simulation result and economic evaluation supports the original hypothesis that the broad view of a high level modeling framework helps to understand the relevance of specific simulation or optimization approaches and scenarios. In the presented concrete simulation scenario, only two power management strategies on two architectural layers were implemented, determining the current 'technical potential'. Modeling more strategies and using other power market and cost conditions might have increased both the technical and the economic potential of demand response in this specific case.

Threats to validity of the presented approach mostly relate to the concrete simulation:

- The difference between the time series power representation of the job data trace and the IT data trace is unspecified, so that it had to be modeled coarsely.
- The CPU frequency data relate to the maximum allowed frequency, not to the executed frequency; and the job data trace did not contain information on the applications, which both might have lead to further inaccuracies.
- The simulation has a high computational weight so that only one week could be simulated.
- Apart from the fact that not the total range of all possible simulation parameters could be tested, also the system uses historic data so that uncertainty of the future development both of the workload and of power flex market conditions were excluded.

Shortcomings of the modeling framework mostly relate to the fact that it is static and does not include uncertainty. Also the different levels of contractual bondage between the explicit and implicit power flex markets have not been expressed in the theoretical model yet. However, the advantage of the current version is the clarity of the approach that, notwithstanding the lack of detail, helps at putting concrete examples of demand response with data centers into context so that untapped potentials can be easier identified and limitations understood.

Outlook

Data Center demand response is still in its infancy, not only looking at its realization under probably unfavourable circumstances but also with regards to research which fails to offer a complete picture instead of shedding a coup d'oeil on different aspects. The presented modeling framework is a step in this direction that needs both further development and more evaluations.

In order to enhance the presented optimization framework, as hinted above, uncertainty and temporal dynamics should be included as an additional version in order not to reduce the clarity of this first, here presented modeling framework.

Strengthening the evaluation of this approach can be implemented on two different levels. On the one hand, different model instances of the framework can be created. This has been undertaken and published [131] for a linear optimization instance that builds on the same scenario, using the same data, power management techniques, and power flex markets. Also, the impact of the human factor on decision making , e.g. risk propensity or inertia of behavioural patterns, might be further explored. In the framework, this is currently expressed through the option to formulate alternative cost functions by adding a risk adversity index RI. As of now this was not included in either evaluation instance due to the lack of data. In order to collect a first data set, plans to issue a questionnaire targeting data centers across Europe are under way.

And finally, the generic simulation architecture Sim2Win can be applied in different scenarios and/or with other data centers and markets. For instance, alternative markets and new power management strategies could be added as e.g. analysing the options of geographical shifting or shutting down servers into the current instance of the architecture. It is further planned to model and integrate the concept of GreenSLAs using publicly available REN data. As it is not possible to receive more detailed data for instance with regards to cooling, a different option is to use workload, server and cooling data from a different data center. The only limitation, which proved to be one major obstacle on the way to simulation, is data availability.

Bibliography

[1] 50Hertz, Amprion, Tennet, and TransnetBW. Bericht der deutschen Übertragungsnetzbetreiber zur Leistungsbilanz 2018-2022. Technical report, 2020.

[2] M. Acton, P. Bertoldi, and J. Booth. 2020 Best Practice guidelines for the EU Code of Conduct on data centre energy efficiency. *Publications Office of the European Union, Luxembourg, Tech. Report. EUR 29103 EN, 2018*, 2020.

[3] I. Ahmed, H. Okumura, and K. Arai. Analysis on existing basic SLAs and Green SLAs to define new sustainable Green SLA. *International Journal of Advanced Computer Science and Applications*, 6(12):100–108, 2015.

[4] K. Ahmed, M. A. Islam, and S. Ren. A contract design approach for colocation data center demand response. In *Proceedings of the IEEE/ACM International Conference on Computer-Aided Design*, pages 635–640. IEEE Press, 2015.

[5] K. Ahmed, J. Liu, and X. Wu. An energy efficient demand-response model for high performance computing systems. In *2017 IEEE 25th International Symposium on Modeling, Analysis, and Simulation of Computer and Telecommunication Systems (MASCOTS)*, pages 175–186. IEEE, 2017.

[6] D. Aikema, R. Simmonds, and H. Zareipour. Data centres in the ancillary services market. In *Green Computing Conference (IGCC), 2012 International*, pages 1–10. IEEE, 2012.

[7] D. Aikema, R. Simmonds, and H. Zareipour. Delivering ancillary services with data centres. *Sustainable Computing: Informatics and Systems*, 3(3):172–182, 2013.

[8] B. Aksanli and T. Rosing. Providing regulation services and managing data center peak power budgets. In *Proceedings of the conference on Design, Automation & Test in Europe*, page 143. European Design and Automation Association, 2014.

[9] M. H. Albadi and E. El-Saadany. Demand response in electricity markets: An overview. In *2007 IEEE power engineering society general meeting*, 2007.

[10] H. A. Alissa, K. Nemati, B. G. Sammakia, M. J. Seymour, R. Tipton, D. Mendo, D. W. Demetriou, and K. Schneebeli. Chip to chiller experimental cooling failure analysis of data centers: The interaction between IT and facility. *IEEE Transactions on Components, Packaging and Manufacturing Technology*, 6(9):1361–1378, 2016.

[11] A. Amokrane, R. Langar, M. F. Zhani, R. Boutaba, and G. Pujolle. Greenslater: On satisfying green slas in distributed clouds. *IEEE Transactions on Network and Service Management*, 12(3):363–376, 2015.

[12] A. S. Andrae. Projecting the chiaroscuro of the electricity use of communication and computing from 2018 to 2030. Technical report, Huawei Technologies Sweden AB, 2019.

[13] M. D. W. Andreu Mas-Colell and J. R. Green. *Microeconomic Theory.* Oxford University press New York, 1995.

[14] A. I. Aravanis, A. Voulkidis, J. Salom, J. Townley, V. Georgiadou, A. Oleksiak, M. R. Porto, F. Roudet, and T. Zahariadis. Metrics for assessing flexibility and sustainability of next generation data centers. In *2015 IEEE Globecom Workshops (GC Wkshps)*, pages 1–6, 2015.

[15] D. Arnone, A. Barberi, D. La Cascia, E. R. Sanseverino, and G. Zizzo. Green data centres integration in smart grids: New frontiers for ancillary service provision. *Electric Power Systems Research*, 148:59–73, 2017.

[16] ASHRAE TC 9.9. Thermal guidelines for liquid cooled data processing environments. Technical report, 2011.

[17] A. Auweter, A. Bode, M. Brehm, L. Brochard, N. Hammer, H. Huber, R. Panda, F. Thomas, and T. Wilde. A case study of energy aware scheduling on SuperMuc. In *International Supercomputing Conference*, pages 394–409. Springer, 2014.

[18] M. Avgerinou, P. Bertoldi, and L. Castellazzi. Trends in data centre energy consumption under the European Code of Conduct for data centre energy efficiency. *Energies*, 10(10):1470, 2017.

[19] S. Bahrami, V. W. Wong, and J. Huang. Demand response for data centers in deregulated markets: A matching game approach. In *2017 IEEE International Conference on Smart Grid Communications (SmartGridComm)*, pages 344–350. IEEE, 2017.

[20] S. Bahrami, V. W. Wong, and J. Huang. Data center demand response in deregulated electricity markets. *IEEE Transactions on Smart Grid*, 10(3):2820–2832, 2018.

[21] C. Baier, S. Klueppelholz, H. de Meer, F. Niedermeier, and S. Wunderlich. Greener bits: Formal analysis of demand response. In C. A. et al., editor, *ATVA 2016*, volume 9938 of *LNCS*, pages 1–17. Springer International Publishing, 2016.

[22] O. Balci. Verification, validation, and certification of modeling and simulation applications. In *Proceedings of the 35th conference on Winter simulation: driving innovation*, pages 150–158. Winter Simulation Conference, 2003.

[23] M. Banja and M. Jégard. Renewable technologies in the EU electricity sector: trends and projections. *Publication Office of the EU*, 2017.

[24] L. A. Barroso and U. Hölzle. The case for energy-proportional computing. *Computer*, (12):33–37, 2007.

[25] L. A. Barroso and U. Hölzle. The datacenter as a computer: An introduction to the design of warehouse-scale machines, second edition. *Synthesis lectures on computer architecture*, 4(1):1–135, 2013.

[26] L. Barth, N. Ludwig, E. Mengelkamp, and P. Staudt. A comprehensive modelling framework for demand side flexibility in smart grids. *Computer Science-Research and Development*, 33(1-2):13–23, 2018.

[27] R. Basmadjian, J. F. Botero, G. Giuliani, X. H. Serra, S. Klingert, and H. De Meer. Making data centres fit for demand response: Introducing greenSDA and greenSLA contracts. *IEEE Transactions on Smart Grid*, 2016.

[28] R. Basmadjian, C. Bunse, V. Georgiadou, G. Giuliani, S. Klingert, G. Lovasz, and M. Majanen. Fit4green - energy aware ict optimization policies. In *Proceedings of the COST Action IC0804 on Energy Efficiency in Large Scale Distributed Systems1st Year*, pages 88–92. IRIT, 2010.

[29] R. Basmadjian, G. Lovasz, M. Beck, H. De Meer, X. Hesselbach-Serra, J. F. Botero, S. Klingert, M. P. Ortega, J. C. Lopez, A. Stam, et al. A generic architecture for demand response: The ALL4Green approach. In *2013 International Conference on Cloud and Green Computing*, pages 464–471. IEEE, 2013.

[30] R. Basmadjian, F. Niedermeier, G. Lovasz, H. De Meer, and S. Klingert. GreenSDAs leveraging power adaption collaboration between energy provider and data centres. In *Sustainable Internet and ICT for Sustainability (SustainIT), 2013*, pages 1–9. IEEE, 2013.

[31] N. Bates, G. Ghatikar, G. Abdulla, G. A. Koenig, S. Bhalachandra, M. Sheikhalishahi, T. Patki, B. Rountree, and S. Poole. Electrical grid and supercomputing centers: An investigative analysis of emerging opportunities and challenges. *Informatik-Spektrum*, 38(2):111–127, 2015.

[32] A. Beloglazov, R. Buyya, Y. C. Lee, and A. Zomaya. A taxonomy and survey of energy-efficient data centers and cloud computing systems. In *Advances in computers*, volume 82, pages 47–111. Elsevier, 2011.

[33] C. Bergaentzlé and C. Clastres. Demand side management in an integrated electricity market: What are the impacts on generation and en-

vironmental concerns? In *2013 10th International Conference on the European Energy Market (EEM)*, pages 1–8. IEEE, 2013.

[34] M. Berkelaar, K. Eikland, and P. Notebaert. lp_solve 5.5, open source (mixed-integer) linear programming system. software, may 1 2004.

[35] A. Berl, S. Klingert, M. T. Beck, and H. de Meer. Integrating data centres into demand-response management: A local case study. In *Industrial Electronics Society, IECON 2013-39th Annual Conference of the IEEE*, pages 4762–4767. IEEE, 2013.

[36] A. Berwald, T. Faninger, S. Bayramoglu, B. Tinetti, S. Mudgal, L. Stobbe, and N. Nissen. Ecodesign preparatory study on enterprise servers and data equipment. Technical report, European Commission, 2015.

[37] A. A. Bhattacharya, D. Culler, A. Kansal, S. Govindan, and S. Sankar. The need for speed and stability in data center power capping. *Sustainable Computing: Informatics and Systems*, 3(3):183–193, 2013.

[38] J. F. Botero, S. Klingert, X. Hesselbach-Serra, A. Falcone, and G. Giuliani. GreenSLAs: Providing energy consumption flexibility in data centers through energy-aware contracts. In *Proceedings of the International Conference of Smart Cities and Green ICT Systems (SMARTGREENS)*. SciTePress, 2013.

[39] Broadgroup. Data centre market Europe. Whitepaper, 2016. `https://www.broad-group.com/reports/data-centres-europe-6`.

[40] Bundesnetzagentur für Elektrizität, Gas, Telekommunikation, Post und Eisenbahnen. Monitoring report 2018. Technical report, 2019.

[41] Bundesnetzagentur für Elektrizität, Gas, Telekommunikation, Post und Eisenbahnen. Monitoringbericht 2019. Technical report, 2020.

[42] Bundesverband der Energie- und Wasserwirtschaft. BDEW-Strompreisanalyse Februar 2018. Technical report, BDEW, 2018.

[43] Bundesverband der Energie- und Wasserwirtschaft. BDEW-Strompreisanalyse Juli 2019: Haushalte und Industrie. Technical report, BDEW, 2019.

[44] Bundesverband der Energie- und Wasserwirtschaft. Nettostromverbrauch in Deutschland in den Jahren 1991 bis 2018. Technical report, BDEW, 2019.

[45] M. Calzarossa and G. Serazzi. Workload characterization: A survey. *Proceedings of the IEEE*, 81(8):1136–1150, 1993.

[46] M. C. Calzarossa, L. Massari, and D. Tessera. Workload characterization: A survey revisited. *ACM Computing Surveys (CSUR)*, 48(3):48, 2016.

[47] A. Capozzoli, M. Chinnici, M. Perino, and G. Serale. Review on performance metrics for energy efficiency in data center: The role of thermal management. In *International Workshop on Energy Efficient Data Centers*, pages 135–151. Springer, 2014.

[48] C. Cappiello, N. T. T. Ho, B. Pernici, P. Plebani, and M. Vitali. CO2-aware adaptation strategies for cloud applications. *IEEE Transactions on Cloud Computing*, 4(2):152–165, 2016.

[49] CEN-CENELEC-ETSI, Smart Grid Coordination. Smart grid reference architecture. Whitepaper, 2012. `https://ec.europa.eu/energy/sites/ener/files/documents/xpert_group1_reference_architecture.pdf`, accessed 02/05/2020.

[50] H. Chen, M. C. Caramanis, and A. K. Coskun. The data center as a grid load stabilizer. In *2014 19th Asia and South Pacific Design Automation Conference (ASP-DAC)*, pages 105–112. IEEE, 2014.

[51] H. Chen, M. C. Caramanis, and A. K. Coskun. Reducing the data center electricity costs through participation in smart grid programs. In *Green Computing Conference (IGCC), 2014 International* [50], pages 1–10.

[52] H. Chen, Y. Zhang, M. C. Caramanis, and A. K. Coskun. Energyqare: Qos-aware data center participation in smart grid regulation service re-

serve provision. *ACM Transactions on Modeling and Performance Evaluation of Computing Systems (TOMPECS)*, 4(1):1–31, 2019.

[53] Y. Chen, A. Das, W. Qin, A. Sivasubramaniam, Q. Wang, and N. Gautam. Managing server energy and operational costs in hosting centers. In *ACM SIGMETRICS performance evaluation review*, volume 33, pages 303–314. ACM, 2005.

[54] T. Cioara, I. Anghel, M. Bertoncini, I. Salomie, D. Arnone, M. Mammina, T.-H. Velivassaki, and M. Antal. Optimized flexibility management enacting data centres participation in smart demand response programs. *Future Generation Computer Systems*, 2016.

[55] T. Cioara, I. Anghel, I. Salomie, M. Antal, C. Pop, M. Bertoncini, D. Arnone, and F. Pop. Exploiting data centres energy flexibility in smart cities: Business scenarios. *Information Sciences*, 476:392–412, 2019.

[56] A. Clausen, G. Koenig, S. Klingert, G. Ghatikar, P. M. Schwartz, and N. Bates. An analysis of contracts and relationships between supercomputing centers and electricity service providers. In *Proceedings of the 48th International Conference on Parallel Processing: Workshops*, pages 1–8, 2019.

[57] Consentec. Beschreibung von Regelleistungskonzepten und Regelleistungsmarkt. Studie im Auftrag der deutschen Übertragungsnetzbetreiber, Consentec, 2014.

[58] Council of European Energy Regulators. Status review on the implementation of transmission system operators unbundling provisions of the 3rd energy package - CEER status review. Technical report, CEER, 2016.

[59] P. Cristian, P. Eugen, A. Marcel, C. Pop, T. Cioara, I. Anghel, and I. Salomie. Coolcloudsim: Integrating cooling system models in CloudSim. In *2018 IEEE 14th International Conference on Intelligent Computer Communication and Processing (ICCP)*, pages 387–394. IEEE, 2018.

[60] L. J. Cupelli, T. Schutz, P. Jahangiri, M. Fuchs, A. Monti, and D. Muller. Data center control strategy for participation in demand response programs. *IEEE Transactions on Industrial Informatics*, 2018.

[61] M. Dayarathna, Y. Wen, and R. Fan. Data center energy consumption modeling: A survey. *IEEE Communications Surveys & Tutorials*, 18(1):732–794, 2016.

[62] P. De Martini. DR 2.0 future of customer response. Newport consulting prepared for the association for demand response and smart grid, ADS & LBNL, 2013.

[63] C. Dupont, F. Hermenier, T. Schulze, R. Basmadjian, A. Somov, and G. Giuliani. Plug4green: A flexible energy-aware VM manager to fit data centre particularities. *Ad Hoc Networks*, 25:505–519, 2015.

[64] C. Dupont, M. Sheikhalishahi, F. M. Facca, and F. Hermenier. An energy aware application controller for optimizing renewable energy consumption in data centres. In *Utility and Cloud Computing (UCC), 2015 IEEE/ACM 8th International Conference on*, pages 195–204. IEEE, 2015.

[65] C. Eid, E. Koliou, M. Valles, J. Reneses, and R. Hakvoort. Time-based pricing and electricity demand response: Existing barriers and next steps. *Utilities Policy*, 40:15–25, 2016.

[66] E. N. Elnozahy, M. Kistler, and R. Rajamony. Energy-efficient server clusters. In *PACS*, volume 2325, pages 179–196. Springer, 2002.

[67] M. Etinski, J. Corbalán, J. Labarta, and M. Valero. Understanding the future of energy-performance trade-off via DVFS in HPC environments. *Journal of Parallel and Distributed Computing*, 72(4):579–590, 2012.

[68] ETSO. Demand response as a resource for the adequacy and operational reliability of the power systems. Technical report, ETSO, 2007.

[69] European Commission. Incorporing demand side flexibility, in particular demand response, in electricity markets: Delivering the internal electricity market and making the most of public intervention. Communication from the Commission, SWD(2013) 442 final, November 2013.

[70] European Commission. A policy framework for climate and energy in the period from 2020 to 2030. Communication from the Commission to the European Parliament, the Council, the European Economic and Social Committee and the Committee of the Regions, 2014.

[71] X. Fan, W.-D. Weber, and L. A. Barroso. Power provisioning for a warehouse-sized computer. In *ACM SIGARCH Computer Architecture News*, volume 35, pages 13–23. ACM, 2007.

[72] S. Federal Energy Regulatory Commission. Assessment of demand response and advanced metering. *FERC, Docket AD-06-2-000*, 2006.

[73] S. Federal Energy Regulatory Commission. Assessment of demand response and advanced metering. *FERC*, 2018.

[74] Federal Ministry of Economic Affairs and Energy. Draft of the Integrated National Energy and Climate Plan. Technical Report, 2019.

[75] Federal Ministry of Economics and Technology. Germanys new energy policy. Technical report, BMWi, 2012.

[76] D. G. Feitelson. *Workload modeling for computer systems performance evaluation*. Cambridge University Press, 2015.

[77] A. Fernández-Montes, D. Fernández-Cerero, L. González-Abril, J. A. Álvarez-García, and J. A. Ortega. Energy wasting at internet data centers due to fear. *Pattern Recognition Letters*, 67:59–65, 2015.

[78] S. Frey, C. Reich, and C. Lüthje. Key performance indicators for cloud computing SLAs. In *The fifth international conference on emerging network intelligence,*, pages 60–64, 2013.

[79] G. Fridgen, R. Keller, M. Thimmel, and L. Wederhake. Shifting load through space - The economics of spatial demand side management using distributed data centers. *Energy Policy*, 109:400–413, 2017.

[80] Frontier Economics Europe. Dezentrale Leistungsverpflichtungssysteme: Eine geeignete Alternative zu zentralen Kapazitätsmechanismen? Technical report, Frontier Economics Europe, 2013.

[81] E. Fryer. Data centre business models: The sherry trifle. Technical report, TechUK, 2014.

[82] S. K. Garg, A. N. Toosi, S. K. Gopalaiyengar, and R. Buyya. SLA-based virtual machine management for heterogeneous workloads in a cloud datacenter. *Journal of Network and Computer Applications*, 45:108–120, 2014.

[83] N. Gast, J.-Y. Le Boudec, and D.-C. Tomozei. Impact of demand-response on the efficiency and prices in real-time electricity markets. In *Proceedings of the 5th international conference on Future energy systems*, pages 171–182. ACM, 2014.

[84] C. W. Gellings and W. M. Smith. Integrating demand-side management into utility planning. *Proceedings of the IEEE*, 77(6):908–918, 1989.

[85] German Federal Minstry for Economic Affairs and Energy. Die Energie der Zukunft - Berichtsjahr 2017. Zweiter Fortschrittsbericht zu Energiewende, 2019.

[86] M. Ghamkhari and H. Mohsenian-Rad. Data centers to offer ancillary services. In *Smart Grid Communications (SmartGridComm), 2012 IEEE Third International Conference on*, pages 436–441. IEEE, 2012.

[87] M. Ghasemi-Gol, Y. Wang, and M. Pedram. An optimization framework for data centers to minimize electric bill under day-ahead dynamic energy prices while providing regulation services. In *Green Computing Conference (IGCC), 2014 International*, pages 1–9. IEEE, 2014.

[88] G. Ghatikar. Demand response opportunities and enabling technologies for data centers: Findings from field studies. 2012.

[89] G. Ghatikar, M. A. Piette, S. Fujita, A. McKane, J. H. Dudley, A. Radspieler, K. Mares, and D. Shroyer. Demand response and open automated demand response opportunities for data centers. *Lawrence Berkeley National Laboratory*, 2010.

[90] H. C. Gils. Assessment of the theoretical demand response potential in Europe. *Energy*, 67:1–18, 2014.

[91] J. Glanz. Power, pollution and the internet. *The New York Times*, 22, 2012.

[92] P. Godfrey-Smith. *Theory and reality: An introduction to the philosophy of science*. University of Chicago Press, 2009.

[93] L. A. Greening. Demand response resources: Who is responsible for implementation in a deregulated market? *Energy*, 35(4):1518–1525, 2010.

[94] S. Y. Hadush and L. Meeus. DSO-TSO cooperation issues and solutions for distribution grid congestion management. *Energy policy*, 120:610–621, 2018.

[95] G. Hager, J. Treibig, J. Habich, and G. Wellein. Exploring performance and power properties of modern multi-core chips via simple machine models. *Concurrency and Computation: Practice and Experience*, 28(2):189–210, 2016.

[96] M. Hall, E. Frank, G. Holmes, B. Pfahringer, P. Reutemann, and I. H. Witten. The WEKA data mining software: An update. *ACM SIGKDD explorations newsletter*, 11(1):10–18, 2009.

[97] J. Hamilton. Cooperative expendable micro-slice servers (CEMS): low cost, low power servers for internet-scale services. In *Conference on Innovative Data Systems Research (CIDR09)(January 2009)*. Citeseer, 2009.

[98] M. S. Hasan, Y. Kouki, T. Ledoux, and J.-L. Pazat. Exploiting renewable sources: when green SLA becomes a possible reality in cloud computing. *IEEE Transactions on Cloud Computing*, 5(2):249–262, 2015.

[99] Y. He, S. Elnikety, J. Larus, and C. Yan. Zeta: Scheduling interactive services with partial execution. In *Proceedings of the Third ACM Symposium on Cloud Computing*, page 12. ACM, 2012.

[100] M. Healy. The Eco enterprise and the reality of green IT. Technical report, InformationWeek Analytics, 2007.

[101] A. Hevner and S. Chatterjee. *Design research in information systems: Theory and practice*, volume 22. Springer Science & Business Media, 2010.

[102] A. R. Hevner, S. T. March, J. Park, and S. Ram. Design science in information systems research. *MIS quarterly*, pages 75–105, 2004.

[103] R. Hintemann. Consolidation, colocation, virtualization, and cloud computing: The impact of the changing structure of data centers on total electricity demand. In *ICT Innovations for Sustainability*, pages 125–136. Springer, 2015.

[104] R. Hintemann. Update 2017: Rechenzentren in Deutschland: Eine Studie zur Darstellung der wirtschaftlichen Bedeutung und der Wettbewerbssituation. Technical report, Borderstep Institute, 2017.

[105] R. Hintemann. Digitalisierung treibt Strombedarf von Rechenzentren: Boom führt zu deutlich steigendem Energiebedarf der Rechenzentren in Deutschland im Jahr 2017. Technical report, Borderstep Institute for Innovation and Sustainability, 2018.

[106] R. Hintemann, S. Beucker, and S. Hinterholzer. Energieeffizienz und Rechenzentren in Deutschland: Weltweit führend oder längst abgehängt? Technical report, Borderstep Institute for Innovation and Sustainability, Berlin, 2017.

[107] R. Hintemann and J. Clausen. Rechenzentren in Deutschland: Eine Studie zur Darstellung der wirtschaftlichen Bedeutung und der Wettbewerbssituation, 2014.

[108] R. Hintemann and J. Clausen. Bedeutung digitaler Infrastrukturen In Deutschland: Sozioökonomische Chancen und Herausforderungen für Rechenzentren im internationalen Wettbewerb. Technical report, Borderstep Institute for Innovation and Sustainability, Berlin, 2018.

[109] L. Hirth and I. Schlecht. Zusammenspiel von Markt und Netz im Stromsystem - Eine Systematisierung und Bewertung von Ausgestaltungen des

Strommarkts. Study for German Ministry of Economic Affairs and Energy, Consentec, 2018.

[110] Höchstleistungsrechenzentrum Stuttgart. Lesefassung der HLRS Entgeltordnung 2017. Technical report, HLRS, 2017. accessed 10.01.2020.

[111] C.-H. Hsu and U. Kremer. The design, implementation, and evaluation of a compiler algorithm for CPU energy reduction. In *ACM SIGPLAN Notices*, volume 38, pages 38–48. ACM, 2003.

[112] D. Hurley, P. Peterson, and M. Whited. Demand response as a power system resource. *Regulatory Assistance Project: Montpelier, VT, USA*, 2013.

[113] Intel. Techical resources: Intel xeon processors. `https://www.intel.com/content/www/us/en/processors/xeon/xeon-technical-resources.html`. Accessed: 2020-02-06.

[114] M. A. Islam, H. Mahmud, S. Ren, and X. Wang. Paying to save: Reducing cost of colocation data center via rewards. In *2015 IEEE 21st International Symposium on High Performance Computer Architecture (HPCA)*, pages 235–245. IEEE, 2015.

[115] M. A. Islam, X. Ren, S. Ren, A. Wierman, and X. Wang. A market approach for handling power emergencies in multi-tenant data center. In *High Performance Computer Architecture (HPCA), 2016 IEEE International Symposium on*, pages 432–443. IEEE, 2016.

[116] C. Jahns and C. Weber. Probabilistic forecasting of reserve power prices in Germany using quantile regression. In *2019 16th International Conference on the European Energy Market (EEM)*, pages 1–5. IEEE, 2019.

[117] A. K. Jain. Data clustering: 50 years beyond K-means. *Pattern Recognition Letters*, 31(8):651–666, June 2010.

[118] H.-P. Jiang, D. Chuck, and W.-M. Chen. Energy-aware data center networks. *Journal of Network and Computer Applications*, 68:80–89, 2016.

[119] Y. Jiang, Z. Huang, and D. H. Tsang. On power-peak-aware scheduling for large-scale shared clusters. *IEEE Transactions on Big Data*, 2018.

[120] E. Jochem, A. Adegbulugbe, B. Aebischer, S. Bhattacharjee, G. Gritsevich, I.and Jannuzzi, and T. Jaszay. *Energy and the Challenge of Sustainability. World Energy Assessment.*, chapter Energy end-use efficiency, pages 173–217. UNDP/UNDESA/WEC: Energy and the Challenge of Sustainability. World Energy Assessment., 2000.

[121] S. Just and C. Weber. Strategic behavior in the German balancing energy mechanism: Incentives, evidence, costs and solutions. *Journal of Regulatory Economics*, 48(2):218–243, 2015.

[122] S. Keshav. *Mathematical foundations of computer networking.* Addison-Wesley, 2012.

[123] J.-H. Kim and A. Shcherbakova. Common failures of demand response. *Energy*, 36(2):873–880, 2011.

[124] B. Kirpes and S. Klingert. Evaluation process of demand response compensation models for data centers. In *Proceedings of the 5th International Workshop on Energy Efficient Data Centres*, page 4. ACM, 2016.

[125] D. Kliazovich, P. Bouvry, and S. U. Khan. Greencloud: a packet-level simulator of energy-aware cloud computing data centers. *The Journal of Supercomputing*, 62(3):1263–1283, 2012.

[126] S. Klingert. Mapping data centre business types with power management strategies to identify demand response candidates. In *Proceedings of the Ninth International Conference on Future Energy Systems*, pages 492–498. ACM, 2018.

[127] S. Klingert, A. Berl, M. Beck, R. Serban, M. Di Girolamo, G. Giuliani, H. de Meer, and A. Salden. Sustainable energy management in data centers through collaboration. In *International Workshop on Energy Efficient Data Centers*, pages 13–24. Springer, 2012.

[128] S. Klingert, F. Niedermeier, C. Dupont, G. Giuliani, T. Schulze, and H. de Meer. Introducing flexibility into data centers for smart cities. In *Smart Cities, Green Technologies, and Intelligent Transport Systems*, pages 128–145. Springer, 2015.

[129] S. Klingert, F. Niedermeier, C. Dupont, G. Giuliani, T. Schulze, and H. de Meer. Renewable energy-aware data centre operations for smart cities the DC4Cities approach. In *International Conference on Smart Cities and Green ICT Systems (SMARTGREENS)*, pages 1–9. IEEE, 2015.

[130] S. Klingert, T. Schulze, and C. Bunse. GreenSLAs for the energy-efficient management of data centres. In *Proceedings of the 2nd International Conference on Energy-Efficient Computing and Networking*, pages 21–30. ACM, 2011.

[131] S. Klingert and S. Szilvas. Spinning gold from straw - evaluating the flexibility of data centres on power markets. *Energy Informatics*, 3(1):1–34, 2020.

[132] S. Klingert, N. Wilken, and C. Becker. Sim2win: How simulation can help data centers to benefit from controlling their power profile. *Energy Efficiency*, 13(5):1007–1029, 2020.

[133] M. Klobasa, S. von Roon, T. Buber, and A. Gruber. Load management as a way of covering peak demand in Southern Germany. *Agora Energiewende, Berlin*, 2013.

[134] M. Kolenc, N. Ihle, C. Gutschi, P. Nemček, T. Breitkreuz, K. Goedderz, N. Suljanović, and M. Zajc. Virtual power plant architecture using OpenADR 2.0b for dynamic charging of automated guided vehicles. *International Journal of Electrical Power & Energy Systems*, 104:370–382, 2019.

[135] E. Koliou, C. Eid, J. P. Chaves-Ávila, and R. A. Hakvoort. Demand response in liberalized electricity markets: Analysis of aggregated load

participation in the German balancing mechanism. *Energy*, 71:245–254, 2014.

[136] J. Koomey, K. Brill, P. Turner, J. Stanley, and B. Taylor. A simple model for determining true total cost of ownership for data centers. *Uptime Institute White Paper, Version*, 2:2007, 2007.

[137] S. Lavrijssen and A. Carrilo. Radical innovation in the energy sector and the impact on regulation. TILEC Discussion Paper No. DP 2017-017, 2017.

[138] T. N. Le, Z. Liu, Y. Chen, and C. Bash. Joint capacity planning and operational management for sustainable data centers and demand response. In *Proceedings of the Seventh International Conference on Future Energy Systems*, page 16. ACM, 2016.

[139] P. D. Leedy and J. E. Ormrod. *Practical research: Planning and design.* Pearson Education, 2014.

[140] Y. Li, D. Chiu, C. Liu, L. T. Phan, T. Gill, S. Aggarwal, Z. Zhang, B. T. Loo, D. Maier, and B. McManus. Towards dynamic pricing-based collaborative optimizations for green data centers. In *2013 IEEE 29th International Conference on Data Engineering Workshops (ICDEW)*, pages 272–278. IEEE, 2013.

[141] Z. Liu, Y. Chen, C. Bash, A. Wierman, D. Gmach, Z. Wang, M. Marwah, and C. Hyser. Renewable and cooling aware workload management for sustainable data centers. In *ACM SIGMETRICS Performance Evaluation Review*, volume 40, pages 175–186. ACM, 2012.

[142] Z. Liu, M. Lin, A. Wierman, S. H. Low, and L. L. Andrew. Geographical load balancing with renewables. *ACM SIGMETRICS Performance Evaluation Review*, 39(3):62–66, 2011.

[143] Z. Liu, M. Lin, A. Wierman, S. H. Low, and L. L. Andrew. Greening geographical load balancing. In *Proceedings of the ACM SIGMETRICS*

joint international conference on Measurement and modeling of computer systems, pages 233–244. ACM, 2011.

[144] Z. Liu, I. Liu, S. Low, and A. Wierman. Pricing data center demand response. In *ACM SIGMETRICS Performance Evaluation Review* [145], pages 111–123.

[145] Z. Liu, A. Wierman, Y. Chen, B. Razon, and N. Chen. Data center demand response: Avoiding the coincident peak via workload shifting and local generation. In *Performance Evaluation* [141], pages 770–791.

[146] R. V. Lopes and D. Menascé. A taxonomy of job scheduling on distributed computing systems. *IEEE Transactions on Parallel and Distributed Systems*, 27(12):3412–3428, 2016.

[147] D. Magalhães, R. N. Calheiros, R. Buyya, and D. G. Gomes. Workload modeling for resource usage analysis and simulation in cloud computing. *Computers & Electrical Engineering*, 47:69–81, 2015.

[148] P. Mahadevan, P. Sharma, S. Banerjee, and P. Ranganathan. A power benchmarking framework for network devices. In *International Conference on Research in Networking*, pages 795–808. Springer, 2009.

[149] A. H. Mahmud and S. Ren. Online capacity provisioning for carbon-neutral data center with demand-responsive electricity prices. *ACM SIGMETRICS Performance Evaluation Review*, 41(2):26–37, 2013.

[150] A. Markandya, A. Bigano, and R. Porchia. The social cost of electricity. scenarios and policy implications. 2010.

[151] M. Mäsker, L. Nagel, A. Brinkmann, F. Lotfifar, and M. Johnson. Smart grid-aware scheduling in data centres. *Computer Communications*, 96:73–85, 2016.

[152] V. Mathew, R. K. Sitaraman, and P. Shenoy. Energy-efficient content delivery networks using cluster shutdown. *Sustainable Computing: Informatics and Systems*, 6:58–68, 2015.

[153] G. Migliavacca, M. Rossi, D. Six, M. Džamarija, S. Horsmanheimo, C. Madina, I. Kockar, and J. M. Morales. SmartNet: H2020 project analysing TSO–DSO interaction to enable ancillary services provision from distribution networks. *CIRED-Open Access Proceedings Journal*, 2017(1):1998–2002, 2017.

[154] J. D. Moore, J. S. Chase, P. Ranganathan, and R. K. Sharma. Making scheduling" cool": Temperature-aware workload placement in data centers. In *USENIX annual technical conference, General Track*, pages 61–75, 2005.

[155] D. Moss. Facility cooling failure: How much time do you have? *Dell White Paper*, 1:5, 2011.

[156] S. Nada and M. Said. Effect of CRAC units layout on thermal management of data center. *Applied thermal engineering*, 118:339–344, 2017.

[157] N. Nasiriani, G. Kesidis, and D. Wang. Public cloud differential pricing design under provider and tenants joint demand response. In *Proceedings of the Ninth International Conference on Future Energy Systems*, pages 21–32, 2018.

[158] F. Niedermeier, F. Kazhamiaka, and H. de Meer. Energy supply aware power planning for flexible loads. In *Proceedings of the 5th International Workshop on Energy Efficient Data Centres*, page 2. ACM, 2016.

[159] A. M. Novikov and D. A. Novikov. *Research methodology: From philosophy of science to research design.* CRC Press, 2013.

[160] E. Oró, V. Depoorter, A. Garcia, and J. Salom. Energy efficiency and renewable energy integration in data centres. strategies and modelling review. *Renewable and Sustainable Energy Reviews*, 42:429–445, 2015.

[161] E. Oró and J. Salom. Data centre overview. *Advanced Concepts for Renewable Energy Supply of Data Centres*, page 1, 2017.

[162] P. Palensky and D. Dietrich. Demand side management: Demand response, intelligent energy systems, and smart loads. *IEEE transactions on industrial informatics*, 7(3):381–388, 2011.

[163] G. Papaefthymiou and K. Dragoon. Towards 100% renewable energy systems: Uncapping power system flexibility. *Energy Policy*, 92:69–82, 2016.

[164] J. Patel, V. Jindal, I.-L. Yen, F. Bastani, J. Xu, and P. Garraghan. Workload estimation for improving resource management decisions in the cloud. In *2015 IEEE Twelfth International Symposium on Autonomous Decentralized Systems*, pages 25–32. IEEE, 2015.

[165] T. Patki, N. Bates, G. Ghatikar, A. Clausen, S. Klingert, G. Abdulla, and M. Sheikhalishahi. Supercomputing centers and electricity service providers: A geographically distributed perspective on demand management in europe and the united states. In *International Conference on High Performance Computing*, pages 243–260. Springer, 2016.

[166] M. K. Patterson. The effect of data center temperature on energy efficiency. In *Thermal and Thermomechanical Phenomena in Electronic Systems, 2008. ITHERM 2008. 11th Intersociety Conference on*, pages 1167–1174. IEEE, 2008.

[167] K. Peffers, T. Tuunanen, M. A. Rothenberger, and S. Chatterjee. A design science research methodology for information systems research. *Journal of management information systems*, 24(3):45–77, 2007.

[168] M. G. Pollitt and I. Shaorshadze. The role of behavioural economics in energy and climate policy. 2011.

[169] B. F. Postema, N. J. Geuze, and B. R. Haverkort. Fitting realistic data centre workloads: A data science approach. In *Proceedings of the Ninth International Conference on Future Energy Systems*, pages 486–491. ACM, 2018.

[170] G. Prettico, M. G. Flammini, N. Andreadou, S. Vitiello, G. Fulli, and M. Masera. Distribution System Operators observatory 2018 - Overview of

the electricity distribution system in Europe. EUR 29615 EN, Publications Office of the European Union, Luxembourg, 2019.

[171] A. Qureshi, R. Weber, H. Balakrishnan, J. Guttag, and B. Maggs. Cutting the electric bill for internet-scale systems. In *ACM SIGCOMM computer communication review*, volume 39, pages 123–134. ACM, 2009.

[172] R. Rahmani, I. Moser, and M. Seyedmahmoudian. A complete model for modular simulation of data centre power load. *arXiv preprint arXiv:1804.00703*, 2018.

[173] L. Rao, X. Liu, L. Xie, and W. Liu. Minimizing electricity cost: Optimization of distributed internet data centers in a multi-electricity-market environment. *Proceedings - IEEE INFOCOM*, 2010.

[174] A. Rawson, J. Pfleuger, and T. Cader. Data center power efficiency metrics: PUE and DCiE. *The Green Grid*, page 120, 2007.

[175] S. Ren and M. A. Islam. Colocation demand response: Why do I turn off my servers? In *11th International Conference on Autonomic Computing (ICAC 14)*, pages 201–208, 2014.

[176] S. Rivoire, P. Ranganathan, and C. Kozyrakis. A comparison of high-level full-system power models. *HotPower*, 8(2):32–39, 2008.

[177] H. Rong, H. Zhang, S. Xiao, C. Li, and C. Hu. Optimizing energy consumption for data centers. *Renewable and Sustainable Energy Reviews*, 58:674–691, 2016.

[178] F. D. Rossi, M. Storch, I. de Oliveira, and C. A. De Rose. Modeling power consumption for DVFS policies. In *Circuits and Systems (ISCAS), 2015 IEEE International Symposium on*, pages 1879–1882. IEEE, 2015.

[179] B. Rountree, D. K. Lowenthal, M. Schulz, and B. R. De Supinski. Practical performance prediction under dynamic voltage frequency scaling. In *Green Computing Conference and Workshops (IGCC), 2011 International*, pages 1–8. IEEE, 2011.

[180] B. Rountree, D. K. Lownenthal, B. R. De Supinski, M. Schulz, V. W. Freeh, and T. Bletsch. Adagio: making DVS practical for complex HPC applications. In *Proceedings of the 23rd international conference on Supercomputing*, pages 460–469. ACM, 2009.

[181] S. Samedi. *The social costs of electricity supply: types of costs, their dynamics over time and how energy models take these costs into account.* PhD thesis, Faculty II, University of Oldenburg, 2018.

[182] A. J. Schwab. Elektroenergiesysteme, Verbundsysteme. In *Elektroenergiesysteme*, pages 11–47. Springer, 2015.

[183] A. Shehabi, S. Smith, D. Sartor, R. Brown, M. Herrlin, J. Koomey, E. Masanet, N. Horner, I. Azevedo, and W. Lintner. United States data center energy usage report. Technical report, Lawrence Berkeley National Laboratory, 2016.

[184] M. H. Shoreh, P. Siano, M. Shafie-khah, V. Loia, and J. P. Catalão. A survey of industrial applications of demand response. *Electric Power Systems Research*, 141:31–49, 2016.

[185] H. Shoukourian, T. Wilde, A. Auweter, and A. Bode. Power variation aware configuration adviser for scalable HPC schedulers. In *High Performance Computing & Simulation (HPCS), 2015 International Conference on* [186], pages 71–79.

[186] H. Shoukourian, T. Wilde, A. Auweter, A. Bode, and D. Tafani. Predicting energy consumption relevant indicators of strong scaling HPC applications for different compute resource configurations. In *Proceedings of the Symposium on High Performance Computing* [185], pages 115–126.

[187] H. Shoukourian, T. Wilde, H. Huber, and A. Bode. Analysis of the efficiency characteristics of the first high-temperature direct liquid cooled petascale supercomputer and its cooling infrastructure. *Journal of Parallel and Distributed Computing*, 107:87–100, 2017.

[188] H. Shoukourian, T. Wilde, D. Labrenz, and A. Bode. Using machine learning for data center cooling infrastructure efficiency prediction. In *Parallel and Distributed Processing Symposium Workshops (IPDPSW), 2017 IEEE International*, pages 954–963. IEEE, 2017.

[189] L. Šikšnys and T. B. Pedersen. Dependency-based flexoffers: Scalable management of flexible loads with dependencies. In *Proceedings of the Seventh International Conference on Future Energy Systems*, page 11. ACM, 2016.

[190] L. Šikšnys, E. Valsomatzis, K. Hose, and T. B. Pedersen. Aggregating and disaggregating flexibility objects. *IEEE Transactions on Knowledge and Data Engineering*, 27(11):2893–2906, 2015.

[191] M. Skach, M. Arora, C.-H. Hsu, Q. Li, D. Tullsen, L. Tang, and J. Mars. Thermal time shifting: Decreasing data center cooling costs with phase-change materials. *IEEE Internet Computing*, 21(4):34–43, 2017.

[192] Smart Energy Demand Coalition. A demand response action plan For Europe: Regulatory requirements and market models. Technical report, SEDC Brussels, 2013.

[193] Smart Energy Demand Coalition. 10 recommendations for an efficient European power market design. Technical report, SEDC, Brussels, 2016.

[194] Smart Energy Demand Coalition. Demand response at the DSO level: - enabling DSOs to harness the benefits of demand-side flexibility. Technical report, SEDC, Brussels, 2016.

[195] Smart Energy Demand Coalition. Explicit demand response in Europe - Mapping the markets 2017. Technical report, SEDC, Brussels, 2017.

[196] Smart Grid Task Force - EU. Regulatory recommendations for the deployment of flexibility. EU SGTF-EG3 Report, 2015.

[197] I. Sommerville. Software engineering 9th edition. *ISBN-10137035152*, 2011.

[198] G. L. Stewart, G. A. Koenig, J. Liu, A. Clausen, S. Klingert, and N. Bates. Grid accommodation of dynamic HPC demand. In *Proceedings of the 48th*

International Conference on Parallel Processing: Workshops, pages 1–4, 2019.

[199] W. Ströbele, W. Pfaffenberger, and M. Heuterkes. *Energiewirtschaft: Einführung in Theorie und Politik.* Walter de Gruyter, 2012.

[200] C.-J. Tang, M.-R. Dai, and C.-C. Chuang. Exploring the potential benefits of demand response in small data centers. In *Proceedings of the International MultiConference of Engineers and Computer Scientists*, volume 1, 2013.

[201] X. Tang, X. Liao, J. Zheng, and X. Yang. Energy efficient job scheduling with workload prediction on cloud data center. *Cluster Computing*, 21(3):1581–1593, 2018.

[202] The Agency for the Cooperations of Energy Regulators. Capacity renumeration mechanisms and the internal market for electricity. Report Pursuant to Article 11 of Regulation (EC) No 713/2009, July 2013. Whitepaper.

[203] C. Tipantuña and X. Hesselbach. Demand-response power management strategy using time shifting capabilities. In *Proceedings of the Ninth International Conference on Future Energy Systems*, pages 480–485, 2018.

[204] J. Torriti, M. G. Hassan, and M. Leach. Demand response experience in Europe: Policies, programmes and implementation. *Energy*, 35(4):1575–1583, 2010.

[205] N. H. Tran, C. Pham, S. Ren, Z. Han, and C. S. Hong. Coordinated power reduction in multi-tenant colocation datacenter: An emergency demand response study. In *2016 IEEE International Conference on Communications (ICC)*, pages 1–6. IEEE, 2016.

[206] Uptime Institute. Data center site infrastructure Tier standard: Operational sustainability. Whitepaper, 2014.

[207] Uptime Institute. Data center site infrastructure Tier standard: Topology. Whitepaper, 2018.

[208] B. Vanderveken and J. Trzcinski. Insight energy & environment: Demand response: A study of its potential in europe. Sia Partners SAS, Belgium, dec 2014.

[209] G. Von Laszewski, L. Wang, A. J. Younge, and X. He. Power-aware scheduling of virtual machines in DVFS-enabled clusters. In *Cluster Computing and Workshops, 2009. CLUSTER'09. IEEE International Conference on*, pages 1–10. IEEE, 2009.

[210] S. von Roon and T. Gobmaier. Demand Response in der Industrie–Status und Potenziale in Deutschland. *München: Forschungsstelle für Energiewirtschaft eV (FfE)*, 2010.

[211] T. M. W. von Roon, S.; Gobmaier. Durchführung eines Messprogramms - Forschungsvorhaben 0327246E im Verbundprojekt EnOB - Optimierung der Bausubstanz - OASE. Technical report, Forschungsstelle für Energiewirtschaft e.V., 2007.

[212] D. R. Wallace and R. U. Fujii. Software verification and validation: an overview. *Ieee Software*, 6(3):10–17, 1989.

[213] C. Wang, B. Urgaonkar, Q. Wang, and G. Kesidis. A hierarchical demand response framework for data center power cost optimization under real-world electricity pricing. In *Modelling, Analysis & Simulation of Computer and Telecommunication Systems, 2014 IEEE 22nd International Symposium on*, pages 305–314. IEEE, 2014.

[214] R. Wang, N. Kandasamy, and C. Nwankpa. Data centers as demand response resources in the electricity market: Some preliminary results. In *Intl. Workshop on Feedback Computing*, 2012.

[215] R. Wang, N. Kandasamy, C. Nwankpa, and D. R. Kaeli. Datacenters as controllable load resources in the electricity market. *Proceedings - International Conference on Distributed Computing Systems*, pages 176–185, 2013.

[216] J. Whitney, P. Delforge, E. Masanet, G. Peridas, M. Stamas, N. Jimenez, P. Remick, J. Clinger, and S. M. T. Brown. Scaling up energy efficiency across the data center industry: Evaluating key drivers and barriers. *Issue Paper No. IP*, pages 14–08, 2014.

[217] A. Wierman, Z. Liu, I. Liu, and H. Mohsenian-Rad. Opportunities and challenges for data center demand response. In *Green Computing Conference (IGCC), 2014 International*, pages 1–10. IEEE, 2014.

[218] T. Wilde, A. Auweter, H. Shoukourian, and A. Bode. Taking advantage of node power variation in homogenous HPC systems to save energy. In L. T. Kunkel J., editor, *International Conference on High Performance Computing*, volume Lecture Notes in Computer Science, vol 9137, pages 376–393. Springer, Springer, Cham, 2015.

[219] T. Wilde, T. Clees, H. Shoukourian, N. Hornung, M. Schnell, I. Torgovitskaia, E. L. Alvarez, D. Labrenz, and H. Schwichtenberg. Increasing data center energy efficiency via simulation and optimization of cooling circuits-a practical approach. In *DA-CH Conference on Energy Informatics*, pages 208–221. Springer, 2015.

[220] M.-A. Wolf. Environmentally sound data centres: Policy measures, metrics, and methodologies. Technical report, European Commission Directorate-General for Communications Networks, Content and Technology (CONNECT), 2014.

[221] H. Xu and B. Li. Reducing electricity demand charge for data centers with partial execution. In *Proceedings of the 5th international conference on Future energy systems*, pages 51–61. ACM, 2014.

[222] J. Yao, X. Liu, and C. Zhang. Predictive electricity cost minimization through energy buffering in data centers. *IEEE Transactions on Smart Grid*, 5(1):230–238, 2014.

[223] H. Zhang, S. Shao, H. Xu, H. Zou, and C. Tian. Free cooling of data centers: A review. *Renewable and Sustainable Energy Reviews*, 35:171–182, 2014.

[224] Y. Zhang, I. C. Paschalidis, and A. K. Coskun. Data center participation in demand response programs with quality-of-service guarantees. In *Proceedings of the Tenth ACM International Conference on Future Energy Systems*, pages 285–302, 2019.

[225] K. Zhu, Z. Cui, Y. Wang, H. Li, X. Zhang, and C. Franke. Estimating the maximum energy-saving potential based on it load and it load shifting. *Energy*, 138:902–909, 2017.

[226] C. Zöphel and T. Müller. Flexibilitätsoptionen am Strommarkt – Eine Analyse zu Hemmnissen und Erlösmöglichkeiten.

Appendix

A. Processing the Data Traces

The considered HPC data center provided 3 data traces, of which the first, 'Job Data' needed to be cleaned in order to avoid inconsistent simulation results (see section A.1). The total facility power of the data center that provided the traces, was unfortunately not available but had to be generated artificially (see section A.2).

A.1. Job Data Trace

Description of the Job Data Trace

'JobData' contains information for every job in 2014 that was executed in the considered HPC environment, in total 406980 jobs. Each record consists of the following 10 fields:

Job id: an individual job id for each job assigned by the scheduling system

Submission time: the time at which the job was submitted to the scheduling system

Start time: the time at which the actual execution of the job started

End time: the time at which the actual execution of the job finished

Status: the status of a job within the LoadLeveler system which is either *Completed* or *Removed*

Energy tag: a user specified job tag which should be unique for each application; however, only rarely any other tag than the default tag is used, so that the information is meaningless

CPU frequency: the maximum allowed CPU frequency for this specific job; however, it is not known whether the job was actually executed using this frequency

Number of utilized nodes: the number of compute nodes which were utilized for the execution of the job; a compute note is the smalles unit assigned, which implies that the two CPUs of each node always process the same job

Energy to solution (EtS): the amount of energy in kWh consumed by the job during execution; this value is directly measured by the LoadLeveler system during execution

Average power consumption (APC): the average power consumption in W of the corresponding job; this value is calculated from the measured runtime and the measured EtS values of the job

Data Cleaning

The job data trace contained faulty jobs so that it had to be cleaned before being processed. This was done usinge the following procedures:

- Jobs with zero values of frequency and EtS were deleted in order not to distort simulation results. A reason for these errors might have been the premature abortion of a job or measuring mistakes.
- For the same reason jobs with a negative runtime were deleted.
- All jobs with an APC/node value below 40W were deleted. The reason is that the according to [95] the computing power of each node is approximately 23W, so that the idle power of the node should be at least 46W. It was assumed that the corresponding jobs contain measuring mistakes and might have been aborted, as the vast majority of these records had a runtime of less than 5 seconds,

  After the data cleaning, the job data trace contained 389968 job records. Unfortunately, as the HPC data center is a productive environment it is not possible to give information about general data statistics for the whole data trace.

A.2. Total Facility Power

Unfortunately the data center considered could not provide a data trace for the total facility power. The reason is that there are additional server rooms with a different technical set-up than the one used as a data source for this thesis. Therefore an artifical total facility power needed to be constructed. This was done using the information of the IT room and the PUE data assuming that the *Total Facility Power* equals the sum of the *IT power* and the *Cooling Power.* Only if this assumption holds, equation (6.1) can be used to calculate the *Total Facility Power*: $TotalFacilityPower = PUE * ITPower$.

Using the total facility power constructed from the PUE values and the IT data, the cooling power consumption can be constructed accordingly.

The artifical data traces generated based on this are part of the basis against which the validation in section is compared. The derived total facility power trace is rather stable; the cooling power data center exhibits more peaks as it is not only influenced by the job load but also by the outside temperature.

B. Simulation Results Summary

This section displays the statistics of the simulation runs with Sim2Win-HPC: first the evalutation metrics are introduced and explained (table B.1). Subsequently the results of the first simulation set are displayed in tables B.2 and B.3. The results of the variations of the SLA simulated in the second set of scenarios are given in tables B.4 for the SCR and B.5 for EPEX. Finally results of simulating the artificial workloads generated through the job classes with 'Short Jobs' and 'Long Jobs' are presented in tables B.6 and B.7 accordingly.

Table B.1.: Explanation of the evaluation metrics.

All values relate to the week starting on 03/03/2014 and ending on 09/03/2014; the result tables contain both absolute and relative values	
Electricity Items	
Total Facility Electricity Consumption (TFE)	TFE is calculated based on the power values of the total facility power (TFP) per timestep (5 mins): $TFE = \sum TFP * 0.05$
Average Total Facility Power Consumption (ATFP)	AFTP is calculated by averageing the power values of TFP: $ATFP = /timesteps$; the simulation period consists of 2016 timesteps
Peak Total Facility Power Consumption (PTFP)	PTFP is the maximum of the TFP power values: $PTFP = maxTFP$
Job Electricity Consumption (JE)	JE is the electricity consumption of the artificially created job power data trace (JP); calculated in the same way as TFE: $JE = \sum JP * 0.05$
Average Job Power Consumption (AJP)	AJP is the averaged power value of the artifically created job power data trace: $AJP = JP/timesteps$ (2016)
Job Items	
Average Runtime (ART)	Job runtime (RT) is logged and averaged over the number of timesteps $ART = \sum RT/timesteps$
Workload executed (WL)	WL is measured by the average number of active jobs J of the time series Job Power data trace: $WL = \sum J/timesteps$
Power Management	
Ratio Workload Shifting (RWL)	RWL is expressed in terms of shifted Jobs in relation to shiftable Jobs: $RWL = shiftedJ/shiftableJ$
Average Frequency (AF)	Frequency F is logged and averaged over the number of timesteps $AF = \sum F/timesteps$
Cost Items	
Energy Cost - static (ECS)	Energy cost is calculated as price/kWh * kWh consumed: $EC = TFE * p^e$; EC^0, EC^1 are energy cost before and after the adaptation; static electricity tariff
Energy Cost - dynamic (ECD)	Energy cost is calculated as price/kWh * kWh consumed: $EC = TFE * p^e$; EC^0, EC^1 are energy cost before and after the adaptation; EPEX hourly prices
SLA Cost (SLA_C)	SLA cost is calculated based on execution time according to the SLA runtime model : $uP * rD$, where uP is the node hour usage price, and rD the relative delay
Benefit Items	
Benefit SCR Energy (SCR_E)	SCR_E is calculated multiplying the SCR energy reward EP with the offered power, based on the event time (15mins): $SCRE = Events * EP * PF_{DC} * 0.25$
Benefit SCR Power (SCR_P)	SCR_P is calculated multiplying the SCR energy reward EP with the offered power flexibility: $SCRP = PP * PF_{DC}$
Gros Benefit -static (GBS)	For SCR GBS is calculated adding up income and substracting cost: $SCR_E + SCR_P - SLA_C - (ECS^1 - ECS^0)$ For EPEX: $EPEX = \sum \Delta p^e_{static} * PF_{DC} * 0.25$
Gros Benefit -dynamic (GBD)	For SCR GBD is calculated adding up income and substracting cost: $SCR_E + SCR_P - SLA_C - (ECD^1 - ECD^0)$ For EPEX: $EPEX = \sum \Delta p^e_{dynamic} * PF_{DC} * 0.25$
Net Benefit SCR-static (NBS)	NBS is GBS reduced by aggregator fee of 30%: $NB = GB - 0.3 * (SCR_E + SCR_P)$
Net Benefit SCR-dynamic (NBD)	NBD is GBD reduced by aggregator fee of 30%: $NB = GB - 0.3 * (SCR_E + SCR_P)$

Table B.2.: Results of the MaxSLA bids and the EPEX engagement with original SLAs and workload.

	BL	**MaxSLA0.2**		**MaxSLA0.4**		**MaxSLA0.5**		**MaxSLA0.6**		**EPEX**	
		absolute	% BL	absolute	% BL	absolute	% BL	absolute	% BL	absolute	% BL
Power											
TFE	347,804	344,390	-0.98%	342,429	-1.55%	341,848	-1.71%	341,565	-1.79%	320,657	**-7.81%**
ATFP	2,070	2,050	-0.98%	2,038	-1.55%	2,035	-1.71%	2,033	-1.79%	1,909	-7.81%
PTFP	2,408	2,423	0.53%	2,467	2.47%	2,486	3.24%	2,499	3.77%	2,505	**4.05%**
JE	210,833	209,244	-0.75%	208,556	-1.08%	208,580	-1.07%	208,906	-0.91%	184,474	**-12.50%**
AJP	1,255	1,245	-0.75%	1,241	-1.08%	1,242	-1.07%	1,243	-0.91%	1,098	-12.50%
PJP	1,546	1,533	-0.85%	1,566	1.31%	1,566	1.31%	1,583	2.43%	1,621	4.87%
Jobs											
ART	16,319	19,791	21.28%	19,897	21.93%	20,026	22.72%	20,127	23.34%	17,567	7.65%
WL	190.9	192.5	0.86%	194.2	1.73%	195.3	2.34%	197.6	3.54%	168.2	**-11.88%**
RWL	0		3.24%		3.79%		3.90%		6.00%		
AF	2.35	2.33	-0.92%	2.30	-2.14%	2.28	-2.81%	2.26	-3.73%		
Cost											
ECS	53,284	52,761	-0.98%	52,460	-1.55%	52,371	-1.71%	52,328	-1.79%	49,125	-7.81%
ECD	10,339	10,216	-1.20%	10,144	-1.89%	10,124	-2.09%	10,108	-2.24%	9,202	**-11.00%**
SLA_C	0	176	n.a	1,443	n.a	699	n.a	2,501	n.a	1,082	n.a
SCR_E	0	284	n.a	568	n.a	710	n.a	852	n.a	0	n.a
SCR_P	0	76	n.a	153	n.a	191	n.a	229	n.a	0	n.a
GBS	0	707	1.33%	102	0.19%	1,114	**2.09%**	-464	-0.87%	3,077	5.77%
GBD	0	308	2.98%	-526	-5.09%	418	4.04%	-1,188	-11.49%	56	0.54%
NBS	0	599	1.12%	-115	-0.22%	844	**1.58%**	-789	-1.48%	3,077	**5.77%**
NBD	0	200	1.93%	-743	-7.18%	147	1.43%	-1,513	**-14.63%**	56	**0.54%**

Table B.3.: Results of the MaxBids without SLAs and MinBids with original SLAs, both with original workload.

	BL	**Max0.2**		**Max0.5**		**Max0.6**		**MinSLA0.2**		**MinSLA0.5**		**MinSLA0.6**	
		absolute	% BL	absolute	% BL	absolute	% BL	absolute	% BL	absolute	% BL	absolute	% BL
Power													
TFE	347,804	342,495	-1.53%	341,408	-1.84%	341,519	-1.81%	347,650	-0.04%	347,541	-0.08%	347,541	-0.08%
ATFP	2,070	2,039	-1.51%	2032	-1.84%	2,033	-1.81%	2,069	-0.04%	2,069	-0.08%	2,069	-0.08%
PTFP	2,408	2,474	2.73%	2,474	2.75%	2,499	**3.78%**	2,408	0.00%	2,408	0.00%	2,408	0.00%
JE	210,833	208,606	-1.06%	208,307	-1.20%	208,844	-0.94%	210,761	-0.03%	210,734	-0.05%	210,737	-0.05%
AJP	1,255	1,242	-1.06%	1,240	-1.20%	1,243	-0.94%	1,255	-0.03%	1,254	-0.05%	1,254	-0.05%
PJP	1,546	1,543	-0.17%	1,566	1.31%	1,566	1.34%	1,546	0.00%	1,546	0.00%	1,546	0.00%
Jobs													
ART	16,319	19,967	22.36%	20,209	23.84%	20,291	24.34%	19,591	20.05%	19,606	20.15%	19,614	20.20%
WL	190.9	194.5	1.90%	195.7	2.55%	197.6	**3.54%**	190.9	0.04%	191.1	0.13%	191.2	0.16%
RWL	0		0.00%		1.35%		3.68%		0.00%		0.02%		0.04%
AF	2.35	2.30	-1.99%	2.28	-2.80%	2.26	-3.65%	2.35	-0.04%	2.35	-0.12%	2.35	-0.15%
Cost													
ECS	53,284	52,470	-1.53%	52,304	-1.84%	52,321	-1.81%	53,260	-0.04%	53,243	-0.08%	53,240	-0.08%
ECD	10,339	10,151	-1.20%	10,114	-1.20%	10,111	-1.20%	10,334	-1.20%	10,331	-1.20%	10,330	-1.20%
SLA_C	0	0	n.a	0	n.a	0	n.a	10	n.a	14	n.a	10	n.a
SCR_E	0	284	n.a	710	n.a	852	n.a	13	n.a	32	n.a	39	n.a
SCR_P	0	76	n.a	191	n.a	229	n.a	54	n.a	136	n.a	163	n.a
GBS	0	1,174	2.20%	1,881	3.53%	2,044	3.84%	81	0.15%	194	0.36%	234	0.44%
GBD	0	548	5.30%	1,126	10.89%	1,310	12.67%	62	0.60%	162	1.57%	200	1.93%
NBS	0	1,066	2.00%	1,610	3.02%	1,720	3.23%	61	0.11%	144	0.27%	174	0.33%
NBD	0	440	4.26%	856	8.28%	986	9.53%	42	0.41%	112	1.08%	140	1.35%

Table B.4.: Results comparing the MaxSLA and MinSLA runs using 'Hard SLA' versus 'Soft SLA', both with original workload.

	MaxH-SLA0.2		MaxH-SLA0.4		MaxH-SLA0.5		MaxH-SLA0.6		MinH-SLA0.2		MinH-SLA0.5		MinH-SLA0.6	
	absolute	% BL	absolute	% BL	absolute	% BL	absolute	% BL	absolute	% BL	absolute	% BL	absolute	% BL
Power														
TFE	344,404	-0.98%	341,326	-1.86%	342,027	-1.66%	341,599	-1.78%	347,652	-0.04%	347,544	-0.07%	347,523	-0.08%
ATFP	2,051	-0.98%	2,033	-1.86%	2,037	-1.66%	2,034	-1.78%	2,070	-0.04%	2,070	-0.07%	2,070	-0.08%
PTFP	2,423	0.63%	2,473	2.72%	2,473	2.70%	2,475	2.79%	2,408	0.00%	2,408	0.00%	2,408	0.00%
JE	209,252	-0.75%	207,802	-1.44%	208,712	-1.01%	208,919	-0.91%	210,762	-0.03%	210,735	-0.05%	210,738	-0.05%
AJP	1,246	-0.75%	1,238	-1.44%	1,243	-1.01%	1,244	62.02%	1,255	-0.03%	1,255	-0.05%	1,255	-0.05%
PJP	1,533	-0.85%	1,566	1.29%	1,588	2.71%	1,593	3.08%	1,546	0.00%	1,546	0.00%	1,546	0.00%
Jobs														
ART	19,752	21.04%	20,020	22.68%	19,999	22.55%	20,211	23.86%	19,568	19.91%	19,580	19.98%	19,588	20.03%
WL	192.6	0.85%	192.7	0.92%	196.0	2.65%	197.7	3.53%	191.0	0.04%	191.2	0.13%	191.3	0.16%
RWL		4.50%		6.26%		6.73%		7.26%		0.05%		0.07%		0.07%
AF	2.33	-0.92%	2.30	-2.20%	2.28	-2.87%	2.26	-3.76%	2.35	-0.04%	2.35	-0.12%	2.35	-0.15%
Cost														
ECS	52,763	-0.98%	52,291	-1.86%	52,398	-1.66%	52,333	-1.78%	53,260	-0.04%	53,244	-0.07%	53,241	-0.08%
ECD	10,216	-1.19%	10,105	-2.27%	10,127	-2.06%	10,108	-2.23%	10,334	-0.05%	10,331	-0.08%	10,330	-0.09%
SLA_C	501	n.a	3,881	n.a	3,532	n.a	4,270	n.a	10	n.a	11	n.a	11	n.a
SCR_E	284	n.a	568	n.a	710	n.a	852	n.a	13	n.a	32	n.a	39	n.a
SCR_P	76	n.a	153	n.a	191	n.a	229	n.a	54	n.a	136	n.a	163	n.a
GBS	380	0.71%	-2,168	-4.07%	-1,746	-3.28%	-2,239	-4.20%	80	0.15%	197	0.37%	233	0.44%
GBD	-18	-0.17%	-2,926	-28.30%	-2,418	-23.39%	-2,958	-28.61%	62	0.60%	165	1.60%	199	1.93%
NBS	272	0.51%	-2,384	-4.47%	-2,016	-3.78%	-2,563	-4.81%	60	0.11%	146	0.27%	172	0.32%
NBD	-126	-1.22%	-3,142	-30.39%	-2,689	-26.00%	-3,282	-31.75%	42	0.41%	115	1.11%	139	1.34%

Table B.5.: Results comparing the EPEX 'Hard SLA' and 'Soft SLA' runs, both with original workload.

	BL	**EPEX**		**H_EPEX**	
		absolute	% BL	absolute	% BL
Power					
TFE	347,804	320,657	**-7.81%**	313,071	**-9.99%**
ATFP	2,070	1,909	-7.81%	1,864	-9.99%
PTFP	2,408	2,505	**4.05%**	2,384	-0.99%
JE	210,833	184,474	**-12.50%**	180,235	**-14.51%**
AJP	1,255	1,098	-12.50%	1,073	-14.51%
PJP	1,546	1,621	4.87%	1,529	-1.11%
Jobs					
ART	16,319	17,567	7.65%	17,540	7.49%
WL	190.9	168.2	**-11.88%**	166.4	**-12.88%**
RWL	0				
AF	2.35				
Cost					
ECS	53,284	49,125	-7.81%	49,211	-7.64%
ECD	10,339	9,202	**-11.00%**	9,258	-10.46%
SLA_C	0	1,082	n.a	1,518	n.a
SCR_E	0	0	n.a	0	n.a
SCR_P	0	0	n.a	0	n.a
GBS	0	3,077	5.77%	2,555	4,79%
GBD	0	56	0.54%	-436	-4,22%
NBS	0	3,077	**5.77%**	2,555	4,79%
NBD	0	56	**0.54%**	-436	-4,22%

Table B.6.: Results of 'Short Jobs' workload for MaxSLA and EPEX engagement, both using original SLAs.

	BL Short		MaxSLA0.05SHORT		MaxSLA0.1SHORT		MaxSLA0.2SHORT		EPEXSHORT	
	absolute	% BL	absolute	% BL	absolute	% BL	absolute	% BL	absolute	% BL
Power										
TFE	216,340	-37.80%	215,148	-0.55%	214,735	-0.74%	214,058	-1.05%	215,737	-0.28%
ATFP	1,288	-37.80%	1,281	-0.55%	1,278	-0.74%	1,274	-1.05%	1,284	-0.28%
PTFP	1,630	-32.29%	1,647	1.00%	1,649	1.12%	1,691	3.70%	1,965	20.52%
JE	95,058	-54.91%	94 543	-0.54%	94,393	-0.70%	94,375	-0.72%	94,452	-0.64%
AJP	566	-54.91%	563	-0.54%	562	-0.70%	562	-0.72%	562	-0.64%
PJP	890	-42.40%	901	1.14%	903	1.44%	942	5.81%	1.271	42.71%
Jobs										
ART	15,282		14,149	-7.41%	14,281	-6.55%	14,403	-5.75%	13,253	-13.28%
WL	93.2		93.8	0.65%	94.1	1.04%	95.5	2.50%	91.4	-1.92%
RWL				3.00%		2.84%		4.30%		n.a
AF	2.42		2,33	-3.67%	2,32	-4.16%	2,28	-5.73%		
Cost										
ECS	33,143	-37.80%	32961	-0.55%	32,897	-0.74%	32,794	-1.05%	33,051	-0.28%
ECD	6,441	-37.70%	6397	-0.69%	6,382	-0.92%	6,357	-1.31%	6,263	-2.77%
SLA_C	0	n.a	156	n.a	222	n.a	376	n.a	3	n.a
SCR_E	0	n.a	71	n.a	142	n.a	284	n.a	0	n.a
SCR_P	0	n.a	19	n.a	38	n.a	76	n.a	0	n.a
GBS	0	n.a	116	0.35%	204	0.62%	334	1.01%	95	0.29%
GBD	0	n.a	-22	-0.34%	17	0.27%	69	1.06%	178	2.77%
NBS	0	n.a	89	0.27%	150	0.45%	225	0.68%	95	0.29%
NBD	0	n.a	-49	-0.76%	-37	-0.57%	-40	-0.61%	178	2.77%

Table B.7.: Results of 'Long Jobs' workload for MaxSLA and EPEX engagement, both using original SLAs.

	BL Long		**MaxSLA0.05LONG**		**MaxSLA0.1LONG**		**MaxSLA0.2LONG**		**EPEXLONG**	
	absolute	% BL	absolute	% BL	absolute	% BL	absolute	% BL	absolute	% BL
Power										
TFE	194,406	-44.10%	193,494	-0.47%	193,000	-0.72%	192,591	-0.93%	20,0781	3.28%
ATFP	1,157	-44.10%	1,152	-0.47%	1,149	-0.72%	1,146	-0.93%	1,195	3.28%
PTFP	1,438	-40.29%	1,436	-0.12%	1,436	-0.11%	1,454	1.12%	1,693	**17.75%**
JE	64,907	-69.21%	64,449	-0.70%	64,245	-1.02%	64,250	-1.01%	70,422	8.50%
AJP	386	-69.21%	384	-0.70%	382	-1.02%	382	-1.01%	419	8.50%
PJP	652	-57.85%	652	0.00%	652	0.02%	653	0.21%	831	**27.59%**
Jobs										
ART	30,703		30,691	-0.04%	31,002	0.97%	31,294	1.92%	30,223	-1.56%
WL	94.9		95.4	0.47%	96.1	1.26%	97.9	3.09%	95.5	0.66%
RWL				1.16%		2.84%		*5.57%*		
AF	2,43		2,34	-3.39%	2,32	-4.28%	2,25	-7.16%		
Cost										
ECS	29,783	-44.10%	29,643	-0.47%	29,568	-0.72%	29,505	-0.93%	30,760	3.28%
ECD	5,719	-44.68%	5,687	-0.57%	5,669	-0.88%	5,658	-1,07%	5,727	0.14%
SLA_C	0	n.a	7	n.a	92	n.a	676	n.a	5	n.a
SCR_E	0	n.a	71	n.a	142	n.a	0	n.a	0	n.a
SCR_P	0	n.a	19	n.a	38	n.a	0	n.a	0	n.a
GBS	0	n.a	223	0.75%	304	1.02%	0	n.a	-981	**-3.30%**
GBD	0	n.a	116	2.03%	139	2.43%	0	n.a	-12	**-0.22%**
NBS	0	n.a	196	0.66%	250	0.84%	0	n.a	-981	-3.30%
NBD	0	n.a	89	1.56%	85	1.48%	0	n.a	-12	-0.22%

C. Publications in this Thesis

- S. Klingert, S. Szilvas. Spinning Gold from Straw - Evaluating the Flexibility of Data Centres on Power Markets. *Energy Informatics 3.1*: 1-34, 2020.
- S. Klingert, N. Wilken, C. Becker. Sim to Win: How Simulation can Help Data Centres to Benefit from Controlling their Power Profile. *Energy Efficiency 13.5*:1007-1029, 2020.
- A. Clausen, G. Koenig, S. Klingert, G. Ghatikar, P. M. Schwartz, and N. Bates. An analysis of contracts and relationships between supercomputing centers and electricity service providers. In *Proceedings of the 48th International Conference on Parallel Processing: Workshops,* pages 1-8. ACM, 2019.
- G. L. Stewart, G. A. Koenig, J. Liu, A. Clausen, S. Klingert, and N. Bates. Grid accommodation of dynamic HPC demand. In *Proceedings of the 48th International Conference on Parallel Processing: Workshops,* pages 1-4. ACM, 2019.
- S. Klingert. Mapping Data Centre Business Types with Power Management Strategies to Identify Demand Response Candidates. In *Proceedings of the Ninth International Conference on Future Energy Systems,* pages 492-498. ACM, 2018.
- S. Klingert and C. Becker. Economics-inspired Modeling of Data Centre Power Flexibility. *Computer Science-Research and Development, Springer*: 247â“249, 2017.
- R. Basmadjian, J. F. Botero, G. Giuliani, X. Hesselbach Serra, S. Klingert, and H. De Meer. Making Data Centres Fit for Demand

Response: Introducing GreenSDA and GreenSLA Contracts. *IEEE Transactions on Smart Grid 3(1)*: 3453-3464, 2016.

- B. Kirpes and S. Klingert. Evaluation process of demand response compensation models for data centers. In *Proceedings of the 5th International Workshop on Energy Efficient Data Centres,* pages 1-6. Springer, 2016.
- T. Patki, N. Bates, G. Ghatikar, A. Clausen, S. Klingert, G. Abdulla, and M. Sheikhalishahi. Supercomputing Centers and Electricity Service Providers: A geographically distributed perspective on demand management in Europe and the United States. In *Proceedings of the International Conference on High Performance Computing,*pages 243-260. Springer, 2016.
- S. Klingert, F. Niedermeier, C. Dupont, G. Giuliani, T. Schulze, and H. de Meer. Renewable energy-aware data centre operations for smart cities the DC4Cities approach. In *Proceedings of the International Conference of Smart Cities and Green ICT Systems (SMARTGREENS), 2015 International Conference on,* pages 1-9. IEEE, 2015.
- S. Klingert, F. Niedermeier, C. Dupont, G. Giuliani, T. Schulze, and H. de Meer. Introducing flexibility into data centers for smart cities. In *Smart Cities, Green Technologies, and Intelligent Transport Systems,* pages 128-145. Springer, 2015.
- R. Basmadjian, G. Lovasz, M. Beck, H. De Meer, X. Hesselbach Serra, J. F. Botero, S.Klingert, M. Perez-Ortega, J. C. Lopez, A. Stam, and others: A generic architecture for demand response: the ALL4Green approach. In *2013 International Conference on Cloud and Green Computing,* pages 464-471. IEEE, 2013.
- R. Basmadjian, F. Niedermeier, G. Lovasz, H. De Meer, and S. Klingert. GreenSDAs leveraging power adaption collaboration between energy provider and data centres. In *Sustainable Internet and ICT for Sustainability (SustainIT),* pages 1-9. IEEE, 2013.

- A. Berl, S. Klingert, M. Beck, and H. de Meer. Integrating data centres into demand-response management: A local case study. In *Industrial Electronics Society, IECON 2013-39th Annual Conference of the IEEE,* pages 4762-4767. IEEE, 2013.
- J.F. Botero, S. Klingert, X. HesselbachSerra, A. Falcone, and G. Giuliani. GreenSLAs: providing energy consumption flexibility in Data Centers through energy-aware contracts. In *Proceedings of the International Conference of Smart Cities and Green ICT Systems (SMARTGREENS),* pages 119-122. SciTePress, 2013.
- C. Bunse, S. Klingert, and T. Schulze. Greenslas: Supporting energy-efficiency through contracts. In *International Workshop on Energy Efficient Data Centers,* pages 54-68. Springer, 2012.
- S. Klingert, A. Berl, M. Beck, R. Serban, M. Di Girolamo, G. Giuliani, H. de Meer, H., and A. Salden. Sustainable energy management in data centers through collaboration. In *International Workshop on Energy Efficient Data Centers,* pages 13-24. Springer, 2012.
- S. Klingert, T. Schulze, and C. Bunse. GreenSLAs for the energy-efficient management of data centres. In *Proceedings of the 2nd International Conference on Energy-Efficient Computing and Networking,* pages 21-30. ACM, 2011.
- R. Basmadjian, C. Bunse, V. Georgiadou, G. Giuliani, S. Klingert, G. Lovasz, and M. Majanen. Fit4green -Energy aware ICT optimization policies. In *Proceedings of theCOST Action IC0804onEnergy Efficiency in Large Scale Distributed Systems1st Year,* p. 88-92. IRIT, 2010.

D. Lebenslauf

seit 03/2016	Akademische Mitarbeiterin Lehrstuhl für Wirtschaftsinformatik II Universität Mannheim
01/2010-02/2016	Akademische Mitarbeiterin Lehrstuhl für Softwaretechnik Universität Mannheim
08/2006-12/2009	Projektleiterin School of Information Technology International University in Germany
08/2006-07/2008	Projektassistenz School of Information Technology International University in Germany
01/1997-12/1998	Freie wissenschaftliche Mitarbeiterin Abteilung Stoffströme Wuppertal Institut für Klima, Umwelt, Energie
10/1990-09/1996	Hauptdiplom Volkswirtschaftslehre Universität Karlsruhe
10/1988-09/1990	Vordiplom Volkswirtschaftslehre Universität Kiel

www.ingramcontent.com/pod-product-compliance
Ingram Content Group UK Ltd.
Pitfield, Milton Keynes, MK11 3LW, UK
UKHW022001190726
13853UKWH00004B/1669

9 783736 973305